THE

Advanced
Citizen

How Thought Leaders Serve,
Lead and Succeed

DR. DENNIS PERMAN

Kindness Media
c/o Dennis Perman DC
129 East Neck Road Huntington, NY 11743
www.theadvancedcitizen.com
email dpermandc@hotmail.com
Phone 631-742-7571

Layout and Printing by BookBaby.com
The Advanced Citizen/Dr. Dennis Perman—1st ed.

ISBN: 978-0-98639-772-1

Contents

Change, The Only Constant   August 2008 1

The Rewards Of Leadership   September 2008 4

Alive and Well   December 2008 6

The Basics and Your Standards of Excellence   January 2009 8

What Price Freedom?   February 2009 10

Self Esteem and Leadership   March 2009 12

Drive   April 2009 15

The Six Human Needs   May 2009 18

Commitment   June 2009 20

Prosperity Consciousness   July 2009 22

Relationships   August 2009 24

Personal Power   September 2009 26

Vision   October 2009 28

Gratitude   November 2009 30

Identity   December 2009 32

Honoring Your Standards   January 2010 35

Communication   February 2010 37

Risk   March 2010 39

Shut Up and Speed Up   April 2010 42

The Power of Full Engagement   May 2010 44

Measurement   June 2010 46

Courage   July 2010 48

Family   August 2010 50

Willingness   September 2010 52

Thinking Big   October 2010 54

Expectation Management   November 2010 56

Winners Circle Identity 58

Self-Discipline   December 2010 59

Community   January 2011 61

The Passage of Pain   February 2011 64

The Unknown   March 2011 66

Long Term Relationships and Short Term Relationships   April 2011 68

A Matter Of Principle   May 2011 71

Adjusting   June 2011 73

Practice Philosophy   July/August 2011 77

Going Global   September 2011 80

Growth and Function   October 2011 83

Doing Good   November 2011 85

Knowing Who You're Dealing With   December 2011 88

Adventure   January 2012 91

Synergy   February 2012 94

Cause and Effect   March 2012 97

Lucky or Smart?   April 2012 100

Consistency   May 2012 102

Responsibility   June 2012 105

Fun   July 2012 107

Dealing With Adversity   August 2012 110

The Four Adjustments   September 2012 113

Braving The Unknown   October 2012 115

Creative Genius   November 2012 117

The MasterMind Principle   December 2012 119

Presence   January 2013 121

Motivation   February 2013 124

Profitability   March 2013 127

Clarity   April 2013 130

Ownership   May 2013 132

Tall Poppies   June 2013 135

Recognition   July 2013 137

Love Bomb   August 2013 140

Troubleshooting With the PFQ   September 2013 143

Goal Setting   October 2013 146

Seven (Plus Two) Kinds Of Smart   November 2013 148

Determination   December 2013 151

Integrity   January 2014 154

Mindfulness   February 2014 157

Hope   March 2014 160

Enthusiasm   April 2014 162

Making A Difference   May 2014 164

Balancing Tradition and Innovation   June 2014 167

How Talent Becomes Command   July 2014 170

Simplicity   August 2014 172

Questions   September 2014 175

Contrast   October 2014 178

The Enneagram   November 2014 182

Generosity   December 2014 185

On Writing A Book   January 2015 188

Continuing Dedication   February 2015 191

Progress   March 2015 193

Planning   April 2015 196

Loss   May 2015 199

Self-Indulgence   June 2015 202

The Innate Practice   July 2015 206

Kindness   August 2015 209

Loyalty   September 2015 212

Looking For A Miracle   October 2015 215

Resilience   November 2015 217

Givingness   December 2015 219

Target Orientation   January 2016 222

Compassion   February 2016 225

Optimization   March 2016 228

Transcendence   April 2016 230

Perfection and Excellence   May 2016 233

Stress   June 2016 236

Fear and Faith   July 2016 239

Empathy   August 2016 242

Common Sense   September 2016 245

Legacy   October 2016 248

Imagination   November 2016 250

Grit   December 2016 253

Colors of the Rainbow   January 2017 256

Decisiveness   February 2017 259

Positive Expectancy   March 2017 262

Love and Precision   April 2017 265

Alignment   May 2017 268

Self-Awareness   June 2017 271

Grace   July 2017 274

Bereavement   August 2017 277

First Responders   September 2017 280

Hospitality   October 2017 283

Coping   November 2017 286

Dreaming   December 2017 289

The Second Puzzle   January 2018 292

World Class   February 2018 295

Inertia   March 2018 298

Structure   April 2018 301

Authorship   May 2018 304

Zero-Sum   June 2018 307

Priorities   July 2018 310

Stress Patterns   August 2018 313

Brain-Based Wellness   September 2018 316

Violence   October 2018 319

Polarity   November 2018 322

Evolution   December 2018 325

Fitness   January 2019 328

Winning   February 2019 331

Surprise   March 2019 334

The Curse Of Knowledge   April 2019 337

Elegance   May 2019 340

Endurance   June 2019 343

Completion   July 2019 346

Epilogue: Accountability and Truth   August 2019 349

Final Reflections   September 2019 352

Acknowledgments 353

Foreword

What are the virtues and values of a life well lived? What are the organizing principles of a servant entrepreneur, an advanced citizen who does as much good as possible and develops an optimally satisfying career and lifestyle?

These essays are excerpts from the 8/08-7/19 editions of "The Advanced Citizen," the newsletter of the Winners Circle, the personal growth and high achievement club within The Masters Circle Global, a premier coaching and seminar company for chiropractors, wellness professionals and their staff.

The intention was to capture distinctions that would serve to inspire, motivate and train leaders to lead, healers to heal, and doctors to succeed. For that reason, the subject matter is diverse but wound around a core of resources you can apply to your life, your work and your relationships.

Some readers may prefer to read these passages in chronological order as they were written, while others may open to any page and see what guidance good fortune brings. Either way, read, learn and enjoy this time lapse stream of consciousness chronicle of self-development for high achievers over the last eleven years.

Dennis Perman DC

Co-Founder of The Masters Circle Global

Change, The Only Constant   August 2008

I was editing the new Guy Riekeman album we're releasing in Washington this month (which is killer by the way) and I heard him say that in his father's time, the amount of known information doubled every forty years, and now it doubles every three and a half years, an astounding rate of new ideas and concepts.

We all have to be ready for the twists and turns that happen as a result of this accelerated pace. Shifts in finances, relationships, health, and self-image require us to think on our feet, and respond as the world frantically whirls around us at breakneck speed. And many of these decisions we're called upon to make in such stressful circumstances may have huge impact on our outcomes, which means that to succeed, we have to step up and face the issue resourcefully, optimistically and with certainty.

As The Winners Circle, you have a bit of an insider's view of The Masters Circle, seeing Bob and myself with our guards down a bit, trading more at shoulder level with other top achievers like you, risking to reveal our own frailties so you can see that, as Sue Morter showed us in Portland, excellence is not perfection.

Tony Robbins teaches about CANI – Constant and Never-ending Improvement, the notion that you can continue along a path of growth for as long as you are committed to do so. But to follow such an intention is to be willing to embrace change, because you cannot grow and stay the same, it's as simple as that.

Change is uncomfortable and inconvenient. It doesn't feel good. Yet, it is the only way to make things better, and as long as you value making things better, you must be willing to let go of what was in favor of what could be.

I remember when I was a senior consultant for Markson Management Services in 1992, at the height of its success, and I presented to Larry the models that became The Masters Circle's technology – Identity-Based Consulting, the Practice Fulfillment Quotient, The PVA Skills, The Financial Master Plan, How To Target Your

Ideal Patient, Resource-Building, I tried to give it all to him, but he already had a model that was working, and he was at the top of the game, why should he listen to me?

So I went out on my own, and it turned out well, the Identity-Based approach was the way to expand on the strategy-based perspectives of the 80's and early 90's. I built a company called Consultant on Call, blazed some new trails that caught Larry's attention, and parlayed that into Larry's first partnership ever. If I hadn't been willing to go out on my own fifteen years ago and test my ideas, I never would have gotten the opportunity to share what I have with you today.

In this spirit, it is with great pride and just a little sadness that I announce that Janice Hughes has submitted her letter of resignation, effective shortly after the Washington seminar. She has decided to explore new opportunities, and while we will miss her terribly, we support her endeavors, and look forward to a warm and mutually beneficial relationship going forward.

I will be taking over The Winners Circle, and my intention is to create a Winners Circle Identity that we can all be passionate about. Let's choose a path together that inspires us, to raise our standards and our consciousness so we become truly advanced citizens. Each of us has a right to express ourselves as we wish, and a responsibility to invest the right amount of our time and energy in helping others.

Through our role as chiropractors and as successful businesspeople and leaders, we can use our influence to do good, however we define it. It is my hope that you will help me define the specifics of our mission, while we keep our vision in mind – The Winners Circle as role models of excellence in our profession, our communities and beyond, leading by example and inspiring others to wellness and higher achievement.

I know some of you better than others, but I want to know each and every one of you, because my belief is that our lives are coming together because I have gifts for you, and you have gifts for me, and it's time to exchange them. For example, Bob and I have been doing Mid Year Reviews with Winners Circle Members, as a special way to share our views and suggestions with you. (If you haven't had yours yet, please call and schedule soon.)

We want more engagement with you, those who care about developing leadership and advanced citizenry (an odd but pithy phrase derived from the Riekeman project), because our profession is in dire need of on-site in-the-trenches role models who can then rise to regional and national prominence. We believe that The Winners Circle is the training ground for that, building leaders and advanced citizens.

Change is hard, but the only way to make things better is to change. Uncomfortable, inconvenient, but learning to embrace it and make the best of it is the least difficult and most efficient way to get where you want to be. Buddha said that life is painful, but the suffering is optional.

You decide the meaning of your experiences, and when you face change, be flexible, stay light on your feet, and notice the trends that serve you from your current vantage point. Information is doubling as we speak, don't try to manage it all with your left brain, it's like trying to drink off a fire hose – dial in to your purpose, and you'll be amazed at the stamina and resiliency you can exhibit. Expect the best, prepare for the worst, and aim down the middle, and don't get caught up in how you feel at any given moment – just like a patient, you can be duped by your symptoms into thinking that they are the problem.

Pay attention, and you'll be more likely to see the value in withstanding the discomforts of change – because they are worth it, if you only look at it right. Please let me help you look at it right, to minimize your suffering and maximize the great results you deserve in your practice and your life. I look forward to being your guide in some small or large way along your path to victory, success and fulfillment. I appreciate your loyalty, and now, let's roll up our sleeves and get to work.

The Rewards Of Leadership   September 2008

Oh, it's not easy, I realize that – accepting the responsibility of leadership requires more of us, sometimes more than we feel like giving -- more focus, more self-discipline, more certainty, more attention to detail, and often more patience and determination than we feel we can muster – but the willingness to pay the price of leadership brings with it significant rewards.

First, and most obviously, is the feeling of being in control – having the self esteem and confidence to assume a leadership role means that you will be granted the right to decide, a necessary precondition for all success – and so, refining your decision-making ability and perspective is a bonus that comes along with being a leader, an advantage you take with you to all future circumstances.

Next, you have the opportunity to test your vision in actuality, to see your intention come to fruition, and calibrate it against your expectations, the ultimate reality check. Power is the ability to translate intention into reality, and the leader gets to orchestrate that process, and see it up close and personal.

You also get to choose your team and assign their roles, to select those support players who increase the likelihood of success and get them in the right seats on the bus. Surrounding yourself with the right team makes your work that much more pleasurable and effective, and the leader gets to call the shots on assembling and guiding them to generate the optimal results – the buck stops with you.

But there are more subtle benefits to being in command, like guiding and nurturing those in your charge toward higher achievement, developing them so they too can taste the sweetness of victory and freedom. Whether you lead your staff, your patients, your community or your family, seeing the light go on in someone's eyes and recognizing the metamorphosis that occurs when someone awakens to their greatness is by itself worth the price of admission.

If leadership feels like an inconvenient burden, or a job someone else is probably better suited for, consider this – your reluctance is more likely a defense your left brain is creating to protect you from unnecessary pain, and in that regard, it serves you – but only up to a point. Seeing the landscape clearly, you will arrive at the same conclusion all winners eventually do – that while stepping up to take the helm can be intimidating, frightening, or just challenging, the alternative is less desirable still – having someone you feel less qualified or less loving than you are running the show, and you being obligated to follow.

This points out one of the reasons we have a Winners Circle in the first place – it's designed to be a training ground for leaders, for advanced citizens who want to have impact and make the biggest difference possible, through their practices, their public service, and the expression of their lives as examples of excellence.

Carefully examine your feelings about leadership, as they are a window into your beliefs about yourself as a leader. Write down the qualities you think a leader should exhibit, and rate yourself in each of these areas, not to judge yourself, but to plot a course you could reasonably follow that would take you to a place of greater authority, greater self-respect, greater self-acceptance, and greater accomplishment, too.

You'll be amazed to discover that deep down, even our greatest leaders are no different from you – they just found ways to access their best and put it in play, which is not and has never been beyond you. You have what it takes too -- look at yourself objectively, congratulate yourself for your strengths, and roll up your sleeves to tackle your weaker areas. It will come back in the form of progress, service, and the deliciously satisfying movement along the path to your own fulfillment.

Alive and Well   December 2008

The Winners Circle is alive and well and moving forward with passion, certainty and a renewed sense of purpose. With the enthusiasm demonstrated through my survey, and the obvious desire on the part of those who responded, I'm doubly committed to making your Winners Circle experience uplifting, transformational and of course, fun!

The Winners Circle is a leadership pipeline, focusing empowered chiropractors and their significant others on productive displays of advanced citizenry. Our vision is to establish a mastermind designed to generate top level players in health and wellness, who go beyond their own successes to inspire others to greatness.

Each Winners Circle member is unique and adds something special to the mix, and your input and contribution make a difference – don't be shy about it. The days of elitism, good old boys and girls clubs and exclusionary tactics are history, part of Winners Circle lore but no longer appropriate or necessary. Young and not so young, large practices and more modest, wellness or otherwise, our profession is in dire need of fresh leadership, and The Winners Circle is the source.

Some of you have been growing rapidly and have lofty aspirations for the New Year. Others are stalled at a substantial (or not so substantial) level and face the crossroads – are you green and growing or brown and rotting? Still others have adversities to address, and can use the power of the mastermind to break through limitation and blaze new trails. Bring your issues to the mastermind, and if you're cruising in an issue-free zone, then bring your best vision-creating and problem-solving vibes, and be there to support your Winners Circle colleagues.

"Why Is God Laughing?"

Deepak Chopra has a new novel out, with the above title, and I found it to be relevant to the transformation of the Winners Circle. It's the story of a comedian who surprisingly finds himself on a quest for self discovery, and his adventures make his vision clear and his course obvious to him. It's a quick and entertaining read, but like most of Chopra's work carries a deeper meaning too.

2009 Goals

If you're not early, you're late – what's the status of your goal structure for the coming year? This is as good a time as any to revisit your 6 P's – purpose, personal goals, professional goals, people goals, prosperity goals, and play goals. You can write as many as you like, though I recommend you select the top three in each category and focus on them. This keeps your attention on the most important objectives, and avoids majoring in minors.

The Basics and Your Standards of Excellence   January 2009

Well, it's a new year and time to buckle down and look at our expectations and goals for the year. If you've been holding yourself to a high standard, your goals have been written since October 1, reviewed on Thanksgiving Eve (a time to reflect on all we have to be grateful for) and finalized New Year's Eve, leaving you poised and ready to launch yourself into the next cycle.

If you have not followed this pattern, don't despair – just don't drag your feet. The best time to set goals may be October 1, but the second best time is… right now. You can't go back, only forward, so if you haven't established the assorted objectives you want to aim at this year, now is the time.

Remember, you can't hit a target if you don't aim at it, and you can't aim at a target if you don't know what it is – get a grip, write down what you want to accomplish, and you dramatically increase the likelihood of achieving what you desire.

Once you write your goals, it's essential not to just trust to luck – tip the odds in your favor by constructing specific plans, to create a road map to your outcome. Most of us think this process is only a matter of picking action steps, and of course this is essential, but looking at your success from the identity-based approach, there's a bit more to it.

What beliefs would you need in place to hit your goals? What resources would you need? What people would you want as part of your support mechanism? What materials would you need to pull off the logistics of your goal? These questions will help you produce a more complete plan, not only based on actions that may or may not be within your grasp, but including the inner work necessary to develop absolute certainty. Combined with a thorough game plan, your strategies will take on new life as you add the X-factor – the best you possible!

I remember when I was in chiropractic college, hungry for distinctions about healing technique, I had the privilege of studying with some of the most influential pioneers in healing, including Richard Van Rumpt (Directional Non Force Technique, DNFT,) M.L. Rees (Soft Tissue Orthopedics and Harmonics,) Vern Pierce (Thompson Terminal Point,) George Goodheart (Applied Kinesiology) and top ranking instructors in SOT (though I never met DeJarnette, I did study with Dave Denton and Jim Cima,) full spine technique (Joe Stuckey was about the best adjuster I ever met) and upper cervical technique (Thomas Leroy Whitehorne, who ran the BJ Palmer Clinic in the 60's) – I was intent on never having a patient come in my door with a subluxation complex I couldn't solve.

And do you know what I learned from each and every one of these masters? It's the basics that address the huge majority of their challenges. The fancy footwork was only necessary in those rare occasions that the fundamentals needed to be expanded upon. The majority of the time, they handled the task at hand by applying the elements of their particular method.

How about you? Are you taking care of the simple behaviors that form the foundations of success? Are you setting goals, affirming your success with a consistent morning routine, taking care of your body and your relationships, meeting regularly with your coaches and showing up big in your practice and your life?

Don't make this more complicated than it is – if you do the things you know you need to do, with a great attitude, resiliency and persistence, you have an excellent chance of doing what you set out to do.

What Price Freedom?   February 2009

As Winners Circle members, you are invited to look at the world not only as a source of opportunity to grow, but also to serve at the highest level possible. It's easy to fall into the traps of success, where money is flowing, and we may lose focus or forget what got us there. It is this very freedom to continually and consistently re-invent yourself that is the topic of this month's newsletter.

Look at the people you know, and I believe without exception, those with the most freedom are those with the most happiness and satisfaction. But what is the price of freedom? Along with it comes… responsibility.

You see, the freer you are, the more options you have to choose from, and more options usually includes some that take you away from your objective. Yes, I know it seems like a good idea to open an organic foods restaurant in town, but running two businesses takes more time, energy and capital, Yes, I know it looks sexy to have multiple offices, but it's not for someone who isn't willing to spend more time marketing, training, and administering to both businesses. Yes, I see the value of exotic hobbies, but they may devour resources you might invest otherwise in retrospect.

The point is, as you get more and more successful, you'll have more freedom and more options tugging on you, and that requires presence, awareness, flexibility and discernment.

Leaders have yet another challenge, on top of managing their own freedom – leadership includes helping others learn to deal with their freedom. From making sure your kids do their homework to overseeing the training of an associate doctor or assistant, people will tend to find their level, and it falls to those in command to tend the flock and guide their charges toward optimization.

How are you dealing with the freedom you've earned? It's a tricky question, because many of you may not be feeling very free right now, from financial issues to family conflicts to philosophical frustrations and so on. If so, this is the time to seize control of your thinking and realize that your decisions about being and doing can NEVER be taken from you, no matter what the circumstances.

If you've been victimized a bit by your freedom, and you notice that a little discipline may be required to balance it better, then organize your thoughts on paper, where you can be more objective about them, and apply this simple four part process – first, get the big rocks in order, by making sure that the most important values and obligations are met. Second, be present where you are, and use your present time consciousness to get the most out of yourself, whatever you happen to be doing at the time. Be flexible, light enough on your feet to shift when necessary, and with enough latitude built into your schedule so you don't have to run from chore to chore without a chance to breathe and enjoy your progress. And finally, be discerning, decisive and discriminating enough to notice where your time and energy are best invested.

Maybe freedom's just another word for nothing left to lose, but to the entrepreneurial advanced citizen, freedom is an outcome that manifests from serving well – with a little freedom management, it's really wealth without the strings attached.

Self Esteem and Leadership   March 2009

People who naturally tend toward being leaders share numerous qualities, not the least of which is self esteem. If you don't feel good about who you are, it's unlikely you can guide others to maximum accomplishment, but with a great self-concept, you can easily shape your talents and abilities and share yourself as a healer, director, educator, or CEO.

Dr. Nathaniel Branden, foremost expert on this topic, says in his landmark book "The Six Pillars of Self Esteem," that self esteem is "confidence in our ability to think, confidence in our ability to cope with the basic challenges of life, and confidence in our right to be successful and happy, the feeling of being worthy, deserving, entitled to assert our needs and wants, achieve our values, and enjoy the fruits of our efforts."

Notice how these qualities enhance the likelihood of effective leadership.

Confidence in our ability to think: clear and practical thinking is a necessary precondition for every kind of success, and in leadership, it's essential to be able to formulate compelling visions, effective game plans, and passionate action steps and to motivate followers to respond accordingly

Confidence in our ability to cope with the basic challenges of life: when problems arise as obstacles to growth and progress, a positive sense of self is the platform from which the corrective adjustments and resolving refinements are launched, so leaders must be well-versed in sizing up situations, evaluating the best course to move along, and energizing the team to push forward even in times of great adversity

Confidence in our right to be successful and happy: inspiration occurs when people see the relationship between their deepest desires and the identity that leads to fulfillment, and leaders understand the power of connecting your purpose with your paycheck

The feeling of being worthy, deserving: before you can lead, you have to feel good about you, so when you face difficult decisions you can default to previous reference experiences in which you performed well, and bring forward these sensations not only for yourself, but as an example to those who may not yet have such references to draw upon, so they can borrow upon your certainty and execute better because of it

Entitled to assert our needs and wants: proclaiming your desires is intimately interwoven into the process of both personal success and leadership, since unless you are able to convey what you want to others, the probability of them complying is reduced or eliminated

Achieve our values: accomplishment, whether for an individual or a group, depends on consistent focus on what's important, and reminders as needed to keep yourself and those you lead on the path to realization

And enjoy the fruits of our efforts: the reason victory has a sweet smell is because arriving there is the fruition of your ideas, goals, plans, and actions, and the manifestation of your objectives is pointless if you can't appreciate the ground you've covered and what you've invested to get there

This is a road map for aspiring leaders, and at the same time provides a formula for a lifetime of happiness and satisfaction. In fact, Tony Robbins says that relationships, of which leadership is a good example, occur in four categories, of increasing complexity.

First, we must master our relationship with ourselves. Second, we learn to produce a relationship with another. Third, we extrapolate to create relationships with groups, and finally, our outreach becomes strong enough so that we can have relationships with and influence others even if we're not physically present. It is in these third and fourth categories that we discover the way to invest our self esteem – by making ourselves available, once we feel secure inside ourselves and with others one-on-one, to become leaders who influence others in groups, whether we have current physical contact with them or not.

The reason The Masters Circle works from an Identity-Based™ perspective is contained in these thoughts and concepts – by building yourself up in strong and noble thought, you can help others at the deepest level and lead them to their own definition of success, limited only by your vision and willingness to do what it takes.

Drive   April 2009

If you had to take a test on what you needed to do to make your life great, you would probably get a high grade. Wake up early with a great attitude, conduct an empowering and uplifting morning routine, eat a satisfying healthy breakfast, structure your mission around carefully constructed goals based on a meaningful vision, work steadily and passionately, return home for a delicious dinner and enjoyable evening activities – a life of fulfillment, by your design. It doesn't really seem that complicated, on the surface.

So why do so few of us actually achieve this model existence, settling instead for some pretty close matches on some of these habits and not so close on others? Why do we accept less than we feel we really deserve, instead of taking it to the limit?

I have previously illustrated the role self esteem plays in this equation, but there is another component that seems to be missing or at least underdeveloped in many of us – and that is the resource I call drive.

Drive can be defined as an inner urge, a basic or instinctive need, a vigorous onset or onward course toward a goal or objective, a united effort to accomplish some specific purpose with energy and initiative.

Drive is of particular interest to me, because it is not a natural default position for me. Some might call me lazy, other might say preoccupied, but ordinarily I don't just "feel like" working really hard and getting important things done. I have to spur myself into action and overcome the inertia of inactivity, and I bet many of you have the same experience, at least some of the time.

The root of this is most often not in our underlying character, which tends to be consistent with our ethics at our best, and that is the reason why most of us believe we are working to capacity even when we aren't. We intuitively sense that we are good people, and good people do the right thing, so what we are doing must be the right thing, by virtue of the fact that we are doing it. This subtle self-hypnosis is one of the prime detractors from productivity, where we believe our own press clippings and ignore the opportunities and clues that success is constantly leaving for us.

No, lack of drive typically isn't a core issue, it's usually a result of insufficient state management, which allows us to opt out of our best behaviors in favor of more convenient ones. This complacency prevents us from taking our game to another level, so it is useful to notice how we can awaken our drive and reset our course for even more excellence.

So how can you initiate more drive? Start by evaluating yourself at times you feel driven – you have a particular mindset and a particular bodyset that you call drive, and the simplest way to access those patterns is to imagine a time you experienced drive, or a situation in which you would, and calibrate how you are using your machinery – is there a facial expression, a posture, or a pace of movement that contributes to drive for you?

Are there mental pictures you visualize, self-talk that pushes you from inside, or feelings and sensations you get in a particular place in your body that is always there when you feel compelled to take massive action?

By tapping into your personal formula for drive, you can master the mechanics of this essential quality, and if that's all you need to do, then commit to reinforcing this resource as a habit and it will reward you many times over.

For some of us, though, it is a bit more complex, because we may have mixed neuro-associations, in other words, mixed feelings about what we are driving toward. This is where coaching comes in, because we cannot always see ourselves clearly in this regard. I personally count on Bob and others on my team to reel me in if I get too far off course, and while it rarely feels good while they're doing it, I'm grateful to have the support, and it invariably helps. A little clarity goes a long way.

The tool that helps most in this context is reframing, in other words, shifting the meanings and perceptions so you reshape your view on the goal you're moving toward and your strategies for achieving it. This new way of looking at your challenges sparks a new enthusiasm and persistence that manifests as a determination to succeed, and a willingness to do whatever it takes.

If you feel you need some reframing on the importance and value of your objectives, so you feel a greater desire to pursue them, please make sure to ask me or your coaches. In fact, if you feel that drive has been an issue for you, and you feel you've done your due diligence in introspection and inner work and you still feel a little stuck on this, your next movement in the direction you seek is to call me and get some ideas on how to get yourself in gear.

The Six Human Needs   May 2009

As you know, I have been studying, reformatting and applying the technology of Anthony Robbins for well over twenty years, and with all his research into anchoring, reframing, personal power, neuro-associative conditioning, and a host of other immensely practical breakthroughs, one of the most underappreciated aspects of his work is his repackaging and repurposing of Maslow's distinctions on human needs, referred to by Tony as "The Six Human Needs."

Hidden in this work are many answers to success, in practice and in life.

The Six Human Needs are usually addressed in pairs, the first of which is the need for Certainty, coupled with the need for Variety. Certainty is required for basic sanity – I mean, you need to be sure the floor with hold you up when you step on it, that when you take a breath air will be available, but Certainty also includes pleasure, comfort, faith, and predictability. Yet, if all was comfortable and predictable, then life would be boring, so the pair is completed and balanced by the need for Variety, for things to be different sometimes. This need includes excitement, adventure, and new experiences. Finding the right balance between Certainty and Variety allows for proper decision-making about interpreting your reality and knowing which actions to take.

The second pair of human needs is the balance between Significance and Connection. Significance means importance, individuality, being special and standing out, and includes concepts like success, power, and uniqueness. Connection is the opposite balancer, because while we need to feel special, separate and distinct, we also need to feel appreciated and connected to others. Connection includes love, family, friendship, and bonding. Finding the right balance between Significance and Connection sets the stage for leadership, parenting, masterminding, and developing worthwhile relationships.

The third pair of needs addresses Growth and Contribution. Growth refers to personal accomplishment, where contribution refers to accomplishment on behalf of others. Growth includes learning, expansion, philosophical thought and personal development, while Contribution includes service, generosity, educating others, and other forms of making a difference. Finding the balance between Growth and Contribution allows for investment of resources, accumulation of all forms of wealth (both tangible and esoteric,) service orientation, and meaningful achievement based on higher purpose.

Following these guidelines gives you a game plan for happiness, satisfaction and fulfillment. If you look at the things you love to do or people you love to be around, you'll probably find that they go a long way toward meeting these six needs. Further, you can establish a better practice and a better life in general by noticing how you are getting these needs met yourself, and how you are meeting them with your patients, family and friends, and you can use your observations to troubleshoot those relationships and improve them.

Experiment with these ideas, and notice how you can get your needs met through your practice, your family and other aspects of your life. The willingness to explore these concepts will lead to a deeper understanding of the way things work and the way people tick – dig in, you'll find a whole new angle of your communication, with yourself and those you care about.

Commitment   June 2009

In the pages of the Advanced Citizen so far this year, we've talked about standards of excellence, freedom and responsibility, self esteem and leadership, drive, the six human needs, all fundamentals for success and fulfillment.

Now it's time to talk about… commitment.

Too many of our colleagues inherently know how vital it is to spread the word and help as many people as possible to discover the miraculous healing benefits of chiropractic, yet for whatever reason under-engage and therefore deliver something less than their best.

It's an empty feeling, a recognition that opportunities have been missed, options left unconverted, money left on the table. Ironically, no one ever needs to feel this way – if you understand the sequence of events leading to commitment.

First, as always, there must be awareness, a sense of the landscape before you. Next comes willingness, an openness to experience what is there. Third, there must be engagement, so you are present and connected to the circumstances and the task at hand. Fourth, passion, desire and energy invested in fanning the flames until they are blazing. Finally, determination, so nothing can stop you from moving toward what you want.

In your practice and your life, you are invited constantly to commit, and when you are able to execute these patterns, it takes you to uncharted territory of happiness and achievement. So why do so few of us commit?

Because it usually involves some degree of sacrifice. Commitment is easy to talk about, not as easy to do. It takes the momentum of starting with awareness, being willing, getting fully engaged, demonstrating the passion and persisting until you get there, in order to overcome the inertia of the status quo.

How can you amplify your level of commitment? Look at the recipe, and notice where you may be falling short. To establish the big frame, connect with your purpose, and think about why it is important to you in the first place.

Then, to get the mechanics in place, you can use some personal growth technology, like a resource builder, belief shift or a reframe of some sort to address the weaker area -- and if you need some support in identifying the desired patterns, breaking down resistance to them and installing them, ask me or your coach to help.

Commitment will help you move toward your vision, based on your purpose. It serves no one for you to play smaller than you really are – raise your standards, dial into your optimal beliefs, and hold yourself on course with the top strategies to accomplish that which you set out to do. It's a formula for success and fulfillment we can all benefit from.

Prosperity Consciousness   July 2009

When things are going well, it's easy to feel prosperous – just look around, everything reminds you of the abundance available to tap into. In times of plenty, prosperity is a default position.

But when belts are tightening and the media offers up an ongoing litany of doom, it's not so easy to maintain your prosperous outlook – yet, this is the time when it's most necessary, and ironically, the time when there is most opportunity, since so many have bought into lack thinking, it makes it possible for someone upbeat to shine and stick out amongst the competition.

Even affluent people can fall into the trap of the poverty complex (I confess that I have), so don't think you're immune because you have a few bucks put away – prosperity consciousness is a habit as much as any other, one that requires consistent implementation to remain in force, and getting into the habit of thinking success is a necessary precondition for creating success. It comes from you, not to you, so if you have not been holding yourself to the highest standard here, let me share a few tips that may streamline your thoughts.

First, honestly assess your current thought process – have you dialed into the dark side, pessimistic and gloomy, or have you taken the responsibility to focus your attention on pure potentiality? In Chopra's "Seven Spiritual Laws of Success," he is careful to start the process with an awareness and acceptance that the potential for creating literally anything you desire already exists without you doing anything.

Built into this notion is a sense of positive expectancy, and you and I cannot afford the luxury of thinking otherwise. Optimism lubricates the system to reduce the friction of temporary setbacks, and helps us to see that there really is no failure except giving up. If you're in the game and taking your best shot, you have a chance to come back and succeed, as so many have before you, but if not, there is no chance

– so, the first order of business is an attitude check, to make sure you believe it's possible to win, and you expect to do so.

Get yourself into an empowered state, with affirmation, visualization, resource building, or some other tool you would use in such circumstances – develop and concentrate on patterns that inspire you on the inside to shift toward prosperity, or to accentuate your abundant feelings. Notice that these feelings may describe the future, not the present, and they are no less potent when they do. At this point, you should be feeling better, having accessed positive resources on this topic.

Now that you're in a more empowered state, write your current beliefs about prosperity, and notice if they are supportive or detrimental to the process of achieving success. If they are constructive, then emphasize them by reading them daily or more frequently, until they feel like a conscious part of you.

If any of the beliefs are limiting, then use some reframing tools to dismantle them and replace them with uplifting ones. These beliefs may be interfering with your ability to see the landscape clearly, and addressing them will make it easier and smoother to move forward.

Using state and belief management techniques is a tried-and-true methodology for changing your internal and external environment. By managing your state and establishing an empowering belief system, you can show up in your practice and your life with a prosperous outlook, and this invariably leads to more prosperous results.

Prosperity consciousness sets the stage for manifesting actual prosperity, in that it triggers the law of attraction and utilizes the vibrational field in a focused, productive fashion – dial in, use the power of plenty, think and act abundantly.

Relationships   August 2009

Your practice, your family, your spirituality, your prosperity – so much of our lives depends on the quality of relationships we develop. Mentors, friends, relatives, patients, team, Winners Circle brothers and sisters -- in so many ways, our happiness and success relies on the type and intensity of relationships we create. Here are some nuts and bolts about forging world class relationships.

There are two factors that go into making a relationship – the ability to generate rapport, and the ability to generate a commonality of values. Let's look at each of these factors and see how we can use them.

Rapport is a feeling of connection, comfort, or liking. It seems like it should be based on emotions, but it really stems from creating a neuro-mechanical connection, where the other person's nerve system detects a familiarity in you, and feels a connection because of it. People who are like each other tend to like each other, and people who are not like each other tend to not like each other – so rapport occurs when there is a perception of "being like someone."

This leads to the skill of matching and mirroring, a method of observing someone's traits and giving them back so there is a feeling of sameness established. Simple as it may seem, this is one of the most powerful things you can do, whether with a new patient, significant other or friend – in fact, you'll notice that the people you already feel comfortable around will tend to "get in sync" with you more easily than those who aren't such a natural fit.

But even for those who don't naturally fall into rhythm with you, you can cause rapport by noticing some of their communications style and returning it – for example, matching their facial expression, posture, pace or common word choice. This leads to a stronger connection, and paves the way for the second critical factor in developing relationships, a commonality of values.

The concept of "values" refers to what's important to someone, in other words, what they "value" – this can be a resource, like honesty, respect, or love, or it can be based on a behavior, like neatness, timeliness, or communication.

It is important to note that it isn't necessary to share the exact same values to make a great relationship – it's somewhat rare to find someone who has all these things in alignment with you. Rather, we need to be aware of and understand someone's values to have a great relationship with them, because you may be called upon to support them, and the evolution of the relationship may depend on that. Obviously, the relationship-mate must be willing to create the same commonality with you, supporting you in achieving what's important to you as well.

So, if you want to enjoy outstanding relationships, focus on these two factors – or, if there's a relationship you'd like to improve, look at these two factors to deduce where the conflict or violation may be. If it's a matter of not having comfort and ease around each other, it's probably a rapport violation. If it's a matter of disagreement over ideas, concepts, and issues, it's probably a values conflict.

If you notice a rapport violation, use your matching and mirroring skills to produce a sense of comfort and familiarity, and it should improve. If you notice a values conflict, identify which values are not being supported, in yourself or the relationship-mate, and examine what has to happen for that support to manifest -- in other words, what do you or they have to do to feel supported in this particular value?

Including such relationship skills in your toolbox can help in every aspect of your life and practice – at least the ones that require other people! Try these techniques out, and see for yourself what breakthroughs you experience!

Personal Power   September 2009

As most of you know, I was in the right place at the right time and caught pretty much the entire ascent of Anthony Robbins, from addressing 40 people at a high school in the Bronx to wowing 3700 Europeans through ten translators in five languages who scrambled to keep up with him at the Fila Forum in Milan, Italy.

Woven throughout all of the Robbins lore is the basic theme that is the topic of this Advanced Citizen – personal power. Rather than being one thing, personal power is a spectrum of attributes that formulate the distinguishing factor between those who accomplish at a high level and those who do not – and ironically, it isn't as much about talent and potential as it is about application and implementation of that talent and potential. Personal power is not about ability, it's about getting things done.

People who demonstrate personal power have a magical x-factor that resonates from deep inside them, and seem to have a "Midas touch" – but they are no more charmed than anyone else, they have just synthesized a winning recipe for success, an ability to access their best at will so they can show up big when they need to.

Everyone has had some experiences like this, where you find yourself in the groove, in the zone, firing on all cylinders – but true personal power is being able to turn it on when the situation calls for it, so it becomes willful instead of just serendipitous.

Developing your personal power is not unlike establishing any other constructive habit – it takes awareness first, so you identify the patterns of physiology and thought that you desire – and then, like any other identity chunk, you have to align the beliefs, values, and personality tendencies so you can get at the potential you have beneath the surface, to get it into play.

When you are at your most effective, most powerful, most productive, what qualities are you applying? Are you focused, disciplined, enthusiastic, passionate, energized? Think of a time when you showed up at your best, a specific time, and consider what was true about you when you were in that place – notice your facial expressions, your posture, your breathing and movement, and identify the mental pictures, sounds and voices, self talk, and feelings or sensations you had. As you access these component parts of your personal power pattern, you'll begin to feel that power swell inside you – notice those sensations too, so you can tell when you're getting closer.

Rate your degree of personal power from just doing this simple exercise, where you start building it as a resource. If you feel you can get to level 8 or better just by doing this, you may not need to dig into your beliefs and values, but if not, look at your beliefs surrounding personal power, and see if you have any limiting factors preventing you from expressing your personal power. Do you believe yourself worthy, capable, and competent? Do you think of yourself as a leader, a motivator, a success? Beliefs like these add to your personal power.

Examine your values – what's in it for you to express your personal power? What does it cost you if you don't? Asking questions like this gains you entry into your inner power centers, so you can apply all you have to work with.

Finally, look at your personality patterns, and see if your tendencies are supportive of demonstrating your personal power – if so, great, but if not, then remember that while the tendency is hard-wired, the behavior itself is always a choice – you can be more confrontational, more decisive, more precise, more creative, just by directing your attention there and choosing that behavior over your typical defaults. That's part of personal power too – resolving to show up a particular way that isn't your normal way, because you can and because the situation calls for it.

Determination, resiliency, strength, presence, willingness, intensity, flexibility and more – personal power takes many shapes, and has many uses, but above all, it lights the way to do as much good as possible, so find your power, put it into action, and do your part to make the world a better place.

Vision   October 2009

Without it, people perish. It is the commodity of kings. It's about skating to where the puck is going to be.

I'm talking, of course, about vision, the ability to imagine or conceptualize the future, based on what you believe the world should look like ideally and how you intend to manifest it in reality.

Ironically, everyone has vision – unfortunately, most people are unconscious to their vision of the future, and therefore their intention doesn't seem to be much different from what's been happening all along. That's why people of vision are at such a premium, and tend to be the movers of society.

Vision is related to purpose and mission -- your vision is what you see in the future, your purpose is why that's important, and your assorted missions produce the pathway to get there.

A vision is like a giant, overriding goal, the consummation of all of your goals, the be-all-end-all final product of all your hopes, wishes, and expectations, all rolled up in a single entity. That's why most people avoid consciously creating and committing to a vision, because the whole concept seems intimidating and overwhelming – unless you realize that it is an essential part of your success and fulfillment to elucidate your vision.

So you can see that formulating your vision can validate your purpose and energize your missions, which makes it worthwhile to crystallize your vision into a vision statement.

Vision statements define ultimate objectives, such as the vision statement of The Masters Circle – "a worldwide quality-of-life driven health care delivery system with chiropractic in the leading role." Notice what goes into this kind of statement

– global consciousness, large scope, singleness of focus, and yet an expansive view-point on that topic that is as close to all-inclusive as possible.

A simple vision for a chiropractor in practice could be... a well world.

In fact, at the Winners Circle Dinner MasterMind in Chicago in July, I challenged the Winners Circle to come up with a vision statement, and it stimulated some excellent discussion, which has manifested so far as follows:

Otto Janke, working with Denise Mathre and Butch Andrion, among others, came up with this model of an ideal Winners Circle member: "A select group of Masters Circle ambassadors who fully embrace the BE-DO-HAVE ideals, who give, love and serve out of abundance, and who continually learn, encourage and promote greatness of themselves, this group, our profession and the world."

Further, they sculpted this vision for the Winners Circle:

To be the shining embodiment of excellence to ourselves, our profession, our clients and the world as a whole; To be ambassadors of the Masters Circle, and to advance their missions in a strong and loving manner; To drive our profession to be the beacon of health and wellness throughout the world.

Which was then refined by Denise to read:

To be recognized worldwide as wellness chiropractic leaders driving the chiropractic profession to the forefront of true health care.

This is still clearly a work in progress – it took me many years to shape my current vision, purpose and mission statements, and each refinement took me a little closer to the clarity and certainty I prefer. We'll keep working on this together – get with your fellow WC members, and voice your ideas!

Gratitude   November 2009

It seems a little absurd that we have to have a special holiday designated as the time to feel gratitude – if you've been paying any attention whatsoever, you probably realize that the gift of life, the opportunity to serve, the incredible opportunities provided for us and the awesome magnitude of the resources we have available, are a constant reminder of all we have to be thankful for.

Yet most of us still fall into the trap of lack, lusting after what we don't have at the expense of appreciating what we do have.

So let's take stock of our abundance, and decide once and for all if we do or do not live in a friendly universe.

If you've ever had a bully hold you under water until you fought your way to the surface, gasping for breath, you know the sweetness and salvation of air itself. While we may take it for granted, we have air to breathe, to metabolize, and to thrive.

If you've ever visited an impoverished place, you saw how so many people live below the poverty line, unable to afford even the most basic human needs, and you realize how fortunate you are to be able to eat every day, usually several times, and clean, healthy foods are always available for you to nourish yourself effectively.

If you've ever encountered a society that isn't based on freedom, you saw how people's will is beaten down, and you can never again take for granted the opportunity that is built into our culture, making it possible for you to choose work you enjoy, select the spouse and friends you prefer, and spend your time doing what you want to do, even if you opt to do nothing at all.

And, most of us having been brought up in a culture that teaches us that you go to the doctor when you're sick and someone else pays for it, we may well get to be the messengers of the new wellness paradigm that will revolutionize the way people perceive their health and usher in an era of better lifestyle decisions and a richer existence, something to be truly grateful for.

Would you put your card back in the deck and pick another? We are truly blessed, and to ignore that perspective flies in the face of our real existence. We have every chance to succeed, every advantage to be comfortable, and every opportunity to share what we have so everyone benefits – and so, it seems to be a friendly universe after all. We just need to be awake to it, and remain present with it, not just at Thanksgiving time, but always.

We are fortunate, and should never take for granted the sacred trust we have in our hands, and the impact we can have on the future of health and wellness. Being a

Winners Circle member means you are sensitive to the need for leadership and advanced citizenry, and that you care enough to learn and grow so you can participate in your own special way. And that is yet another reason to be grateful.

Please don't mistake gratitude for complacency. One of my favorite quotes from Bob is "Always grateful, never satisfied." Appreciate what you have at present, but also stay conscious of the prospect of accomplishing even more, to make it even better and do even more good. The cycle continues, as we do good and experience good, and so on, the circle of life.

Connect with your feelings of gratitude each day – simply ask yourself, who and what am I grateful for, and you'll be delighted with the pleasurable sensations that come up for you, and the incentive to do more good for those you touch and serve. Try it and see!

Identity   December 2009

What better place to end this first full year of writing the Advanced Citizen than by dancing with the girl that brung me – mysterious and meaningful, confounding and revealing, the basis of everything we do, since it makes us who we perceive ourselves to be – of course I'm talking about identity.

The elusive concept of identity permeates everything that happens by, to and for anyone. Who we are is the primary filter through which we experience our reality – and if you've ever heard several accounts of the same occurrence, you know how varied and distorted those filters can be.

That's why we intend to expose Winners Circle members to examples of outstanding people, so you can draw upon their influence to create more impact and reap the appropriate rewards.

For example, those in attendance at our wonderful Louisville Winners Circle Weekend this month were treated not only to the delightful atmosphere in the 21C and all the cool events we participated in, but also the extraordinary privilege to spend the day with Gerry Clum and gather his perspectives on life and leadership.

Gerry's presentation on the Five Levels of Leadership, derived from the work on "Tribal Leadership" from David Logan, illustrated the importance of leading from the foundation of the correct sense of self. Level One leaders cannot lead at all, coming from an entirely negative reality, believing "life sucks." Level Two leaders feel defeated and are suffering, but they see that others could lead and succeed, thinking "my life sucks." Level Three leaders are starting to feel a better sense of self, expressing that "my life's great and yours sucks," a win-lose way of leadership. Level Four Leaders can not only feel successful and prosperous, but can see others being that way too without threat or insecurity, recognizing that "our lives are great." Finally, the Level Five leader believes "life's great," seeing the interconnectedness of all things and responding to the perfection of it, leading by wisdom and inspiration with effortless ease.

The most fascinating and illuminating distinction Gerry made was that people can only move one level at a time, which explains why so many of our patients, who come in at Level Two, in pain and wrapped up in it, have trouble hearing and understanding our Level Four and Five communication. We must learn to lead from the best perspective for the patient, and to do so we must develop the identity that allows us such flexibility and willingness to adapt to the situation in the patient's best interest.

You can use the tools of Capacity Technology™ to calibrate and refine your identity. Evaluate your capacity limitations, by procedure (DO) and by concept and vision (BE) and notice the patterns of the data you collect. Do you need to add hands, days, hours, speed, or systems? Are you bringing the right attitude and energy to what you're doing?

Are you using affirmation, visualization, goal-setting, and resource building to show up your best each day? Are you monitoring and refining your beliefs and values, checking for congruency with your organizing principles and your personality, and developing habits of excellence on the substructure comprised of those foundational elements?

These are the raw materials of your identity – resources, beliefs, values, and personality tendencies. These ideas form the framework of your sense of self, but you can cause yourself to opt in favor of any behavior you choose, no matter what hard-wiring you happen to have. By applying the optimal habits of excellence with the optimal attitude and energy, you can break free of any previous programming and emerge as the kind of leader, professional and person you want to be.

That's one reason Bob and I were so thrilled with the way you showed up in Louisville – veterans and new members alike, you held yourself to high standards of performance and exemplified the character we look for in putting this tribe together. Thank you for validating our efforts with your excellence. And keep working on yourself, it's a gift you give yourself that keeps on giving.

Enjoy the holiday season, and let's look forward to a happy, healthy and prosperous 2010!

Honoring Your Standards   January 2010

As I get older, and maybe a little wiser, I come to grips with some of the key distinctions that separate those who are truly happy and fulfilled. It's not as complicated as it sometimes seems, but there is an inner force that appears to make a huge difference in people's level of happiness.

Sad to say, talk is cheap, and so many of us, with the best of intentions, end up somehow falling short of what we aim at. It's not a lack of talent, nor a lack of desire – what it really boils down to is that most of us, when faced with the real decision times, when the rubber meets the road, just don't hold ourselves to the standards we set. Honoring your standards is a simple but often overlooked key to ultra-accomplishment.

Congruency, accountability, responsibility, willingness, consistency, passion – they're all part of the process of honoring your standards. By exploring which commitments you've made that you're not really committed to, you can learn your patterns of avoidance and your personal technology of excuse-making, and while it may be painfully revealing at times, this kind of introspection bears fruit almost immediately.

Like finding the subluxation and correcting it, there is a release and a rapid return to normal function – in this case, the normalcy of your chosen behavior.

Select an area in which you have a strong desire to succeed, but have not yet accomplished the result you prefer. Look inside and be honest with yourself, where are the places in the process of achievement that you have ignored, deleted, distorted, or otherwise performed less than your capability and expectation? It is in this evaluation process that you uncover the patterns that will lead to fulfillment.

Make a list of the standards you have not yet honored. Are you sloppy with your belongings, unreliable with your time management, lazy in your exercise or energy management, inconsistent with your diet, behind on your paperwork, unimaginative in your marketing and promotion, incongruent in your leadership, or is it something else you have up until now refused to consider?

This is hard, I know – but being part of the Winners Circle means you are willing to look deeper, test yourself with greater challenges, and emerge on the other side performing closer to your ideal. Remember, Capacity Technology, unlike many "feel-good" success methodologies, requires that you ferret out and respond to weaker areas you detect – and not looking for them is really not acceptable, if you are serious about your own growth and success.

Sometimes it's constructive to be bold enough to include someone else in this process, since often we have a scotoma, or blind spot, when it comes to some of these distinctions – trust one of your Winners Circle brothers or sisters enough to mastermind on some of these deep thoughts. You will be astounded how productive it can be to discover even one place you have not yet honored your standards.

Communication   February 2010

Red Motley said "Nothing happens until somebody sells something" – as a publisher and success philosopher, that was the filter he saw his world through – but for our purposes, it can be re-tooled as "Nothing happens until somebody communicates something" – and then, it takes on new meaning for us as chiropractors.

You see, there isn't a single individual in your sphere of influence who wouldn't want what a chiropractor has to offer – they just don't make the connection between glowing health and vitality and chiropractic services, and until they do, we'll be frustrated in our efforts to make the world a healthier place. And that's where communication comes in.

Dictionary.com defines communication as the imparting or interchange of thoughts, opinions, or information by speech, writing, or signs – but it goes on to say that communication in biology is "activity by one organism that changes or has the potential to change the behavior of other organisms," so let's stay on this point for a moment, since we are biological organisms, subject to natural law.

Communication presupposes making a connection with someone to generate influence – to change or potentially change the behavior of another. That sounds like the seeds of leadership, and that's why refining and mastering your communication is a foundational cornerstone of your success.

I learned from Anthony Robbins that communication is 7% words, 38% tonality, and 55% physiology. This breakdown came from an obscure !1970's study at UCLA, but I can tell you that my experience pretty much supports this ratio. Yes, you have to choose good words, and yes, you have to say them with a suitable tonality – but your physiology, closely linked to your perceived congruency, plays the major role. That's why so many successful people may not always be able to articulate elegantly, but can get their point across with their personal power.

To evaluate your communication skill, you can recognize, as students of neuro-linguistic programming are taught, that the meaning of your communication is the response you get. It's not what you thought you said or meant to say, it's what the other person gets that counts. So, learning to calibrate the responses of the person or people whom you're trying to influence can make the difference between communicating and simply speaking – the latter is just organized noise, the former is the way to make the world a better place.

Get feedback from your Winners Circle colleagues and mentors about your communication – any effort you direct toward improving it, especially if it's a weaker area for you, will make a huge difference in your degree of happiness,

success and fulfillment, and increase your impact on those you touch and serve.

This is one of the ways you develop and demonstrate your advanced citizenry and leadership, for the betterment of all.

Risk   March 2010

Those of us who have had experience of putting it all on the line recognize that playing it safe rarely gets us to the levels of accomplishment and fulfillment that we desire – there's always some element of risk involved, and if you understand how to measure and respond to the risks you see before you, you can make more progress more rapidly and with less stress and distraction.

The definition of risk is "exposure to the chance of injury, loss, hazard or danger," and most of us focus too much on the possibility of loss than on the rewards to be gained from being willing to intelligently put ourselves in harm's way. Most often, the return can be calibrated in advance, and the degree of risk measured against that to see if it's worth it to take the shot in the first place. It only makes sense to risk if there's a good likelihood of seeing the investment come to fruition in some worthwhile way, and the downside is not overly devastating.

So this works both ways – first, to be willing to risk enough to gather the benefits you desire – and second, to be wise enough not to risk unnecessarily if the consequences outweigh the optimal results.

The way we perceive risk can be personality-related, for example, Sevens love the thrill of risk, while Sixes shun it (if this number terminology is new to you, see "The Enneagram" November 2014) -- or, it can be experience-related (fool me once, shame on you, fool me twice, shame on me) – and, it can be a barometer of growth, since those willing to evaluate and act on opportunities with the most appropriate risk tolerance are those who will move along the path of success and fulfillment at the swiftest possible rate.

Take a moment to check yourself in this critical area – what is your nature, your typical default position? How risk averse are you most of the time, and what are the conditions that make you more willing to endure risk? How often do you find yourself at the edge, wondering what will happen next? There are no correct or incorrect responses to these questions – it's only a reality check, so you can know yourself that much better.

I thought it would be fun to see how the various enneagram types might deal with risk:

Type One – *"Nothing will ever be attempted, if all possible objections must be first overcome." -- Samuel Johnson, Rasselas, 1759*

"There are those who are so scrupulously afraid of doing wrong that they seldom venture to do anything." -- Vauvenargues

Type Two – *"Today the man who is the real risk-taker is anonymous and nonheroic. He is the one trying to make institutions work." -- John William Ward*

Type Three – *"Only those who dare to fail greatly can ever achieve greatly." -- Robert F. Kennedy*

Type Four – *"I dip my pen in the blackest ink, because I'm not afraid of falling into my inkpot." -- Ralph Waldo Emerson*

Type Five – *"Do not be too timid and squeamish about your actions. All life is an experiment. The more experiments you make the better. What if they are a little coarse and you may get your coat soiled or torn? What if you do fail, and get fairly rolled in the dirt once or twice? Up again, you shall never be so afraid of a tumble." -- Ralph Waldo Emerson*

Type Six – *"A ship in harbor is safe - but that is not what ships are for." -- John A. Shedd, Salt from My Attic*

Type Seven – *"The healthy being craves an occasional wildness, a jolt from normality, a sharpening of the edge of appetite, his own little festival of the Saturnalia, a brief excursion from his way of life." -- Robert MacIver*

"It is only in adventure that some people succeed in knowing themselves - in finding themselves." -- André Gide

Type Eight – *"You'll always miss 100% of the shots you don't take." -- Wayne Gretzky*

Type Nine – "*The knowledge of the world is only to be acquired in the world, and not in a closet.*" *-- Lord Philip Dormer Stanhope Chesterfield*

Shut Up and Speed Up   April 2010

A day doesn't go by that Alan Rousso doesn't come into my office from next door to make some reference to how he has helped one member or another transform his or her practice by insisting that the doctor shut up and speed up.

"I tell them, if you're stuck seeing 4-6 an hour, you can't grow. Then, I tell them if you're stuck seeing 8-10 an hour, you can't grow. Shut up and speed up!"

Ah, that Dr. Rousso, he has a way about him. Through the brusque countenance, he cares deeply about our members and about chiropractic, and you know what? He's right.

Alan has had extraordinary results helping members grow their practices, and one of the critical keys he has been concentrating on is better use of the appointment book and less use of the vocal cords.

We tend to talk way too much, in the guise of patient education sometimes, but if you were to record and listen back to a typical busy hour you'd quickly see if he is right in your case or not. That kind of self-evaluation takes major guts, but if you are willing to do it, you will learn a lot about leadership, or at times, how you may be leading people in the wrong direction, or not leading them at all, without realizing it.

If your conversation is unfocused, or focused on the wrong subject matter, you'll be able to tell at the first objective listening. It doesn't make you a bad person, a bad chiropractor, or even a bad leader – it means you developed some bad habits, and habits can be changed to better suit your circumstances and conditions. But as you know, awareness is the first key, so take note and get a sense of how you usually use that time with a typical patient. The reality check is the first step – what are you actually saying?

There are two possible forms of inefficient behavior here – the first is talking about irrelevant subject matter, and the second is taking too long to say something that is relevant but overstated, fluffy or vague.

One way to stay focused on relevant subject matter is to plan your table talk in advance, like with a Chiropractic Patient Curriculum (CPC) or a thought of the day, remaining flexible enough to shift gears if the patient's situation warrants it. Most often, you can use the time to educate efficiently, and save back time to invest in other patients' care.

You can get quicker and more on point with your table talk by planning scripts that cover the material the way you want to, in a succinct, concise and easily understood manner. A little pre-planning will help, but just being present enough to realize when you're blabbing will make a significant difference.

When I engage people in conversation, generally I connect with them as if they were the only person in the world, and give them my full attention. To me, it's a matter of respect to do so – if you are important enough for me to share time with at all, you are worthy of me fully engaging – and it's the same thing with patients.

Patients don't need a lot of your time – they need to know that the time you are with them, they matter to you, and that you are concentrating on helping them. They don't need a lot of justification, or a lot of small talk, mostly – they just need to know you care, and you can show them that in a few seconds.

Think about the Rousso formula, and decide if you can streamline your patient interactions without compromising the quality of the experience – it's a major key to growth. Say what needs to be said and nothing more, and move with briskness, purpose and passion, not anxiety and rushing, and your patients will feel well-cared-for, and your practice will grow in response.

The Power of Full Engagement   May 2010

Several years ago, I became aware of a book called "The Power Of Full Engagement" by Jim Loehr and Tony Schwartz. It made two very important points, which I will share with you here now, and then I will comment on how I believe we can all take our game to a new level by applying these two ideas.

First is the concept of engage-disengage – in other words, if you are constantly fully engaged, then it becomes stressful – there must be some disengagement time to allow for recovery, rejuvenation, developing perspective, and a return to full engagement with fresh enthusiasm and potential.

Second are the four areas in which we tend to engage and disengage – physical, mental, emotional and spiritual.

The authors are careful to point out that there is a cultural hypnosis in our society that tends to direct us to over-engage mentally and emotionally and to under-engage physically and spiritually.

You can see how these patterns could create an inappropriate lack of balance – here's how to troubleshoot your degree of engagement to be sure you are getting the most out of yourself without jeopardizing your best interests by pushing too hard or too long.

Give yourself a quick evaluation in each of the four areas, as a general scan of your sense of engagement in each. Remember, you may be in a recovery phase with one or more, so this is not meant to be an indictment, but rather a reality check. If you find yourself getting low scores in three or four, that would be a clue. Notice how you can tell if you are engaged or not, those are also clues about how you can keep yourself focused in the places that will serve you best.

If you find that you are under-engaged physically, plan a new routine that emphasizes movement, breathing, yoga, walking, or some other physical activity that you find beneficial. If you are under-engaged mentally, consider sharpening up by reading, masterminding, writing or solving puzzles. If you are under-engaged emotionally, look for opportunities to flex your emotional muscles, through relationship, family, or emotional experiences like movies, novels, volunteering or traveling. If you are under-engaged spiritually, practice your own form of connection with the higher powers, based on your interpretation and experiences, perhaps through meditation, prayer, seeking spiritual guidance or some other form of self-awareness.

If you are over-engaged physically, meaning that your physical self takes more energy than would lead to a proper balance, then moderate your activities accordingly. If you are over-engaged mentally, take a breather on pounding in the information and allow yourself the latitude to coast a little, looking for places to fruitfully apply what you already know. If you are over-engaged emotionally, then chill out, back off, don't take it all quite so seriously, laugh more and see the cosmic joke, even when it doesn't seem so funny. And if there's such a thing as being over-engaged spiritually, it may mean that there's an avoidance of engaging in the other ways to create that proper balance – don't pass your responsibilities along to your Maker, accept those that are yours and act on them consistently, lovingly, and congruently.

Finding the right blend of stress and recovery, engaging and disengaging effectively in these four areas, is one of the secrets to being a great leader – most people have not achieved such a balance, and they can use your example as a model of excellence, so you are not only dealing with your own adversities, but inspiring others to do the same.

Measurement   June 2010

Among the many lofty sentiments that are expressed on these pages, there is occasionally cause for bringing it in for a landing, so we can touch base with some of the basic building blocks of success, leadership and advanced citizenry. For that reason, I direct my attention this month to the concept of… measurement.

Doesn't sound very glamorous, I know, but hidden within this idea is a seed of greatness many overlook. Socrates said, "An unexamined life is not worth living," which means to me that we must notice, calibrate, and respond to the inputs in our lives – we must stay conscious, present and aware, and be willing to evaluate and compare what we experience, to make distinctions that will carry us further toward our objectives.

Goal-setting depends on measurement – so does wealth accumulation. Those are obvious places where being able to quantify your experience adds to it. But there are more esoteric forms of measurement, known as "rules" which are actually beliefs about something's relative value or worth, and this type of measurement is no less important to your ultimate satisfaction.

Rules are your personal measurements for when to feel pleasure and when to feel pain – they may be sensible or arbitrary, extreme or modest, and are highly individualized. My wife hates mushrooms, I love 'em, go figure – mushrooms are neither good nor bad in and of themselves, but our interpretation sets our rules structure. Shakespeare wrote, "There is nothing either good or bad, but thinking makes it so."

That's the way it is with rules, they guide us toward habits and behaviors, and if we choose them wisely, we can keep our standards high and our results optimal. They can trap us, though, if we're not careful – if, for example, we believe that earning $20,000 per month is a good income, but $30,000 is over our heads, then we will find a way to $20,000, even if we have the talent and ability to earn more. The rule that says "30K is more than I deserve" uses measurement to prevent achievement, and this is where we have to be astute and watch for measurements that don't serve us.

Micromanagement is another example of where measurement can interfere with our success. Measuring too intensely, too minutely, or too often can waste time and energy, even take you out of present time consciousness, like checking your gas gauge on your car every three miles, or looking in the rear view mirror every two seconds. The same goes for looking over your team's shoulder constantly – it reeks of distrust, and stops the energy flow at the front desk when your assistant is guarding against distraction and invasion.

But proper measurement is a tremendous asset, giving you feedback that helps you make good decisions. Some examples of places where good measurement makes a difference – driving, establishing your spending plan (some call it a budget), designing your Financial Master Plan, building a Resource Builder, delivering your Report of Findings, renovating your office, choosing the right automobile, choosing the right relationships, juggling, or portrait painting.

Finally, let me share this fascinating quote from scientist Enrico Fermi, commenting on his research:

"There are two possible outcomes: if the result confirms the hypothesis, then you've made a measurement. If the result is contrary to the hypothesis, then you've made a discovery."

By being willing to analyze what you have done and what you are doing, you gather distinctions that guide you to know what you should do next. Measurement is an often overlooked tool that can lead to the best applications of your inner greatness, and manifest as your best success and your finest hours.

Courage   July 2010

Our 2010 Winners Circle Weekend was as fun as it was transformational – we broke through to new levels of personal power by holding ourselves to a high standard on the Adirondack Extreme Adventure Training, an innovative and thrilling ropes course in the beautiful woods near Lake George, NY.

If you think it's easy to harness up, clip yourself to the apparatus and go for it, think again – it's not a typical set of sensations, yet it mirrors the way we show up in our practices and our lives when we get under stress – and that's where it's critical to develop courage.

Courage is nothing more than the willingness to face fear and do what needs to be done anyway. I can make an argument that it is courageous to show up at your office, given the many things that can happen – but when faced with a challenge like balancing on an unstable rope bridge fifty feet in the air, your need for courage is brought to the forefront.

Personality types shone through everywhere I looked – the Sevens and Threes insisted on going all the way to the end, the Sixes were apprehensive, the Nines went with the flow until they hit their avoidance thresholds – events like this are a human laboratory, both observing those around you from the inside out, and also noticing what goes on inside you when you're in the moment. These distinctions are invaluable for preparing for the adversities that manifest throughout each day, which while not usually as intense, are certainly reminiscent. After all, once you've clung to a log in mid-air, how difficult is it to ask a patient to bring her kids in for a check-up?

I thought the Beyond Technique presentation was rich also – breathing techniques (lift your clavicles), postural tips like pressing with the top of your foot instead of the bottom, buffing your nails and putting the energy into your food, squeezing a towel to strengthen your hands, smiling to your organs, lots of take home pointers we can use immediately in practice, whether we master the martial arts aspects or not.

Once again courage is needed to address your own responsibility to keep upgrading your technical approach – it gets comfortable to adjust patients the way you've always done it, yet adding to your armamentarium not only gives you more ideas on how to help those already under your care, it attracts others who are in need of such new and different methods. Expanding your clinical expertise takes a willingness to be "not you" temporarily, and you'll need to be brave enough to dare to adjust people using other tools and technology if you are ever to break free of the status quo.

Look for places to apply what you learned – and please tap into your Winners Circle brothers and sisters and use them as resources, not only to debrief the weekend, but to act as sounding boards, mastermind partners, and friends. We're all in this together!

Family   August 2010

I just got the happiest email from our dear friend and longtime member Kurt Price, recently returned after a short hiatus – Kurt exemplifies everything we look for in a Winners Circle member and Chiropractor of the Year – loving, ethical, driven to do the right thing, willing to roll up his sleeves and get his hands dirty, respectful to everyone he encounters, tremendous capacity, highly attractive, I can't say enough nice things about this outstanding young man.

It seems that he and his lovely wife Angela are expecting their second child, and it made me reflect on how happy I am with this particular incarnation of the Winners Circle – you are creating something truly magnificent, of which you can be immensely proud, and not the least reason for this delicious, stimulating and satisfying energy field is because of the family feel that is developing. I know how thrilled I am and you will all be for Kurt – Stacey Marshall and her wonderful husband Chris, and Heath McKinley and his delightful wife Monica are also expecting, not to mention secret prego Miriam Leean (she said it was okay to tell) – Anton Stas just had a new addition, and most of us are in varying stages of parenthood, even those who have furry kids.

Family does not only mean mommies and daddies and children – family is a concept that transcends friendship to demonstrate a different kind of love – stronger, more concentrated, more unbreakable, even more beautiful. And, it's not limited to people who are technically blood relatives – most of us have had some non-related individual who is as close as family to us, often referred to as "Uncle This" or "Auntie That." We do that out of love and respect, and it means so much to us to have that kind of connection with someone.

That's what I see developing in the Winners Circle. There is a feeling, a bond being created out of love and shared purpose, a kinship based on advanced citizenry and an authentic commitment to things natural and to spreading the word. It is elegant in its simplicity and magnificent in its scope, and is destined to provide guidance for a sick and suffering humanity that longs for a glimpse of what we already own.

We have a responsibility to alert people to the possibilities, and I see clearly how Winners Circle members are accepting that role and shouldering the massive burden of shifting the world toward a paradigm of wellness instead of emergency crisis intervention. Every one of us is making a difference, and every one of us should be proud of our accomplishments and more determined than ever to take it to the next level – not only for us, but for future chiropractors and future generations of citizens whose lives will be better because of what we do today.

That's why we do what we do for our immediate family, for our extended family at The Winners Circle, for our more extended family at The Masters Circle, into our communities and beyond, as a part of the family of humankind. We matter, and that importance is not ego, it's accepting that we are all connected, all part of the same stuff, and when anyone suffers, we all suffer, and likewise, when any of us breaks through to a new level of understanding and love, we all benefit.

Let's keep that in mind when we make our decisions and choices – every one of us counts. We are family.

Willingness   September 2010

There isn't one of us who couldn't improve, not just in one or two areas, but across the board. As humans, we are blessed with a near-infinite potential, limited only by our ability to uncover it and apply it. Most of us have an intuitive sense of this, even get to glimpse it periodically in flashes of brilliance when we are functioning at our best.

That's why we study capacity technology – the more of our potential we gain access to, the better we perform and the more quality of life we experience. Discovering and exploiting your optimal resources to best advantage are necessary preconditions for success and fulfillment.

Why don't we spend more of our time in this peak state of excellence? Some of it is habit, where we acclimate to our own version of "average" which may vary from mediocrity to pretty good performance at times, and some of us even manage to show up excellent for a measurable portion of our time. But there is a subtle key to exposing more of your greatness, and implementing this small distinction can be a game changer for those on the path to mastery.

I'm talking about willingness – see, even after I share it with you, it doesn't seem very impressive – yet learning to be willing can be an open door into everything you hope for and dream of. In "The Ultimate Secret To Getting Absolutely Everything You Want" author Mike Hernacki says, "Real people, with standard human weaknesses and frailties, use this key – willingness – to accomplish real actual miracles. You can too."

There's more to it than meets the eye. For example, to hit your target weight, or set a new record for office visit volume, or to encounter your soul mate, you'd generally need to be willing to do certain things – eat better and exercise more, confront new patient opportunities more effectively, or find the guts to introduce yourself to that very attractive person.

But willingness goes deeper than these superficial "do" steps – there has to be an inner willingness to develop good feelings about yourself, to raise your standards, to catch yourself in unfavorable patterns of behavior and shift them in a constructive direction, and to commit to following through on what you decide upon. This internal processing is a secret advantage big winners utilize to outperform their previous best.

This brand of willingness is driven by purpose and fueled by passion – it is a manifestation of seeing the landscape clearly, and evaluating what is required to take the next steps. It is usually not the most convenient decision, nor is it the easiest to convert on. But the difference that makes the difference is often a simple resolve to show up a certain way and act consistently with that worldview.

Where have you been unwilling to confront something important to your ultimate progress? What habit have you been unwilling to break or develop? What challenge have you been unwilling to address? What significant goal have you been unwilling to plan for and take action on?

The patterns of your own willingness can be revealing, and help you trace weaker areas you may not have been aware of. This kind of introspection and self-assessment is not for the faint of heart, but it can be transformational for those who refuse to settle for less than their very best. And ironically, it takes willingness even to address such issues – find your way there, or get some coaching to overcome your resistance, and you'll be delighted with the results you can manifest.

Thinking Big   October 2010

Being certain about your vision, mission and purpose brings clarity and intensity to your life and practice. The willingness to act consistently with these high standards and values is not only the mark of the winner, it's what all winning is made of, short of some serendipitous occurrences that we cannot control and will never understand. We all need to stop waiting for Santa Claus to come with a sack of goodies, roll up our sleeves and set about to the task of saving the citizens of our world from the fate of things unnatural.

You probably already know that the vision of The Masters Circle is a worldwide quality-of-life-driven health care delivery system with chiropractic in the leading role. Our purpose, the reason this is important to us, is that we intend to achieve happiness, success and fulfillment, through personal growth and professional excellence, and to lead as many people as possible toward this outcome. Our mission is to help as many chiropractors as possible to build great practices and great lifestyles, based on this vision and purpose.

You, beloved Winners Circle members, are the best examples we have of our work along these lines. You are the future (and some present) leaders, you are the role models that inspire the profession, you are the real deal. And so, I acknowledge you, and I share with you that we all have to think bigger in order to reach the mountaintop we aim for.

You can help us reach more of our colleagues with the message you all apparently relate to, since you have chosen to be Winners Circle members. You were invited because of your character, and you joined because you felt something that meant something to you. You have no idea how much that means to Bob and me, how it supports our aspiration to create as many masters as possible to influence the wellness of our planet. Thank you, and please know that we honor you for being so courageous and progressive in your thinking and behavior.

Now, we believe it's time to step up, time for us to step up, and time for you to step up. Our intention is to double the impact of The Masters Circle over the next year, and to double it again the next year. Playing small is exhausting, it's frustrating, it's painful, and it doesn't work, except to keep us playing small.

We hope you see the vision – building a well world The Masters Circle Way, with chiropractors experiencing happiness, success and fulfillment by building great practices and great lives. It's so compelling, we can't sleep at night, and we hope you feel as passionate about it as we do.

Please join us on this quest – bring your friends, and make a difference that goes beyond your four walls.

Expectation Management   November 2010

I have learned a lot from Bob in the ten years we've worked side by side, but no idea he has shared with me is more important and practical than the concept of expectation management. Sometimes called "preframing" in NLP circles, expectation management is a way to foreshadow and encourage what you hope will happen, so you can communicate effectively with your sphere of influence and guide them toward decisions that are in the best interest of all concerned.

I have made some efforts to provide input to this effect, some more successful than others, and that is why I appeal to you to give me some feedback about a few areas in which I have recently reached out to you, beloved Winners Circle members.

Too many of you could not attend the marvelous transformational weekend we enjoyed at The Sagamore, so I asked if you would give me some guidance about which weekends would not work for you – to date I have heard from six of you, and I am faced with making the decision on when we will gather in 2011 with only that information to go on.

I don't want to scold you, you know I adore you, so I hope you hear this as expectation management – I need you to be responsive and timely to my communications, even if it's to tell me you don't agree with what I'm saying or doing. That feedback helps me know what you are thinking and feeling and how I can serve you better, which is the driving force of this discussion. As I'm sure you already know, I want to create superior coaching in leadership and advanced citizenry, and a transformational weekend (or two, if enough people commit to them) and I cannot get that process underway unless I know who is in, who wants to support our future by making a referral, and who can't make which weekends so I don't plan something you want to attend but cannot.

I know from all my experiences that the meaning of my communication is the response I get, and that brings up an important aspect of all communication and expectation management – clarity. To be truly clear is not to think you are clear or to mean to be clear, it's based on the communication being received clearly.

Each of us has a responsibility to lead, to express ourselves and to promote our services with the utmost clarity, if we are to expect those within our reach to respond as desired.

There are two vital parts to this process, first, to have certainty about the actual message we intend to deliver, and second, to deliver it in a language and with an inflection that works for the target audience. So while I have certainty about my message to you, if I have fallen short in communicating it effectively to you, please let me know so I can adjust my approach. If not, then please get on the stick and tell me what works for you, so I can serve you well. Thanks!

Winners Circle Identity

Several months back, Denise Mathre spearheaded a project to define a Winners Circle Identity, Vision and Mission – here are the current statements, for you to consider, accept if they resonate with you and contribute to writing and rewriting if you feel they need some tweaking or even reinvention. Please spend a few moments as 2010 draws to a close to reconnect with your reasons for being in The Winners Circle, and what you plan on bringing to the table for the coming year.

Winners Circle Identity -- "A select group of Masters Circle ambassadors who fully embrace the BE-DO-HAVE ideals, who give, love and serve out of abundance, and who continually learn, encourage and promote greatness of themselves, this group, our profession and the world."

Winners Circle Vision – "To be the shining embodiment of excellence to ourselves, our profession, our clients and the world."

Winners Circle Mission – "To be ambassadors of the Masters Circle, and to advance their missions in a strong and loving manner, to drive our profession to be the beacon of health and wellness throughout the world."

You may also want to work on a Statement of Purpose, which would define why this identity, vision and mission are important to you. What values are met by being part of the Winners Circle? What benefits do you get out of your membership? What consequences do you avoid by participating? What opportunities are provided for you? What pleasures or pains do you experience or avoid? Narrow down what you get, as it will help you write a meaningful statement of purpose. It's a subtle but potent form of expectation management none of us should look past.

Self-Discipline   December 2010

A tumultuous year draws to a close, and there are many lessons and opportunities built into our experiences in 2010. To look back and see only the pleasure or only the pain would be incomplete and inaccurate – everything that goes into a year is significant in its own way, and astute observers recognize the seeds of greatness that manifest along the path, even in the unpleasant and uncomfortable stuff.

Noticing trends and patterns lights the way for us to support our highest values, and the resources that are required for following through are mostly simple and many obvious – yet one of the greatest challenges each of us faces is the willingness to hold ourselves to the appropriate standard, and that requires... self discipline.

Ouch. While it's easy to make a case that such personal integrity and accountability are necessary, it places the onus of responsibility squarely on our own shoulders, to envision, respond, perform and adjust until we are standing with our feet firmly planted in the topsoil of success, our roots deeply engaged with our intentions, and our gaze affixed on the next objective.

Developing self-discipline can be as simple as a decision (I declare that I am a non-smoker) or a reframe (Exercise is like any other habit, it just takes the guts to begin and the will to keep going), but at times we may find ourselves acting out against authority, restriction or perceived unfairness, and as such may require a bit more understanding and leverage to transcend the issue. Such secondary gain is often the reason why our best efforts may fall short at times, because we get stuck in the trap of self-sabotage, and only understand why after we are willing to explore the underpinnings.

Your personal code of conduct will provide powerful leverage that will help you stay on point, and a quick review will give you incentive to keep yourself focused on your desired behaviors. What do you get out of being neat or timely, for example? What does it cost you when you're not?

Learn yourself thoroughly -- your resources, your beliefs, your values, your personality type, and any other qualities or characteristics that may add to the leverage of developing self-discipline. It will keep you on target when nothing else will suffice. Settle for nothing less than the highest degree of execution in this area, and you'll be that much closer to creating the life and practice you really want.

Community   January 2011

I wonder if you realize just how important you are to me, beloved Winners Circle members. Witnessing your blossoming leadership and your outstanding demonstrations of integrity, compassion, creativity and commitment is one of the great joys of my life. Saying I love you is an understatement – I adore you, I honor you, I consider it one of my great privileges to serve you, and I am grateful every day for that opportunity.

Within our tribe, you are the elders who have stepped forward to engage more fully, to explore perspectives and share experiences with other leaders. I see daily evidence of your growth, and cherish the time we spend together. For those I know intimately already, I delight in the subtleties of our relationship. For those I am just getting to know, I open my arms in welcome and invite you to feed on everything I have, for it is my pleasure to be there for you in every way I can.

As a leader of such leaders, I confess that I am highly imperfect, with strengths and weaker areas, like most of us. Yet my respect for you is perfect, as is my appreciation for the chance to know you and help to guide you. You continue to amaze me with your willingness to raise your standards, and your determination to make things better.

Ours is a community unlike most, in that our common bond is health, wellness, and making the world a better place. Lofty as it may seem, it is a chain of love that holds us together, love for each other and love for the vision of a truly well world.

Thank you for being so good to each other, and please keep finding new ways to support each other. You are just realizing your power, and you have so much to offer – the connection between you is growing, and you will be powerful resources for each other going forward. That is the potency and the poetry of community at its best.

The Winners Circle on Facebook

Today's communicators use the social networking platforms as convenient and effective vehicles, and the 800 pound gorilla is Facebook, with over half a billion friends sharing everything from likes and dislikes to philosophy, from cool videos to inspiring quotations.

I am so excited to see that the Winners Circle group is developing – please encourage each other and communicate! It doesn't have to be a full time job like for some, but the chance to share thoughts and pool resources in very timely and worthwhile.

Here are some of the recent entries posted by Denise Mathre, who did the preliminary legwork to launch the page:

"Let your brilliance shine into the world and inspire all who witness you to do the same!"
-unknown

It's not what so called success you achieve that truly matters, it's what you become that does." -- A. Drayton Boylston

"If you're talking with your head, you're going to speak to their heads. If you're talking with your heart, you're going to reach their hearts. If you talk with your life, you're going to reach their lives." -- Italo Magni

"Frustration stems from your inner critic and only serves to make us crazed," LaRoche says. "Have fun. There are no tombstones that say, 'Did everything, died anyway.'"

"Becoming a leader is the most crucial choice one can make- it is the decision to step out of darkness into the light." -- Deepak Chopra; from his book 'The Soul of Leadership"

"The mind has exactly the same power as the hands: not merely to grasp the world, but to change it. " -- Colin Wilson

It's better to look ahead and prepare than to look back and regret."
-- Jackie Joyner-Kersee

"To love what you do and feel that it matters—how could anything be more fun?"
-- Katherine Graham

These are superb thoughts and ideas – thanks to Denise and please keep them coming, and that goes for any Winners Circle member who wants to contribute. If you don't already receive Martha Nessler's motivational messages, make sure to subscribe to those as well.

I loved it when Denise, Otto Janke and Mary Curtis posted their health care classes, and when Heath announced his daughter's birth -- the legacy of the Winners Circle group is gathering momentum. For those who are already reading and contributing, good! Please keep doing so. For those who have yet to participate, come on and jump right in! The water's fine!

The Passage of Pain   February 2011

A fundamental concept that is essential to your understanding of leadership and advanced citizenry can be referred to as the Passage of Pain.

Simply put, the passage of pain is the discomfort you must be willing to withstand in order to go from where you are to where you want to be. If you want to lose weight, the passage of pain is to handle eating differently and increasing your physical activity. If you want more influence in your community, the passage of pain could be the confrontational tolerance you must develop to meet more people and become part of their lives, whether they're looking for you to do so or not. If you want to become a more skillful adjuster, the passage of pain is the time, energy and capital you invest in the process of becoming a master at your chosen technique.

The Masters Guide says, "It is a Passage of Pain because the development of new habits of thought requires abandoning old ones and there is fear of the unknown, of failing, of making mistakes, of being wrong! Do not let these fears prevent you from being the giant you were created to be. Stop the old voices that said, 'Don't try to be someone you are not.' Don't let your MFTP (your Mothers, Fathers, Teachers and Preachers), the environmental conditioning you were exposed to, keep you from being who and what you want to be."

To go from "here" to "there," especially when "there" is someplace better to be, there is inevitably a passage of pain. How can we deal with this challenge, and both minimize unnecessary suffering and optimize our results?

First remember that aiming "at" a target often leaves you short of the mark – you must learn to aim "through" your target, much like striking a board with a karate blow to break it – if you aim at the board, you may hurt your wrist, while aiming through the board breaks it neatly in two with the very same force and speed. Your contact point is beyond the board, and therefore, you blast through it with little effort by comparison.

A difficult task is no different – you must see yourself past it, aim through it, not at it, and you will reduce the discomfort of the process. Begin with the end on mind, and preserve and maintain your momentum of growth with "The 10%/20% Rule" – choose an intermediate target representing about 20% growth, and when you get halfway there, to about 10% growth, that's when you raise the goals, bumping the target up another 20%, thereby aiming through your previous goal. You can repeat this process until you are playing at the optimal level you desire, capitalizing on the natural energy of your forward thrust.

And, you must bring your best – consider which resources you'd need to weather whatever adversities, and be sure you have those qualities available to you. Use affirmation, visualization, resource building, or other personal growth tools to show up in those scenarios fully equipped to deal with whatever comes up.

Managing the passage of pain is one of the overlooked keys to progress – the more discomfort you can handle, and the more elegantly you handle it, the more deliberate and relentless your movement toward your ultimate objectives.

The Unknown　　March 2011

I learned long ago from Anthony Robbins that learning is linking the unknown to the known – in other words, using your current foundation of knowledge and awareness as a platform upon which to build new understanding. By relating new ideas and concepts to ideas and concepts you already grasp, you can establish even newer ideas and concepts that arise from the interplay between the old and the new.

This means that learning requires a willingness to deal with the unknown, even though it may be scary or intimidating. Growth depends on your ability to engage that which is not yet within your reach, and to bring it close enough so you can integrate and apply it. That is the essence of learning, and it demands your participation in things you don't yet comprehend, no matter how uncomfortable or unsettling.

This is one of the reasons we don't reveal the details of our annual Winners Circle Transformational Weekend until it's absolutely necessary. It isn't just me being that way (it is a little of course) but rather, it asks you to commit based on trust and faith, not some left-brain expectation or interpretation.

Since none of these weekends have sucked so far (at least by my calibration), it's a pretty safe bet, but still it asks you to be open enough and flexible enough to decide to play, even in the absence of the clarity that might ordinarily precede this type of engagement. I believe that you are willing to do so, because there's enough of a foundation of already learned ideas and concepts to make it plausible that this coming transformational weekend will also be worthwhile for you to attend, and so you plan to be there, even though you aren't quite certain what you're signing up for. That, to be sure, is part of the fun, but requires that your expectations be tempered with some blend of patience as the process unfolds and optimism that we'll do a good job and make it something you're glad to attend. (I assure you, we are committed to do so.)

This notion of the unknown lurks around every corner, lying in wait for us, if we conceptualize it that way – taken to its logical end, it becomes paranoia, but even as such is recognized as fear of something that isn't really there. No one is really afraid of the dark, they're afraid of what the dark seems to be keeping them from seeing – in other words, the unknown. All the reframing in the world doesn't convince someone who is afraid of the dark that there's nothing there in the dark that isn't there in the light except light itself, but the inability to see clearly causes the imagination to wander and the apprehension to build – that's why it's so important to see the unknown for what it is, and not to hallucinate on what it might be.

The unknown is nothing more than what you don't know yet – it is often no more mysterious or elusive than things you already know, and once you're exposed to it, it seems natural and obvious enough to assimilate immediately. Most of our experiences with the unknown take this shape, out of sight at first and then coming into view, to be utilized quickly. For the minority of situations where the unknown experience is somewhat more complicated, it makes no sense to squander useful resources on unnecessary anxiety or stress – save your energy, invest it wisely, for if there really is something to worry about, conserve your power so you can use it constructively, instead of fretting and spinning. The unknown doesn't demand that of you – in fact, it doesn't care much what you do, generally speaking. That's why it makes more sense to hold your center, discover what you need to know, and then respond accordingly.

Whether you're building a new office, starting a family, hiring your first associate, doing your first presentation or whatever, embracing the unknown and harnessing it to make it work for you is a better strategy than most people adopt. Next time you face some new experience, keep this in mind and see how much better you process your opportunities, and address any adversities that may arise. Learning is linking the unknown to the known – you've been doing it your whole life, keep it up!

Long Term Relationships and Short Term Relationships   April 2011

I wonder if you've ever had this experience – you have a patient who seems to be a great fit with you, follows preliminary recommendations beautifully, gets great results, seems to dial into the why of it, expresses nothing but great feelings, has no apparent problem with you, and then, out of nowhere, the person quickly disengages, often with no reason given, disclaimers about there being anything wrong, just a rapid withdrawal with a brief explanation or no explanation at all, leaving you standing there sputtering, wondering what happened.

You could substitute for the word "patient" with "client," "girlfriend," boyfriend," "assistant," – it turns out that this phenomenon can be interpreted better by examining the pattern than by examining the context. No, you don't have to be confused by what you did or didn't do, because in situations like this it often has nothing to do with it.

You see, some people are short term relationship people, and some people are long term relationship people. Consistent with their names, short term relationship people tend to prefer shorter term relationships, and likewise, long term relationship people prefer longer term relationships.

When a short term relationship person and another short term relationship person create a relationship, it is easily understood that it will tend toward being a short term relationship, and when it lasts longer than a typical short term relationship, it only means that the relationship mates continually redefine the relationship so it never feels long term to them. Short term relationship people usually have no problem moving from relationship to relationship – they're more likely to move on at some point than to linger.

When a long term relationship person and another long term relationship person create a relationship, it sometimes takes a little longer for the relationship to blossom than it would with two short term relationship people, but still, the value on long term relationship tends to predominate, and usually the relationship tends to be long term – even if it changes form, it tends to last.

The big issues occur when a long term relationship person and a short term relationship person get together, both wanting the relationship that matches their particular relationship identity. For example, when a family wellness oriented chiropractor attracts a short term relationship patient, and tries to fit that patient into the long term relationship mold, it rarely works, not because the patient doesn't get it, not because the doctor hasn't given it, but because there's mismatch on the basic structure of an optimal relationship for that individual.

This applies in personal relationships as well. If one relationship mate seeks a long term relationship, but the other is wired for short term, there is most usually eventual conflict and disengagement. I've seen it close up, people who love each other but cannot remain together because one requires a shorter period than the other -- sad at times perhaps, but useful to understand, to avoid a lot of self-flagellation and despair.

In the movie "Good Will Hunting," when Robin Williams repeats to Matt Damon, "It's not your fault, it's not your fault," it produces a cathartic effect on the young man – it can have the same impact on you, when you realize it's not your fault. How many times did I beat myself up, playing the relationship over and over in my mind, wondering what I could have done better to get a patient or member to stay, until I remember it isn't my fault.

Oh, I haven't played these all perfectly, far from it, but mostly, I did the best I could, and I'm sure you mostly do the best you can also. You just can't make a silk purse out of a sow's ear. As Dr. Seuss says, "This is not That." It reminds me of the story of the frog and the scorpion.

The Frog And The Scorpion

A frog and a scorpion sat by the riverside. The scorpion says, "Frog, I need to get to the other side of the river, and I can't swim. Would you please let me ride on your back while you swim across the river?"

The frog retorted, "No way, Scorpion, you'll just sting me and I'll die."

The scorpion replied, "Why would I do that? If I'm on your back and I sting you, we'll both drown."

The frog thought about this, and it seemed to make sense, so he told the scorpion to hop on his back. About halfway across the river, the scorpion stings the frog.

"Hey, what did you do that for?" exclaimed the frog. "Now we're both going to die!"

"I couldn't help it," mused the scorpion. "It's my nature."

This is why the concept of Identity is so crucial – who we believe ourselves to be dictates our nature, and the type of relationships we are likely to enjoy. Our beliefs, values, and organizing principles are outgrowths of our sense of self, hence the reason we follow an Identity-Based course of self-study, inside out.

Next time you have a relationship last a different length of time than you expected or preferred, recall that some people are just short term relationship people, while others are long term relationship people. Move away from the judgment and pain of blaming and misplaced responsibility, and instead, do the best you can, and accept that sometimes, it's not your fault, it's just their nature.

A Matter Of Principle   May 2011

In my mind, I'm basking in the Sarasota sun – what a delightful and meaningful weekend we shared! Thank you one and all for the warmth, the willingness to learn and grow, and the intellectual and emotional curiosity to explore new territory and break new ground together.

I have always had tremendous respect and admiration for BJ Palmer based on his better known accomplishments, but this event uncovered so much more complexity to his character – every step of the way, his course of action seemed so certain, even when blazing new trails.

No doubt you've heard me say, "When your purpose is clear, your decision-making gets black and white," and I've rarely seen that belief illustrated any better than in what we discovered about BJ in Simon Senzon's presentation. I think the driving force behind BJ's entrepreneurial pursuits and marketing genius was his consistency with his values. For him, it was a matter of principle, and he was unyielding in his determination to be the living embodiment of that principle.

What would happen in our lives if we were to clarify and crystallize our sense of purpose, and acted congruently with that purpose? How would our habits and behaviors differ if we were in constant connection with our highest standards, and could therefore check our strategies and intentions against our authentic selves? How would our practices respond to us showing up at our very best every day? How would our patients react to our loving message of health and wellness if we never wavered from our truth?

There isn't one of us who isn't capable of much more – this is not meant to be an accusation, but rather an invitation to break through to another level of thinking and productivity. You are creative and powerful in ways you have not yet discovered, which is one of the reasons the Winners Circle goes to places you might not select on your own – there is magic wherever you look for it, since you bring it with you, to be sure, but certain adventures unlock something wonderful inside of us and tantalize us to outperform our previous best.

Each of us is a mixed bag, with strengths that are magnificent beyond description, and weaker areas that seem to hold us back in frustrating and sometimes imperceptible ways. What would happen if you were to identify several key weaker areas, and to explore how your tolerating them supports or does not support your sense of principle? What if you decided to improve yourself one percent in each of these areas each week or each month, what do you think would happen to your practice and your life?

I remember, thirty years ago when I was in practice, a patient who came in regularly used to stink of cigarette smoke, and I nagged him every single visit, John, when are you going to quit smoking, don't you know it's bad for you? He laughed it off, and never stopped, until one day, he came in, and didn't smell like smoke.

"John, did you quit smoking?" "Yeah, doc," he shook his head sadly, "I had to, I got emphysema."

Is that what it takes to make the decisions we know we need to make – a gun to our heads and the threat of death? For some of us, unfortunately it seems to be the case, but it doesn't have to be that way – we can choose what's right for us based on our principle, if we are willing to embrace it and live by it.

This turns out to be the challenge of all of our lifetimes – and I am the first to admit to my long list of imperfections and frailties. But the choice is right there for those who are willing to recognize it – you can step up to the plate, clear out the contradictions, and make your life a masterpiece, any time you want. It's there for the taking.

That was my thought about the frame for the weekend – what would BJ do? With a role model of chiropractic excellence like him to measure ourselves against, we can only benefit by having that example in mind and heart. When it's a matter of principle, we tend to bring the very best we've got.

Adjusting   June 2011

We spend a lot of time and energy on learning how to communicate the chiropractic message, and of course it's important that we do so. But we must refine not only our communications and leadership, but the way in which we deliver on our promise. We must become excellent adjusters.

It starts with healing consciousness – John Demartini tells us that the four cardinal pillars of healing are certainty, presence, gratitude and love. There are many ways to access and apply these qualities, but the simplest one is "purple dot, green dot."

Here's the way it works – you have healing consciousness inside you, but you need to bring it to the forefront before you put your hands on your patient or practice member. So, you can set up neurophysiological loops known as anchors to manage your states -- in other words, you can learn to link up signals to desired resources so you can draw them forth in response to those signals.

On the doorframe outside your adjusting rooms, or in some convenient spot in your open adjusting area, place a purple dot and a green dot – you know, those colored circular labels like the ones made by Avery, half an inch or an inch in diameter.

These dots act as your anchors to re-center yourself and get into the proper state for adjusting. Touch the purple dot, and think healing – be grateful for the opportunity to do such divine work, and feel love for your patient and for chiropractic. As you sense yourself going into your healing trance, touch the green dot, get present, get certain, and then GO! Catapult yourself into your adjustment, manifesting those four qualities in just the right proportion, and enter into the healing arena as a full expression of your own healing greatness.

Once you've done this a few times, it will become second nature for you. Touch the purple dot, get in touch with your healing consciousness, touch the green dot and GO! All behavior is state-related, and this procedure gets you into a powerful resource state that is conducive to giving your most effective, potent and meaningful adjustment.

Now that you can summon your optimal healing states, it's essential that you do your due diligence and become an expert at the art of chiropractic. Whether you choose an osseous approach, a postural approach, a tonal approach, or whatever flavors or blend you prefer, it behooves you to excel at your technique. You must find and adjust the subluxation to get the results you and the patient desire.

My personal technique journey included many twists and turns – I started as an upper cervical practitioner, toggling atlases with HIO, you know, drop headpiece, tilt bucky, neurocalometer, the whole nine yards. I saw a need to adjust the lower cervicals and the pelvis, and I learned Terminal Point, Pierce-Stillwagon style, using a DermaThermaGraph. Then I discovered muscle testing, and incorporated AK and SOT. I realized I wanted to pursue the gentlest and most non-forceful style, and embraced Van Rumpt's DNFT as my primary technique, persisting to this day. I added cranial adjusting and TMJ, organ techniques to correct hiatial hernias and ileocecal valves, reflex techniques for female disorders, and vibrational balancing with crystal harmonic devices. I was determined that no one would walk into my office with a subluxation complex I couldn't figure out. Even though it took me to some weird places (like holding African violets over patients' heads and sweeping negative energy into them with a quartz resonating wand) I had tremendous certainty, learned to stay present, remained immensely grateful for the opportunity to serve, and of course, felt healing love for my patients and for the blessing of being a chiropractor. I practiced for ten years, between 1978 and 1987.

A few weeks ago, we were out to dinner with dear friends, and one confided in me that she's been suffering from sciatica, and had been trying for a while to get well, including going to chiropractors, without relief. I invited her to come to my home and let me examine her, not really seeking to take responsibility for being her chiropractor, but to give her a little guidance. I examined her, assessed her condition, saw what would be required to get her well, explained to her what I'd found and what I thought it would take to address it, and then I came to a crossroads – do I want to be her chiropractor? It's not really my job, but she needed someone to help her. So I adjusted her each of the next five evenings.

The first visit I blocked her face-up (Category 2) and did a non-force lumbo-sacral sequence (Category 2, really a posterior sacro-iliac sprain, is not necessarily associated with sciatica, but the chronic low back instability and many years of poor bowel function distorted her lumbar spine, hence the need for the non-force sequence.) The second visit, she was holding the Category 2, and I repeated the non-force sequence in her lower spine. Next visit I found a sub-occipital fiber at Area 3, and felt for ipsilateral tenderness at 4D, 5D, and 1L (the vertebrae involved with Area 3, a digestive circuit affecting the gall bladder, stomach and ileocecal valve.) She had reported digestive complaints, reflux and constipation, maybe from the low back, maybe causing it. She's been going to a nutritionist, so I suggested that she ask about taking a probiotic -- she started taking it and her bowel function is starting to improve. I began the CMRT and bloodless surgery for hiatial hernia and ileocecal valve as the patterns of indicators developed.

I don't expect most of you to know all of these techniques -- my point is that I put serious time and energy into my healing work, because it backed up my philosophy and purpose. I put my hands where my mouth was. I don't care which techniques you use. I care that you study hard, learn from masters, and have the self esteem to expect yourself to be excellent at what you do.

Anyway, days later, she was back to her step aerobics class and singing chiropractic's praises, 75% improvement in a week or so after months of unrelenting pain. I've adjusted her regularly since then, about three weeks, and she reported no pain in her exercise today. With her lower spine healing and her gut now starting to work, I can be more aggressive with fixing her hiatial hernia and solve her reflux issue. And now the cervical spine indicators are popping up, she got a great adjustment to her neck this evening, a prone break on 5C, and a supine break to reset her atlas. She seems really happy.

The public will judge us by our results, regardless of how right our philosophy sounds. In fact, it's because of the great results chiropractic patients experience that we are still around to talk about our philosophy. Please, master your chiropractic art. If you need help improving your technique, tap into Bob and myself for some direction. No one but you can take responsibility to become a great adjuster. Continue to expand your knowledge base, don't settle for being pretty good, raise your standards, and establish a reputation for being the one to go to when no one else can help – you'll never have to search for new patients ever again.

Practice Philosophy   July/August 2011

Most veteran Masters Circle and Winners Circle members realize that there are five areas that contribute to the level of fulfillment you experience in practice, the five circles of the Practice Fulfillment Quotient. The inner circles, the operational aspects of practice, are easy enough to comprehend – you need a certain number of a certain type of new patient, trained to comply with your recommendations so they get optimal results, and participating in a fair exchange with you based on the implementation and enforcement of your fee policies.

The Practice Fulfillment Quotient (PFQ)

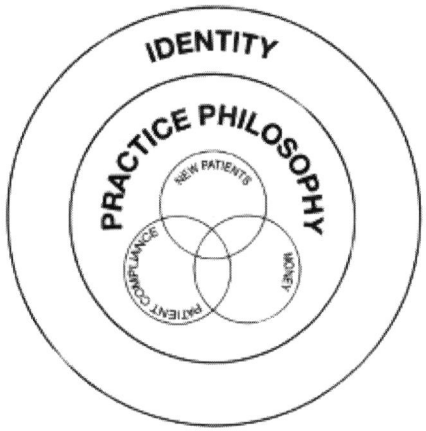

The outermost circle of the PFQ is also easy to understand if not master – your identity determines the boundaries and scope of your inner circles, and governs the magnitude of your fulfillment. With the abundant technology available, there's no excuse for us not to consistently grow ourselves, which makes more room for practice growth.

But the least discussed and understood aspect of the PFQ is Practice Philosophy. It refers to the way your identity is expressed in the context of your practice – in other words, who you are as a chiropractor, and what beliefs, values, resources and patterns of behavior manifest as a result.

I've thought a lot about practice philosophy. At first, I believed that it was mainly a measure of the degree of chiropractic philosophy a particular chiropractor applied in his or her practice. But I have come to understand that it is much more than that. It's a way to determine the level of congruency and authenticity each doctor expresses in the context of his or her practice.

As such, there is no correct or incorrect practice philosophy, any more than there is a correct or incorrect PVA – it's a product of your expression of who you are in your practice, and that means it is somewhat different for each of us.

Sometimes, that makes it a bit difficult for us to wrap our brains around it, so I invented some arbitrary but useful categories for us to consider. There are obviously blends between these, but these are the main chunks, from my point of view.

The first type of practice philosophy is the musculoskeletal practice. If you adopt this practice philosophy, you are interested in helping sick people get well with chiropractic care. You probably tend to attract people with painful problems, use pain management techniques as well as your chiropractic care, and usually need to attract a high volume of new patients to fill your schedule, since patients tend toward short-term relationships with you and with chiropractic. Examples of practices who feature a musculoskeletal practice philosophy are personal injury practices, sports injury practices, and acute care/emergency practices.

The second type of practice philosophy is the traditional practice. If you adopt this philosophy, you are interested in finding and adjusting subluxations, for the purpose of reducing nerve interference. You probably tend to attract people with painful problems, and also people who are interested for some reason in spinal care – either they have a family member who saw the benefits, or they were referred by another doctor of some sort. Or they learned about chiropractic through some outside source and for whatever reason chose to become your patient. Because these patients often stay for correction and not just relief, these practices tend to have higher patient compliance and are somewhat less dependent on a high new patient flow, as each patient stays longer to get their subluxations addressed, not only their symptoms. An example of a traditional practice is a subluxation-based family practice, where patients come in to get their subluxations corrected to remain free of nerve interference.

The third type of practice philosophy is the wellness practice. If you adopt this philosophy, you are interested in maximizing potential for healing, function and expansion, for the purpose of helping patients to experience their optimal performance and health expression. Ironically, you probably still attract many people who have painful problems, and also people who are interested in spinal care, but you also attract people who intend to reach beyond "not sick" to explore what's on the other side, namely, wellness. These practices may use additional services and products, like nutrition, personal training, massage, meditation, and other wellness habits and practices. Because these patients are interested not only in feeling better and getting their subluxations corrected, but also in seeking a higher level of health expression, each patient tends toward a lifetime relationship with chiropractic and their chiropractor. An example of a wellness practice would be an Eight Weeks to Wellness practice, where patients commit to a complete program of health and wellness related services and products, with chiropractic as the centerpiece.

Notice that these distinctions are not mutually exclusive – in fact, almost everyone is a blend, a unique configuration based on their sense of self as a healer. The purest musculoskeletal practice still has some wellness patients, and the most committed wellness doctors have some patients who get relief and are satisfied with that, discontinuing any further services. The question is, is your blend consistent with your intention and desire?

That's where you can influence your results by being congruent – if what you have on the inside is being expressed on the outside, then you are not only successful, but fulfilled, and that's the idea, to experience fulfillment in practice and in life. Your practice philosophy is one of the hidden keys to such consistency with your highest ideals – be honest in your self-assessment, and direct your attention toward making your practice the best possible reflection of yourself. It may be your shortest distance to genuine happiness in practice.

Going Global   September 2011

After much discussion, planning and decision-making, The Winners Circle has gone global. At the Winners Circle Homecoming Reception on Friday evening at SuperConference, six of the twelve new Winners Circle members are from the US and six are from Europe, and we have expanded the WC seminar program by adding a European Transformational Weekend to our traditional North American program.

At SuperConference this year I was reminded of our vision – a worldwide quality-of-life-driven health care delivery system with chiropractic in the leading role. It's more real now than ever to aim at full global access to chiropractic care, extending the benefits of chiropractic services all over the planet.

The work of world chiropractic leaders like Gerry Clum, Brian Kelly and Michael Flynn, in addition to the challenge thrown down by influencers like Patrick Gentempo and Billy DeMoss, clarifies our path – anything less than taking the chiropractic message to every corner of the Earth is incomplete and unacceptable. "Chiropractic for all" needs to be our battle cry, in the most literal sense, and that includes everywhere we can reach.

Dr. Flynn told me that ninety countries are represented at the World Federation of Chiropractic. Ninety countries! Some of them have no chiropractic laws, some of them are attempting to open chiropractic colleges – there is evidence of chiropractic blossoming all over, chiropractic missionaries spreading the word to the far-flung corners of the world, and we have a responsibility to be outstanding role models, and also to support this burgeoning movement wherever it is occurring.

This is one of the reasons The Masters Circle has held seminars in Europe for the last three years. We recognize that chiropractic is sprouting in Europe at a rapid pace, and that people are eager to learn about the miraculous healing benefits of chiropractic. Some of the largest practices in the world are in Europe, some of which have been and are members of The Masters Circle and The Winners Circle.

We want to provide what we have to offer, and also learn from the vast intelligence and experiences of chiropractors all over the world.

Some of you have traveled extensively and sampled other cultures, and some have seen chiropractic taking shape outside the US – others are only now awakening to the extraordinary potential residing in the chiropractors from Europe and beyond. The passion for our philosophy, the drive to excel in every aspect of clinical work, and the service consciousness to reach large segments of the population have all become hallmarks of the European DC, a profile to be proud of, and for all of us to model.

Over the years, Winners Circle members and alumni have gone on to become profound influencers in chiropractic in Europe, outstanding chiropractors like Ross McDonald of Edinburgh Scotland and Haavard Rognerud of Asker, Norway, both of whom have gone on to become world leaders through their own seminars and symposia. Per Munksgaard of Heemstede Netherlands runs one of the largest and most significant practices in Europe, in addition to brand new member Peter Carstens of Aalborg, Denmark and returnee Anton Stas of Valkenswaard, Netherlands – all five of these doctors have been honored as Chiropractor of the Year, all part of the rich heritage of the European chiropractor in The Winners Circle, great examples of the advanced citizenry we all aspire to.

In addition to Peter and Anton, we've also added some young superstars in the making – Jason Gould of Chistlehurst on Kent, UK, Steve Swain from Surrey, UK, and Sindre Daugstad from Oslo, Norway, as well as Manuel Mazzini of Milan, Italy, well-known leader from the Italian Chiropractic Association.

And let's not forget that we also added six outstanding new US members -- Steve Bourdage from Chicago, IL, Brad Miller from Marion IL, Eric Nepute from St. Louis MO, Wes Nyberg from Waukee, IA, Erik Roach from Altamonte Springs FL, and Meridee Lynn Senick from Mill Creek, WA.

Think about it – WC members from California to New York, from Orlando to Seattle, from Dallas to South Dakota, and now, from the UK, Denmark, Norway, Italy, and the Netherlands – the Winners Circle, from sea to shining sea!

Of course, all WC members are encouraged to attend both Transformational Weekends, so we can all share more of our gifts for everyone's benefit. I'm working on a new directory so we can all connect more easily and more frequently. With this influx of outstanding new members, we have dramatically increased our resources – tap into each other, you'll be delighted with what you discover!

Consider the possibilities, and crank up your imagination – think of chiropractic on a global scale, for the betterment of all!

Growth and Function   October 2011

We learn in high school biology that life can be defined as a system that has three basic properties – metabolism, growth and reproduction. Simply said, the energy of each living cell must be directed into one of two areas – growth or function.

The allocation of such cellular energy is a subtle and precise phenomenon – in youth, the cell devotes more energy to growth, as part of the maturation process. When fully developed, the cell turns its attention to function, based on a miraculous and exacting differentiation and specialization managed with infinite control and organization by innate intelligence. This ongoing occurrence, of course, needs no help, as long as there's no interference.

But there can be interference, in the form of some kind of stress on the system – DD Palmer pointed out that this kind of stress was usually a response to physical, chemical or psycho-emotional insult, and that subluxation was a defensive mechanism for protecting against the cumulative impact of these invasive forces.

At the cellular level, this manifests as a shift in the distribution of cellular energies, changing the balance between resources devoted to growth or function. If the energy over-shifts toward function, then it manifests as metabolic disease. If the energy over-shifts toward growth, then it manifests as neoplastic disease.

This pattern can be observed in people, not only cells. Building a great practice, for example, is based on the interplay of two dynamics, capacity and attraction. To increase the magnitude of your practice, you have to create some capacity, some room to grow, and then use attraction to fill the capacity you've created. Then, you'll have to create more capacity to open up more room to attract into, and then attract into it. This repetitively magnificent cycle is the key to reaching the number of people you prefer to serve.

Likewise, if you put too much energy into growth, you attract more new patients, but it becomes overwhelming and difficult to serve them effectively, which compro-

·mises the patient's experience and your reputation. If you put too much energy into function, then you have superior practice management, but probably attract fewer new patients and run the risk of flatness or even boredom.

At the cellular level and in a patient's anatomy, the interference that leads to such imbalances is the subluxation, and that's why it's so important to educate people in your sphere of influence so they can choose their best course of action to address this critical health and wellness factor.

In our lives, though, the interferences are equally important – anything that restricts your capacity or limits your attraction will prevent that normal distribution of energy into growth and function, attraction and capacity. Remember, you can only grow as great as your weaker areas permit, so reduce the interference by identifying weaker areas that have been holding you back and strengthening them enough so your strengths can take you forward.

Analyze your capacity limitations. If your capacity limitations lead to weaker areas in your procedures, you can add hands, add days, add hours, add speed, add systems or technology, or add attitude and energy. If your capacity limitations lead to weaker areas in your sense of self, you can use affirmations, visualization, goal setting, resource building, belief shift, values hierarchies, organizing principles and habits of excellence.

Notice that attitude and energy appear on the procedural list, the "do" list, because they affect every procedure, everything you do. Attitude and energy can be considered "the interface between being and doing from the do side." Likewise, habits of excellence are on the sense of self list, the "be" list, because habits are a result of everything you are. Habits of excellence can be considered "the interface between being and doing from the be side."

Therefore, the interface between being and doing is to perform habits of excellence with optimal attitude and energy, and it turns out that this is the way to balance your capacity and attraction – and also your growth and function. Thus, we see how nature provides us with a template for success and fulfillment, gleaned from watching the tiniest bits of living matter, which holographically and microcosmically contain all we need to know.

Doing Good   November 2011

Bob was talking with new Winners Circle member Manuel Mazzini, well known chiropractic leader in Italy, who told him of a neighboring small town which had seriously flooded and was very much out of commission. Dr. Mazzini and a psychologist friend of his decided to go to the town to see if they could help in any way.

What they found was that the people there were absolutely in shock – the losses were astronomical, the suffering widespread, and he quickly realized that they needed someone to intervene and help.

So, he adjusted 180 people in two days, discovering that the bulk of them were in defense physiology, with labored breathing from their emotional turmoil – by adjusting them, he was able to produce a greater ease, and their respiration improved immediately. This is an example of what Bob calls "release" care, releasing the imprisoned rivulet of energy, and releasing the pent-up stresses held in the structural tissues.

Manuel said he got as much out of it as they did, and I hear this constantly from those of you who have participated in mission trips of all kinds – turning people on to chiropractic has a special atmosphere all its own, and doing it on a large scale, for no ostensible personal gain except the experience of service on a larger scale, well, that is the pinnacle of advanced citizenry.

This boils down to a basic concept in service that I refer to as… doing good. You have the opportunity every day to do as much good as you can, and those who follow through tend to have the most rewarding and fulfilled lives. Every patient who comes to your office offers the possibility of meaningful service, and providing loving care for your patients is consistent with a long-term proud tradition of chiropractors helping in obvious and subtle ways.

Random acts of kindness, paying it forward, The Power of Love as the strongest attractive force – these are all different ways of illustrating the concept of doing good. Tony Robbins taught me that success is evidence of having served well, and this continues to be among my default definitions, since it takes into account not only my benefits from my actions, but the impact and influence my work has on helping others.

Imagine a world where everyone was conscious of the importance of doing good, and intent on looking for opportunities to do as much good as possible as often as possible. I believe that being part of groups like the Winners Circle, who come together in the name of leadership and advanced citizenry, helps us to become role models of excellence for those who want to add value for their fellow man and woman.

One of the most basic of all universal organizing principles is "what goes around comes around," consistent with The Masters Circle core ideology "Circle-Circle," meaning that right intent with right action produces right results, while wrong action or wrong intent will bring about something other than your best result.

This is one reason why doing good is so profound – by acting in a Circle-Circle fashion, you set into motion the wheels of inevitability, and what goes around does indeed come around. It may not seem that way at times, but this is a universal law, and will relentlessly and inexorably express itself on its own time frame. You could no more hurry the orbit of a planet or the germination of a seed – it's a natural process that occurs on its own divinely inspired schedule, regardless of our perception of convenience or inconvenience.

That's a major key to understand the rhythm of doing good. You don't know when the good will manifest, or how, only that it will. This makes playing the game of life so much more momentous, realizing that you can invest in this cosmic bank account and be assured that your interest is compounding. Then you can be delighted when you see the positive results, when you see them.

Maybe it's with a patient, maybe with a friend, maybe with someone who will soon be a patient and/or a friend. Maybe it's for someone you never met, or for someone you know very well. That's part of the fun of doing good – there are an endless series of invitations, all around you every single day, only waiting for you to decide where to point your intentions and make a bit of a difference in someone's life.

Part of being an advanced citizen is to find ways to express your desire to do good, through your practice, your family, your community, our profession, and our planet. Think of some of your favorite ways to do good, and compare notes so we can share our best ideas to make our world a better, healthier, happier place.

Knowing Who You're Dealing With   December 2011

It's only fitting that, going into this coming Transformational Weekend in January, we talk a little about relationships – not only spousal and significant other relationships, but all types of interactions between people – doctor-patient, doctor-staff, doctor-doctor, parent-child, friendships, and all the many permutations and combinations thereof.

We sometimes fall into the trap of thinking that our communication should ultimately be an expression of who we are, but this is misguided in the context of relationship – in fact, it's the opposite, that we must express ourselves in a language the other party will be able to connect with in the way we mean them to.

This, indeed, is the real finesse of relationship – to be able to engage someone in such a way that they prefer to be engaged with you in that way. Those who succeed at this deceivingly complex ability become the movers and shakers of society, the influencers who lead the way and blaze the trails that others can follow.

So therefore, in order to prosper in relationship, you must become astute at interpreting the character and communication traits of the other person – you must know who you are dealing with.

Knowing who you are dealing with means being able to assess the optimal communication style in any given circumstances, and choosing the communications techniques that are most relevant in that particular situation. For a few remarkably talented individuals, this comes naturally, but for those like myself who were not so gifted, I have developed a few models that will help you sort through where you might need to grow, to improve the quality of some or all of your relationships. You can't control what the other person does, but you can learn to select the best way to represent yourself under those conditions, which leads to a better connection and better results with less friction and stress for all involved.

All relationship is built on two factors, the ability to gain and maintain rapport, and the ability to generate a commonality of values. This "relation equation" is the cornerstone of relationship theory, and the usefulness of the following technology rests on these fundamental distinctions.

There are four filters or screens you can look through to ascertain how someone's system is set up, and therefore how they will tend to communicate in certain contexts. This helps you to solve the riddles of how to get rapport and develop consistency with each other's values. Notice that this is not only for spousal and significant other relationships, but for all relationships.

The first filter is representational system, a fancy way of describing which part of their brain they lead with. Some people are visual, some are auditory, some are kinesthetic, and if you can detect which someone favors, by listening to his or her language and recognizing the physiological cues, you can learn to communicate in the right language, which establishes rapport.

Visuals are quick-paced, with erect posture and breathing high in their chest, using seeing words like look, see, focus, viewpoint, or clear. Auditories are moderately paced, with a more relaxed posture and breathing in the midline of their chest, choosing hearing words like sound, hear, resonates, music, or loud. Kinesthetics are slow-paced, with belly-centered posture and breathing lower in their abdomen, picking feeling words like feel, grasp, in touch, or sense. Noticing these cues gives you information about how to gain rapport and enter someone's world with respect.

The second filter is personality style, whether driver, expressive, analytical or amiable. Drivers are certain, directive and tend to be abrupt – communicate with them succinctly and directly. Expressives are verbal, engaged and tend to drop out details, so communicate with them colorfully and emotionally. Analyticals are precise, information-driven and may be exhaustively detail-oriented, so communicate with them with intellectual certainty and abundant detail. Amiables are pleasant, consistent and often overly impressionable, so communicate with them with gentle authority and patience.

The third filter is metaprogram formation, or someone's generalized behavior patterns in specific scenarios. Moving toward pleasure or away from pain, having an internal or external frame of reference, seeing the sameness or the differences in things – these distinctions separate good communicators from great ones, and relationships flourish or wither on your ability to discern someone's likelihood of responding a particular way in a particular situation, and knowing how to cope and/or lead under those circumstances.

The fourth filter is advanced personality type, like the enneagram or Myers Briggs classifications. These deep inner structures of thought and being give shape and color to our existence, pointing us toward major life lessons and the best ways to learn them. In relationship, being aware of someone's tendencies, based on these foundational elements, can help you both avoid land mines and accelerate growth and connection.

This quick synopsis is not intended to lay out every detail on this fascinating work, but rather to entice you to study more about it. Relationship is an important key to happiness and fulfillment, not to mention success – the more skillful and present you become in your relationships, the better you can serve, and frankly, the more joy and inner peace you will discover inside yourself.

Adventure   January 2012

Adventure – even the word itself has a compelling ring to it – yet everyone defines it differently, and everyone experiences it through their own filters and perceptions.

The Sevens are thinking, "yeah, bring it on," while the Sixes are beginning to fret just a little, not knowing what's coming next (if this personality-typing shorthand is new to you, please see "The Enneagram, November 2014.)

I learned from Anthony Robbins that nothing has any meaning but the meaning you give it, and the concept of adventure is no different. For example, he uses the word "picnic" to illustrate this point – some hear the word, and think, "ah, a beautiful day outside, great company, fresh air making everything taste a little better, maybe some chilled white wine or spring water to wash it down," while other hear the very same word and think, "you want to eat sitting on the ground? There's rocks, there's mud, there's bugs, and I have to cook?"

It's the same word, but people filter it through their own perceptions, giving our language infinite color, depth and scope, and giving us an infinite choice of worldviews.

So how we may hear and interpret the word "adventure" plays a major role in our willingness to explore our world and break through to higher and deeper levels of understanding and ultimately success.

Tony tells another story about being called backstage to help Carly Simon. A gifted singer and songwriter, Simon was plagued by stage fright, interfering with her ability to perform and promote her songs. The world's greatest one-stop therapist was called in, and the exchange went something like this:

Tony: Tell me what happens?

Carly: Well, at first I'm looking forward to performing. Then, I get this feeling in my stomach, and then my hands start to sweat, and then I start shaking all over, and then I know I can't possibly go out there.

Tony started to laugh.

Carly: What are you laughing about? This is serious.

Tony: Well I was just backstage a few weeks ago with Bruce Springsteen, and we were talking about how he prepares to perform, and he said, "Tony, I really look forward to going out on stage. Before the show, I get this feeling in my stomach, and then my hands start to sweat, and then I start to shake all over, and that's how I know I'm ready!"

The very same conditions, experienced and defined differently, produce the opposite results – I wonder where you are doing this to yourself in your own life or practice?

Back to adventure. Any time you are about to enter into a situation you cannot predict, it's an adventure. You may choose to enjoy adventure or not, but one thing is for sure – you NEVER know what's going to happen next, so life is really one big moment by moment adventure. If you frame it as a joyful opportunity to investigate new parts of yourself and the world, you will enjoy the process. If you amplify the potential downside risk, react intensely to the worst case scenario in advance, and abhor change, then it will not be near as much fun.

It requires a willingness to be not the same for now, a dread that many suffer, the devil you know vs the devil you don't know. Playing it safe does have its virtues, that cannot be argued, but growth itself depends on making peace with change, so progress is possible. You'll have to try new things somewhere along the line. Adventure is a close cousin to that, once again, depending on how you frame it.

There is no correct or incorrect way to anticipate and address adventure – it's only a matter of how comfortable an experience it turns out to be for you. That, of course, is up to you – you've heard me say it many times, your personality type and fixations are hard-wired, but the ultimate behavior you select is a choice. You may succumb to the natural default, which may or may not be in your best interest, or you can be present enough and values-driven enough to choose the way you prefer to respond, which generally leads to a more liberated life and overall better results.

If you're like me, you are able to do this effectively at times, not so effectively at other times. Let's put some attention on the role adventure plays, so it can be embraced without either over- or under-engaging. Remember, your will is activated when you have a sense of purpose around your crusade, which makes the adventure more meaningful and more enticing still.

Next time you face a challenge or adversity, and you aren't sure what's on the other side of it, take yourself on a "picnic" and decide how to show up instead of just showing up. You'll find you have more control over it than you thought you did, and it is likely to make it easier and more impactful when you do.

Synergy　　February 2012

As far back as classical ancient Greece, where Aristotle taught that what you see is what you get while Plato claimed there was something unseen inside that mattered, there has been a culture-wide dichotomy about the proper definition of things natural.

Does it mean that there are rational, mechanistic explanations for everything, that follow physico-chemical laws, many of which we simply have not yet caught up to understanding but clearly must exist? Or are there mysterious patterns of incomprehensible energy and power that contribute something immeasurable but essential to our existence?

As long as this discussion remains ideological, no progress can be made – each side can easily justify its existence and continued dedication. But In "The 3rd Alternative," Stephen Covey asks the question, "Would you be willing to look for a third alternative we haven't even thought of yet?

In doing so, he exposes the point of his latest book and a critical factor for us to comprehend and embrace – the concept of synergy.

He offers this illustration – "One plus one equals two – except in a synergistic situation. For example, a machine that can exert 60,000 pounds per square inch (PSI) on a bar of iron will break it. A bar of chromium of the same size will break at about 70,000 PSI. A bar of nickel will break at about 80,000 PSI. Added up, that's 210,000 PSI. Therefore, if mixed into one bar, iron, chromium and nickel will withstand 210,000 PSI, right?

Wrong. If I mix iron, chromium and nickel in certain proportions, the resulting bar of metal will withstand 300,000 PSI… the metals together are 43% stronger than they are separately… that's synergy."

The whole is greater than the sum of the parts, teamwork makes the dream work, the mastermind principle – there are many applications of this profound yet accessible tool. Learning to think and act synergistically will heal relationships, families, health care, politics, environmental issues, and more.

Note that synergy does not require that you sacrifice everything that's important to you – as James Collins teaches us, we need to preserve our core values while varying our strategies to suit the changes in the marketplace. Everyone involved needs to be resilient enough and creative enough to think of a new way to consider the options, which leads to a solution all can agree upon.

If we're going to be honest about this, we'll have to admit that sometimes it's easier said than done – but until we begin to consider new solutions, we are stuck in dogma and habit. The willingness to take a fresh look, maybe even through a detractor's eyes, may open new doors of perception and lead to consistent resolution that fits the needs of all concerned.

We saw a lovely example of this, far beneath the earth's surface at Rio Secreto during our tour of the underground river in Playa del Carmen. Remember the roots that penetrated the forest floor to seek water ninety feet down? There were intrepid warrior plants that were strong enough and brave enough to carry out that mission – and their less aggressive, less hardy plant friends and neighbors wound around them and piggy-backed along, using the determination of those warrior roots to find life-giving water, in exchange for some extra protection and support, so their survival was also assured.

We see synergy everywhere in nature – bees pollinating flowers, normal micro-inhabitants aiding in colon function, and of course, people working together in teams to outperform anything they could do individually.

Synergy is one of the reasons we are so particular about whom we invite into the Winners Circle – if you are a member, you can be certain that we believe you add value to the quality of our group vibration, that we want you to be part of what we are building together. Leadership and advanced citizenry have always been at a premium in our profession, not for lack of talented and intelligent people, but due to the paucity of structure and systematic development in a profession composed of rugged individualists who mainly want to be left alone to practice the way they please.

This is one reason why I participate in The Chiropractic Summit, a group of chiropractic leaders who meet quarterly to discuss policy, professional vision, and issues relevant to field practitioners like cultural authority, profitability and professional self esteem. ACA, ICA, Association of Chiropractic Colleges, Congress of Chiropractic State Associations, top vendors like Standard Process and Foot Levelers, top publications like Chiro Econ, DC and The American Chiropractor, top consultants like The Masters Circle, Singer and Breakthrough Coaching, and other selected organizations, 41 entities in all, coming together to facilitate healing and guide the chiropractic profession to its rightful place in health and wellness.

You'd be amazed at the chiropractors who had been adversarial for many years, now rolling up their sleeves and working side by side on committees. You'd be impressed with the level of thinking and the quality of the leadership. But mostly, you'd be proud to be a chiropractor, and optimistic about our future as a profession. These synergistic efforts are forging a better path for all of us.

And, since I have recent reference experiences on this phenomenon and can easily recognize it when I see it, I have to compliment those who participated in the Rivera Maya Transformational Weekend – I saw so many new relationships manifesting and already established ones deepening, and nothing could make me happier. Seeing the bonds of friendship, intimacy and synergy develop is a Winners Circle dream come true.

So, Aristotle and Plato were both right – there are mysterious patterns of incomprehensible energy and power that contribute something immeasurable but essential to our existence, for which there are rational, mechanistic explanations that follow physico-chemical laws, many of which we simply have not yet caught up to understanding but clearly must exist. It's all part of a grand design of things natural which grants us the privilege of life and the opportunity to serve others with what we learn.

Cause and Effect   March 2012

With all the amazing personal growth and success technology available, enthusiasts like me sometimes find themselves sliding down the slick and slippery slope of complexity, for entertainment as well as for expanded intellectual comprehension.

But sometimes it makes sense to return to the basics with profoundly simple universal laws like, for example, the law of cause and effect.

In his classic, "The Seven Spiritual Laws of Success," Deepak Chopra says, "Every action generates a force of energy that returns to us in like kind – what we sow is what we reap. And when we choose actions that bring happiness and success to others, the fruit of our karma is happiness and success." This is why advanced citizenry is at the heart of The Winners Circle – we need to be role models who do as much good as possible and inspire others to do the same.

Chiropractic philosophy tells us that the subluxation is the cause of an effect we call dis-ease. In the "Chiropractic Textbook (1927)" Stephenson tells us, "Every Effect has a Cause, and every Cause has an Effect. The study of Chiropractic is largely a study of the relations between Cause and Effect, and Effect and Cause." He goes on to say "interference with the transmission of Innate forces causes incoordination or dis-ease."

DD Palmer was clear on the cause of disease – in "The Chiropractor's Adjuster (1910)" he says "The determining causes of disease are traumatism, poison and auto-suggestion," and with that simple statement launched the entire wellness movement, encompassing chiropractic approaches to dealing with injury, nutrition and detoxification counseling, and positive psychology and the personal growth industry, all intimately tied into the chiropractic wellness lifestyle and best orchestrated by modern day doctors of chiropractic..

I found this marvelously provocative passage in "The Bigness Of The Fellow Within (1949)," where BJ goes off on a rant:

"Fight cancer! Fight tuberculosis! Fight infantile paralysis!

We have built up an impenetrable wall of medical education of trying to eradicate effects by fighting effects!

There has been built up a medical armamentarium to fight, kill or stamp out disease after it is in existence. "Easter seals to help crippled children." Why become crippled? If cause were known and corrected, there would be no cripples. Medicine does not know the cause. Getting cases in their acute stages, they should know how to correct that which would prevent chronic cripples. Selling or buying Easter seals after children become crip-ples is like putting a horse in the stall after it has been stolen.

It is so easy to help life, health, Innate.

Helping the good is better than fighting the bad. Help God rather than fight the devil.

An ounce of correction of cause is worth a pound of cure of disease. A trifle of internal knowledge is more than a hogshead of external ignorance. A bit of Innate ability is more than a great deal of educated blundering. Thou shalt is better than Thou shalt not!"

Sixty-three years later, the radical philosophies of this visionary are playing out – one by one, drugs are proving more dangerous than the value they provide, and forward thinking healers are aligning with natural law and universal forces – and chiropractors are and should be at the forefront.

In the Winners Circle, we pride ourselves on helping people when the opportunity arises – it's the simplest form of advanced citizenry, to just help someone when you can.

But imagine what would happen if more and more people decided to deliberately and willfully do good? What kind of effect do you think would be set in motion by that kind of cause?

By spreading a message of health and vitality through the chiropractic wellness lifestyle, we can facilitate a groundswell of positive movement toward things natu-ral, and like the rolling waves, we can keep sharing the truth and act as an ongoing source of positive energy, doing good and causing others around you to consider doing good.

Be the cause of wonderful, productive, fruitful effects – the world needs you to do so, and you will enjoy the process, too.

Lucky or Smart?   April 2012

A number of months ago, Bob showed me a book he was reading (as we often do -- I thought I read a lot but I can't possibly keep up with him) called "Lucky or Smart?" written by Bo Peabody.

Peabody is an Internet entrepreneur who timed the bubble perfectly and cashed out for a stupid amount of money. His contention is fairly simple – while there is a type of luck that we may have little control over, such as finding twenty bucks on the ground, we can influence our own luck by surrounding ourselves with the right people, paying attention to our business, and developing a company that is innovative, morally compelling and philosophically positive, which will attract smart, motivated co-workers that will do great things because they are smart and motivated.

In this way, an entrepreneur can make his or her own luck. Peabody makes a specific point of saying that entrepreneurs are often not the "A" students, but tend to draw such extra-intelligent people toward them to participate in their areas of expertise in support of the dream expressed by the leader.

It's a relief to hear someone actually say it – you don't need to be a genius to be successful in practice, or any business. Rather, if you invest your focus in an inspiring vision, concentrate on building a great team, stay humble and sell constantly, you are applying the same rules that have made most businesspeople successful.

While this may seem oversimplified, that's really his point – you make your own luck by directing your energy toward the most important keys, rather than majoring in minors and distracting yourself from the most significant tasks at hand.

How can we apply this in the context of our practices? Here are a few pointers for creating your own luck in a chiropractic office.

1. Take your message seriously, but don't take yourself too seriously. You are a winner, but you won't win every time – lighten up on yourself and

take things in proper stride. Tomorrow is another day, and you will live to thrive again, even if things don't work out immediately. Keep creating your own opportunities.

2. Build a staff of highly trained and committed people who excel at what they do, and care at least almost as much as you.

3. Notice and capitalize on your opportunities to move your practice forward – when you walk down your street, 90% of the people you see have never visited a chiropractor, and 99% have never been to your office – those odds are dramatically in your favor, but only if you take action and engage those candidates for care.

Lucky or smart? Learning to recognize your opportunities and take advantage of them tends to make smart people look lucky. Yes, a little divine intervention is welcome, but you can optimize your results by making your own luck with good judgment, excellence and persistence.

Consistency   May 2012

It may not seem very glamorous, but those among us who are most successful exhibit a quality that is ethereal in its nature but profound in its impact – consistency.

Certainty, predictability, present time consciousness, competence, reliability, trustworthiness – there are many shades to this mystery of consistency. Goal-seeking requires consistent direction of energy and work, and personal growth demands a consistent effort to develop new and better habits – in fact, the very process of habit-formation both relies on and enhances consistency, and in that distinction lies the first trap we must recognize.

Another synonym for consistency is "sameness," so it is important to watch out for the pitfalls of consistency at the expense of growth or change -- in his epic "Self-Reliance," Ralph Waldo Emerson tells us that "foolish consistency is the hobgoblin of little minds," and that "with consistency a great soul has little to do" – this is a warning against confusing consistency with being on auto-pilot, absent and going through the motions, which can rob you of creativity and the power of now.

But there is a credible and attainable balance to be struck, where you can develop rhythm in your habits and behaviors without disappearing into mechanical rote and routine. Developing your ability to consistently show up resourceful and empowered has no such consequences, as you will apply your consistency to valuable and productive endeavors.

Therefore, consistency in its most desirable form is a close relative of unconscious competence, the top level of "Four Levels Of Learning" as defined in the 1970's by Noel Burch at Gordon Training International, though the concept is often attributed to Abraham Maslow.

Here's how we learn – notice how building any new skills passes through these filters on the way to mastery:

1. Unconscious incompetence -- The individual does not understand or know how to do something and is not aware of the deficit. (What's a shoe?")

2. Conscious incompetence -- Though the individual does not understand or know how to do something, the deficit becomes apparent, as well as the value of developing a new skill in addressing the deficit. Making mistakes can be integral to the learning process at this stage. ("Mommy puts on my shoes – I want to do that, how do I do that?")

3. Conscious competence -- The individual understands or knows how to do something, but demonstrating the skill or knowledge requires concentration. ("I can put on my own shoes, but it takes all my attention.")

4. Unconscious competence -- The individual has had so much practice with a skill that it has become "second nature" and can be performed easily. (Of course I put on my shoes.")

So you can see that there is a difference between absent-mindedly going through the motions, and being consistent while consciously expressing your expertise. It is in this "sweet spot" that great successes are made, and is the reason for this focus on consistency – to help you stay conscious of your actions while coming from a deep inner place of natural rightness and integrity.

Monitor your performance to be sure you deliver the same high standard of excellence in those aspects of your life and practice that you can calibrate and evaluate. Something as "simple" as providing a quality adjustment for your patient insists on a level of consistency in analysis, in execution of the adjustive thrust, and in post-analysis to be sure you did what you set out to do. While adjusting may seem at times to be somewhat esoteric, there must be measurable parameters that help you know what to do and when you've done it.

Office procedures are another place that demands consistency – if you "wing it" through your practice day, it takes much more energy and focus, which can lead to fatigue and burnout, as compared to instituting a series of consistent procedures and policies that free you to be flexible and innovative in the circumstances that call for it, because you've built a foundation of structured rules and use them as a platform to push up from in those situations that demand it.

Don't confuse consistency with stagnation – that's the "foolish consistency" Emerson was referring to. Anything you can systematize without interfering with the creative process, please do – you'll find it streamlines your movement toward your ideals, and capitalizes on your current level of mastery to ensure the best results possible.

Responsibility   June 2012

A close cousin of advanced citizenry is responsibility, a word that is often candy-coated to reduce its sting, but nevertheless turns out to be a determining factor in breakthrough and victory of all kinds.

Knowing where the proverbial buck stops is not a burden – in fact, it is liberating to have a firm grasp on what is required of you to succeed, indeed to surpass your wildest expectations. Certainty grows from experience, and taking responsibility tends to grow you by providing experiences you can participate in, evaluate, and make distinctions upon to move you forward.

Often, the concept of responsibility conjures up blame, fault, or culpability – these are the underbelly of responsibility, not unrelated, but not telling the whole story either. Claiming responsibility is not the same as accepting blame or fault – it refers to who needs to take the helm and move the situation toward resolution, not who screwed up and caused problems that weren't there before.

Nor is the threadbare euphemism that responsibility should be written "response-ability," the ability to respond, complete in its perspective – it's one of those "famous reframes that don't work," an insinuation that somehow responsibility itself is too harsh and needs to be softened, another example of the afore-mentioned candy-coating.

No, responsibility is a grown-up word, an invitation to call things the way you see them, and take action and play your role in correction, adjustment, or completion. As such, it is one of our most important and valuable opportunities.

Where in your life could you be taking responsibility where you are not yet doing so? Is it in your own health and wellness, your own prosperity consciousness, your own willingness to serve? Carefully examining your life choices and decisions will often uncover areas where you could improve yourself, and have more positive impact on those you associate with, if you were only prepared to stretch yourself and handle whatever it is that lies right outside your comfort zone, for the betterment of all concerned.

And how can you motivate your team, your patients, and even your family to establish a habit of taking responsibility? What values-driven questions could you ask, what reference experiences could you access, what leverage could you develop to guide those in your sphere of influence to be more responsible?

This is a higher level of advanced citizenry – not only leading, but encouraging those around you to step up to their own greatness and lead in whatever ways their life calls for it. Being responsible in your own right is a cornerstone of personal growth – inspiring responsibility in others makes you a significant influence key and visionary leader who will magnify your impact multifold.

So, when you are asked to take responsibility, don't duck or avoid the circumstances – embrace them whole-heartedly, for hidden in that challenge is a wealth of self-development, as well as a chance to expand your power to do more good and make a bigger difference in the lives of those you touch and serve.

Fun   July 2012

We all want it, but we all define it differently. We're willing to work hard to get to experience it, and when we are in the flow of it, nothing else seems to matter. It's a three-letter word we want to have as much as possible, and when we're not having it, we miss it.

Get your minds out of the gutter – I'm talking about fun. Fun is the vast catch-basin for all of our individual tastes of pleasure and entertainment.

The dictionary tells us that fun is "something that provides mirth, amusement, enjoyment or playfulness." The very word itself evokes sensations and memories of being in places and situations that make us feel good, making it worthy of evaluation – are we structuring our lives with the right amount of fun, and if not, what must we do to reshape that balance?

Too often, it turns out, fun is a throwaway, a default, something we opt into if we have the time and can rationalize "wasting" it – but that's not an ideal way to integrate fun into your lifestyle. Others may swing the pendulum the other way, where the balance is tilted too much toward leisure, so work doesn't have the necessary emphasis to progress meaningfully. We need to be able to evaluate this blend in our own lives so we harmonize the interaction between work time and play time, for optimal lifestyle design.

As most of you already know, Stephen Covey's seventh habit was "sharpening the saw" – in other words, resting, rejuvenating and restoring yourself so you can bring your very best to everything you do. If fun isn't prioritized appropriately, this cannot happen, and the net impact is distraction, fatigue, and ultimately burnout.

But properly orchestrated, fun is an opportunity to celebrate your victories, bask in the glory of your accomplishments, and relax so you can show up for your next set of challenges with maximum capacity available to fill, and the most attraction possible to fill it.

Fun is also a chance to enrich your internal map, to have experiences you might not otherwise have, to explore new territory inside yourself and outside as well. Traveling, participating in uplifting and fascinating activities like concerts or sporting events, or simply communing with nature on walks, runs, or hikes, can bring you up and build you from the inside out.

Some have fun with actively engaged hobbies – playing a musical instrument or singing, collecting stuff that appeals to you, riding a horse or flying a plane, playing a game or sport, or socializing with friends can be a much-needed release after dealing with the stresses of everyday life.

Some people naturally tend toward fun, managing their daily activities to build fun into every day. Others prefer to focus on work, and choose selected times and dates to express their fun side.

But remember, when Bob teaches us about MOA's, major outcome activities, he is careful to remind us that we cannot expect to fill all of our time with such maximum production tasks – it will exhaust us before too very long. Rather, we need to have time both to devote to "neutral" chores, that may not be profit-generating in and of themselves but are necessary to function well, and then to set specific time aside for fun so we are able to appreciate the yield from our endeavors, and recharge to get back into work with our very best energy and focus.

This brings up a comment on this subject by a great philosopher of fun, Dr. Seuss --

"When he worked, he really worked. But when he played, he really PLAYED."

This, I think, is the best way to look at this essential topic – to fully invest yourself in your work, and then to fully invest yourself in not working so that you create the best configuration possible, based on your own values and body rhythms, stress and recovery, engage and disengage..

It is surprising to me when I discover how many of you have a distorted priority on this vital matter. Never taking any time off or taking mass quantities off are both out of balance. Find the right pace that works for you, and implement it – it will reward you many times over.

It reminds me of a favorite movie quote, from "Arthur" where he states categorically:

"Of all the things I have, fun is my favorite!"

So, notice if you have set up the rules of the game so you have the best shot at effectively riding the work-play interface. It will pay you back with more energy, more intensity when called for, and a better worldview overall, where you look forward to both your career and your leisure time with equal enthusiasm.

Dealing With Adversity   August 2012

As many of you already know, I've had a bit of a rocky month – thank you for the tremendous outpouring of loving support, I really needed it and I really appreciate it.

I never would have guessed that a concrete-headed thick-skinned guy like me would be thrown for such a loop, but then again, I never lost my mom, Eileen Perman, before. For those of you who have been through it, I have newfound respect and admiration for you – it was an arduous ordeal, one filled with lessons as well as emotions. For those who have not yet been there, maybe my distinctions will be helpful.

First, I reconnected with the power of family – I saw my roles and responsibilities differently through my mom's demise, recognizing that my input and support were necessary, appreciated and worthwhile, and that in fact, each family member had a part to play.

Next, I observed the relentless, inexorable slide my mom experienced, one month relatively normal, going out to dinner and expressing her opinions as strongly as ever, next month clinging to life by a thread. It's so impermanent, we need to appreciate every breath, every moment of life, as it is a blessing and a gift.

Most of all, though, I felt grateful for all the opportunities I did have to demonstrate my love, for love truly is the most important of all of our values, and the love of a mother is among the most potent there is. I realize many don't have the privilege of growing up with a devoted mother's love, and many others have it only part of the way – the fact that I am 59 years old and had six decades with my mom is a source of great joy and fulfillment – not that I don't miss her, I do, but I feel satisfied that we had so much quality time together, and that she left me with so many valuable perspectives on living a quality life.

We are each going to face our own demons, and have to handle our own unique set of adversities, so I thought a little primer on dealing with adversity might come in handy – here are my thoughts.

1.   Get real. Nothing is ever as good or as bad as it seems – it's our filters and beliefs that make us attach such intensity or lack thereof. Get present in the moment, and be as objective as possible in assessing the landscape – it will keep you from getting too unnecessarily high or low when you stay centered. James Collins recommends that we "confront the brutal facts," and nowhere is it more called for than when we are sorting through our own stresses.

2.   Accept your current circumstances as the slice of life you are engaged in right now, but not necessarily indefinitely. Don't pretend things aren't what they are, acknowledge the conditions you have to address, so you can begin to manifest the resources you need to respond effectively.

3.   Establish a clear target so you know which direction to move in, and when you are moving in it. Knowing your outcome is required to generate the power to change.

4.   Take inventory of your resources, and be sure you face your stresses with the requisite qualities, behavior patterns, values and beliefs – these are the raw materials of confrontation and decision, a personal formula that is custom-tailored just for you. Familiarize yourself with and refine your toolbox so you feel well-equipped to manage your strategies.

5.   Put the wheels in motion – apply your resources to your action plan, and hold your standards up so you bring your very best to the situation.

6.   Stay focused on the desired completion, and don't let up until you are well into creating the results you want. Sometimes we stop short of the finish and try to coast in – not acceptable! Keep going until you have a firm grasp on the intended outcome. Remember to stick to things you can do something about.

This format may seem simple, but it will help you rescue yourself in times of stress and difficulty. I believe that we get the challenges in practice and in life that we can handle, no more, but certainly no less. In times of great pain, I feel grateful that the universe has so much confidence in me, and I do everything within my reach to rise to the occasion.

I know that many of you have had to deal with significant adversities – above all, please resist the impulse to feel persecuted and victimized, because this is never the case. There is always a pony in there under all that horse-flop – you just have to be persistent and determined enough to break through and find it.

The Four Adjustments   September 2012

As you know, the theme for this year's SuperConference was "The Big Adjustment," and it fell to Bob and me to come up with fresh material along these lines. I have long been a fan of the book "The Four Agreements" by Don Miguel Ruiz, and those of you who work with Barry Warren know it as part of his core curriculum.

But I saw within it an opportunity to adapt it to our needs as chiropractors, and so was born… The Four Adjustments.

Be impeccable with your word… with patients, staff, colleagues and community. Your word is your bond, and maintaining a high degree of integrity is essential to develop your relationships effectively. Patients need to know clearly what you plan and why. They need to understand their responsibility in the process as well as yours – be straightforward, while tuning your tone to the best fit for that particular patient. Same with staff – communicate clearly your intentions and expectations. As far as your brother and sister chiropractor, I strongly recommend that you never gossip or speak badly of a colleague – it only cheapens your own reputation and the reputation of chiropractic to besmirch another chiropractor. And presenting an honest and sincere public image sets the stage for patients to engage you with positive expectancy, and positions you for community leadership when the opportunity arises.

Don't take anything personally… with patients, staff, colleagues and community. Patients act based on their own agenda, not based on a validation or rejection of you or what you have recommended. You'll save back a lot of unnecessary pain if you realize this. Same with your team – if they don't perform as you prefer, it isn't about you, it's based on their values and beliefs. You may have to "adjust" your communication to get on the same page, but they are not acting to injure you, only to follow through on their worldview. With your colleagues, it's obvious that there is wide variation from practice to practice, but your neighboring chiropractors and wellness professionals are not out to get you, they are only trying to make their way through the same kinds of challenges you face. And your community will respond or not respond, again, based on their perspectives – it isn't about you personally, it's about their interpretation of your worth to them, which can be changed with education, but not with unpleasantness, hostility or undue sensitivity or defensiveness.

Don't assume anything… with patients, staff, colleagues and community. This is a little trickier – it's easy to slide down the slippery slope of assumption, expecting your patients to know what they haven't yet fully comprehended, or anticipating that staff can deliver without sufficient training, or that your colleagues will understand your point of view without you fully expressing it, or that your community gets the first thing about health and wellness, to be able to appreciate what you have to offer. It is in recognizing that it's up to you to provide the message so they can react properly to it that you save back unnecessary suffering on your part and the part of those you touch.

Always do your best… with patients, staff, colleagues and community. Needless to say, your patient deserves the very finest service and attention you can muster. Likewise, your team will blossom and flourish under your loving hand, so create an environment where good work is rewarded and issues are dealt with skillfully and patiently. Reach out to your fellow chiropractor and share what you know, for the betterment of all. And represent yourself in your community as a person of high vibration, meticulous ethics and great love. It will come back to repay you many times over.

These distinctions are simple and elegant, and they can shape your experience so you contribute the most and also receive the most in return. Consider making them part of your typical thought and action process – it's good for all of us!

Braving The Unknown   October 2012

We come to assorted crossroads in our lives, some of which we can prepare for, others not. When we find ourselves in uncharted territory, our choices are many, but which one is best?

This is the quandary all pioneers confront -- full speed ahead? Proceed with caution? Choose a different path? The moment you leave the usual in favor of the unusual, you will be faced with this kind of creative decision making, and the higher you are on the food chain, the more impact selecting your best options will have.

If you want to play a big game, you must be ready for such opportunities. No one hands you your success -- you must claim it. The rules are the same for everyone, give or take a few advantages that are essentially out of our control. When you find yourself braving the unknown, what are some of the distinctions you will be called upon to make, and how can you tune your responses for the optimal results?

The first checkpoint is outcome clarity -- what do you want to happen? Is it likely, or even possible? It makes no sense to aim at less than what you want, but your mind will play tricks on you if you find yourself aiming higher than you believe you can achieve. Start with a target you are convinced you can hit, and you'll be able to access your resources with more certainty and efficacy. Begin with the end in mind.

Next, you will have to prepare to be uncomfortable, at least temporarily -- things are usually not as good or as bad as they seem, so it isn't much of a stretch to realize that the route to your goal may well be difficult, but not insurmountable. Your attitude will play a major role in supporting or interfering with your progress.

With your prospects conceptualized and your mindset established, now you can construct your plan of attack -- what will reaching this objective require of you, or of those who stand with you? Leaders recognize that this kind of field generalship is the hallmark of the practical visionary, and something as simple and direct as giving understandable instructions and supplying sufficient perspective to carry them out is going to lubricate the forward movement for all concerned.

Now comes the tricky part. You have the wheels in motion -- are you progressing in the direction you desire? Learning to monitor your results, interpret them and make any appropriate course correction will keep you running true to your intentions. It isn't always possible to be perfect in this self-assessment, nor is it probable that the adjustments you make will work every time, but it's worse to see yourself headed for the falls without a paddle and doing nothing at all as you wait to crash and drown. The willingness to try one more time and give it your all is the difference that makes the difference when you are responsible for steering the ship.

Some of you will notice that this is a derivative of the old "how to do anything" format -- get into a resourceful state, know your outcome, notice if your actions are taking you in the right direction, and vary those actions until they do.

There's really no difference between typical problem-solving and braving the unknown, except in common circumstances you have more information, in unfamiliar conditions you have less. But given that, the process is about the same -- decide where you're going, get ready, map out your conquest, take massive action and evaluate as you go, shifting strategies when necessary.

There is one additional element to this approach that has to be figured in, and that is... fear. Fear can reduce even the most competent leader to sputtering ineptitude, unless steps are taken to rise to the occasion. Just keep Denis Waitley's definition of fear in mind -- False Evidence Appearing Real. The huge majority of your apprehensions are ungrounded -- handle your stresses and don't let them take you off your game. Choose physiologies of presence, self-assuredness and power -- even if you make an error in judgment, you'll be able to recover quickly and redirect your attention effectively.

You'll find that just having a format to work with like this one will reward you over and over -- my experience is, we get the challenges we can handle, so if you have big ones to deal with, it's actually a cosmic compliment that the universe feels you are so well-equipped to address even the most daunting situations. Take your best shot!

Creative Genius   November 2012

Those of us who attended the Barcelona event had myriad opportunities to enrich our internal maps – we imprinted wildly on new experiences like oddly shaped and colored buildings, amazing demonstrations of artistic talent, and succulent manifestations of cuisine and winemaking that titillated as much as they inspired.

The theme that ran through this event was… creative genius. Yes, of course it's obvious when brilliance like that expressed by Gaudi in his architecture, or Picasso in his objets d'art comes into view. Sculpture like Miro or world class paella requires a certain flair and expertise that defies explanation, but you know it when you see it.

The question is, can you recognize the same kind of mastery and the wonder that comes along with it in a magnificent adjustment, or an elegant act of leadership, or a supremely clever metaphor that turns on the light for patients who are desperate to find their way out of the darkness?

We chiropractors have our own form of creative genius, based on uniquely applying the philosophy, science and art in our own profoundly individual way, and thereby attracting the right patients who will move toward the answers they in particular need.

The spectrum of chiropractic colors is infinite -- just among techniques, there are hundreds of permutations and combinations, based on patterns we learn and/or notice about the way the body works and heals. Then, on top of the many technical approaches, there is a smorgasbord of office procedures and policies, a special blend each office cooks up in its own way.

And the mixture of philosophical inflections, well, that just guarantees that each chiropractor, like a snowflake, is unlike any other, and the expression of that individuality provides ample opportunity for the culmination of a one-of-a-kind form of creative genius.

Think for a moment about what makes you and your practice stand out – what do you do better than anything else, and what personalized details have you brought to your patient's experience that makes it impossible for them to get such an experience anywhere else?

Every business has its own unique selling proposition, and it is one of the best ways to apply your creativity to develop an enterprise that separates you from the pack. To grow your capacity, you'll need to uncover weaker areas and grow them, but to establish your own practice personality, you'll want to exploit those attributes that make you, well, you. This helps to refine the attractive force that fills your office with the right patients for you.

Looking at your practice like the masterpiece it can be will help you serve more people, and have a more fulfilling career overall. Stay open to learning new things, and to evolving what you already know into an even more sophisticated package. All of the greats we studied had their own fingerprint that made them historically significant – you can do the same and leave a legacy of health and wellness that has your imprimatur on it, if you only work to access the creative genius that is already inside you.

The MasterMind Principle   December 2012

Last week we had our second in a series of mastermind teleconferences – the first one was on profitability, and this past call was about patient compliance and retention, and what ensued was a powerful and productive discussion of PVA, patient visit average, the average number of visits a typical patient comes in to see you.

For those who were in attendance, thank you for your participation, and from the feedback, it was an hour well-invested. Your full engagement is duly noted, and your contribution was significant.

For those of you who were not able to be there for the live event, I hope you will listen to the classes by clicking on the links that were sent to you, where your Winners Circle colleagues generously share some of their innermost secrets. Just one well-placed idea could be worth tens or even hundreds of thousands to you – and each call had many such ideas, waiting to be implemented both for your patients' welfare and for your success.

I first heard about the mastermind principle through reading Napoleon Hill, who boiled down the process of success to three simple steps:

1. Decide exactly where you will be and what you'll accomplish over the next three years.

2. Decide how much money you will make and what you're willing to do to earn it.

3. Form a mastermind alliance with at least one family member and/or at least one friend or business associate.

Many of us have to be dragged kicking and screaming to the mastermind process, and believe me, it's understandable – so many of us have trained ourselves to do our problem-solving individually, for privacy reasons, ego reasons, and for convenience, too.

But when you are willing to engage this priceless principle, to humble yourself before higher powers of relationship and shared leadership, to tap into the vast information fields, and to accept that you may not have all the answers yourself, a confluence of consciousness that far surpasses anything one person can conceptualize is activated, to be used as you see fit.

There will be many opportunities this coming Winners Circle year of 2013 to be part of this mastermind. The more you partake, the more benefit you get and give – there is no limit to the power and magnitude of this universal law, and all it takes is your full engagement to open the floodgates.

Let the mastermind principle prove itself to you – or if it has already been a great asset for you, then thank you for sharing what you have learned with us, and let's move forward.

New Year's Wish

2012 is quickly drawing to a close, and it has been a year of high highs and low lows – a year of transitions and challenges, we saw natural disasters counterbalanced with extraordinary successes, the circle of life in microcosm.

The promise of 2013 is the growth and productivity that follows healing and consolidation. As winter follows autumn, so too does spring follow winter and the seasons of success are no different.

Let the laws of success work for you as well as they work for others – just remember, be loving, and express your love to those you serve and who serve you.

Happy New Year, beloved Winners Circle members!

Presence   January 2013

John Demartini talks about the Four Cardinal Pillars of Healing, where he lists four key qualities that great chiropractors express – certainty, gratitude, love, and… presence.

Certainty is easy to understand – you must demonstrate confidence that you can help the patient and deliver on the chiropractic promise, and be willing to convey any findings, observations or recommendations clearly and authoritatively. Gratitude's role is also apparent -- from the potency of the innate response to the privilege of being a chiropractor and serving that patient, we have so much to be thankful for and to be humbled by. Love is obviously the universal solvent and the most powerful attractive force known, and the unconditional acceptance that comes along with lovingness creates an environment that is most supportive of recovery, health and wellness.

But presence, well, that's a little more challenging to wrap our minds around. Yet, every top shelf chiropractor will tell you, whether they focus on high volume, specialty practice, advanced technical skills or whatever, that being in the moment with that patient is one of the most important elements of their approach.

The dictionary tells us that presence starts with occupancy, residence, inhabitance or attendance, a way of describing physical presence. The meaning of the word evolves as we include presence of mind, like composure, alertness or levelheadedness. Finally, the tone becomes grander as the definition expands, with concepts like existence, awareness, consciousness, potentiality and being.

This scope of meaning points out how important presence can be in practice – first, you must physically be with the patient; next, you must personify presence of mind, so the patient feels trust in you; and finally, you'll find that those upper echelon healers have a certain "it" factor where the quality of their "being" opens the door to increased potential and capacity for advanced healing, which seems to stem from this exceptional quality of being thoroughly and completely where they are. Presence of body, mind and spirit – it's a high vibration way to live and practice.

Forbes writer Jenna Goudreau gives us a practical perspective with her comments on executive presence.

"So what is executive presence? The ability to project gravitas – confidence, poise under pressure and decisiveness — seems to be its core characteristic, according to more than two-thirds of the executives surveyed. Furthermore, communication — including speaking skills, assertiveness and the ability to read an audience or situation — and appearance contribute to a person's perceived executive presence."

In contrast, innerfrontier.org, a website devoted to spiritual presence, offers these distinctions:

"Presence… The very word evokes a depth and potency of character, a gravitas, a charisma based on inner substantiality rather than outward flash, a simple and quiet dignity. All of that, however, only describes the outward signs of presence. Our path addresses its inner manifestation."

True living absolutely requires presence: more presence, more life. Without presence, life passes us by: we neither participate in nor fully experience our life. Presence means being at home in ourselves. Presence means inhabiting our body, heart, and mind, inhabiting our space, inhabiting our actions and inhabiting our life, not just passively letting it all happen.

Consciousness, the distinctive quality of presence, is a timeless energy of wholeness and peace. However, our sensory perceptual experiences, including physical sensations, thoughts and emotions, cover and obscure consciousness, keeping it dispersed, submerged, and mixed with the energies of sensation. For that reason we must learn to focus, to be sensitive and aware, in our whole body, in our emotions and in our minds. This creates a workable and effective foundation for consciousness to crystallize out of sensation.

The foreground of life, the perceptual picture on the screen of consciousness, captivates our attention and we remain unaware of the screen itself. But we cannot find consciousness by concentrating on its contents, on the ever-changing play of sensations. Consciousness possesses entirely different qualities: spacious, timeless, wise and unchanging. However, our contact with consciousness does change. Presence is always available, but by habit, clouded perception, and lack of choice, we are not always available to it."

The more we study this rather complicated subject, the more we grasp the relevance and power of being fully engaged in your current reality. No wonder Dr. Demartini gave it such prominence in his depiction of an optimal healer's toolbox.

Woody Allen joked, "Eighty percent of success is showing up." This turns out to be more profound than it seems at first glance – the better you "show up" the more present you are, and the more present you are, the more likely that you will produce your best possible behaviors, in both your practice and your personal life.

Who you are determines how well what you do works, and when you are fully present, you tend to show up as the best you possible. Discipline yourself to stay in the now, and you'll be a better healer, a better leader – in fact, you'll be a better you.

Motivation   February 2013

Last week we had our monthly telemastermind, and this time we took Denise Mathre's suggestion and discussed motivation – both how we motivate ourselves, and how we act as motivators for our team and patients.

Motivation is invariably some function of the interpretation of pleasure and pain – Tony Robbins has built a career to a large extent on the expansion of this concept. But the definition of pleasure and pain varies so widely from individual to individual, some calibration is required if you're going to use this leverage skillfully and effectively.

"The secret of success is learning how to use pain and pleasure instead of having pain and pleasure use you. If you do that, you're in control of your life. If you don't, life controls you." -- Tony Robbins

After listening to the practical applications shared at the MasterMind, I got curious about some of the underlying philosophy and theory of motivation – when I dug in, I discovered myriad variations and interesting perspectives on this essential field of study. Here are a few of the many distinctions I found:

Frederik Herzberg divided motivation into two factors: intrinsic (internal) motivation and extrinsic (external) motivation. Intrinsic motivation is driven by an interest or enjoyment in the task itself, while extrinsic motivation is an intention to achieve an outcome, whether or not it is accompanied by intrinsic motivation.

Then there's incentive theory, where behavior is positively reinforced with the expectation that the reinforced behavior will be repeated, what Dr. Hoffman refers to as "rewarding the behavior you want."

"Motivation is the art of getting people to do what you want them to do because they want to do it."
-- Dwight D. Eisenhower

A derivative of this is goal-setting theory, which simply states that people have a drive to reach a preferred and specified end state. A goal should meet the SMART criteria – specific, measurable, accurate, realistic, and timely. And if you wonder why the Six P's has purpose before personal, professional, people, prosperity and play goals, it's because the purpose acts as a blanket motivator to pursue the rest of the outcomes you desire. When your purpose is clear, your decision-making gets black and white – either your actions serve your purpose or they don't, and that becomes a prime motivator for your intended achievements.

"Believe in yourself! Have faith in your abilities! Without a humble but reasonable confidence in your own powers you cannot be successful or happy." -- Norman Vincent Peale

Another way of looking at motivation is through the lens of need theory, which suggests that motivation is the process of investing energy to satisfy needs. The best known proponent of need theory is Abraham Maslow, who taught a hierarchy of five needs: physiology (hunger, thirst, sleep, etc.): safety (security, shelter, health); belongingness (love, friendship, connection); self esteem (achievement, recognition); and self actualization (personal growth, identity expansion).

C.P. Alderfer re-chunked Maslow's theory with his ERG theory, which stands for existence, relatedness, and growth. Existence needs are similar to what Maslow called physiological and safety needs, required for simple existence. Relatedness covers social desires and maintaining personal relationships, and growth is the desire for personal development.

Professor Steven Reiss from Ohio State University expanded this theory into sixteen basic desires: acceptance, the need for approval; curiosity, the need to learn; eating, the need for food; family, the need to raise children; honor, the need to be loyal to the traditional values of one's clan/ethnic group; idealism, the need for social justice; independence, the need for individuality; order, the need for organized, stable, predictable environments; physical activity, the need for exercise and fitness; power, the need for influence or will; romance, the need for sex and beauty; saving, the need to collect; social contact, the need for friends and peer relationships; social status, the need for social standing/importance; tranquility, the need to be safe and well; and vengeance, the need to strike back and to compete.

"Our greatest weakness lies in giving up. The most certain way to succeed is always to try just one more time." -- Thomas A. Edison

One more -- cognitive dissonance theory, developed by Leon Festinger, says that people are motivated to reduce dissonance, or conflict in their lives. When someone notices an inconsistency between their actions and something they see in the world around them, they are motivated to resolve the conflict. We chiropractors rely on this theory when we are introducing the concepts of chiropractic philosophy to prospective patients, hoping they will grasp what doesn't work about their previous beliefs and what might work better about these new ones.

"If you don't design your own life plan, chances are you'll fall into someone else's plan. And guess what they have planned for you? Not much." -- Jim Rohn

Profitability   March 2013

The feedback on the First Annual Practice Explosion and Profitability (PEP) Day in Orlando is in, and by all accounts it was a smashing success – each Winners Circle member is powerful in her or his own right, but when we fuse our energies into a confluence of success vibrations, the power is palpable and unmistakably potent.

For those few who were not in attendance, we surely missed you, and look forward to seeing you in June or at SuperConference. But those who were there took their assignments seriously, and developed a litany of themes around the topic of profitability in practice that yielded ample and delicious fruit.

The information ran the spectrum, from the cutting edge coding to innovative marketing and patient compliance systems to space age clinical protocols, with everything in between, but one theme emerged throughout the event – there are myriad ways to be profitable in practice, as long as you act consistently with universal law while you are designing and implementing your strategies for success.

Tony Robbins taught me that wealth is evidence of having served well, and profit is a special kind of wealth, where an individual demonstrates appreciation for your expertise and loving care by giving you money, just for you, above and beyond what it costs you to run your practice. This is a high compliment indeed, and it's only because of the stigma of being a health entrepreneur that this concept isn't more often discussed and explored.

Patients are not dumb, and they surely understand that the doctor is running a business and needs to make a profit. The problem arises when the profit isn't reasonable, like the horror stories about hospital charges and huge markups on pharmaceuticals.

Do a quick analysis – how much does it cost you each month to run your office? Divide that number by your number of office visits, and you know what it costs you per office visit.

For example, if your average monthly office overhead is $16,000, and you see 500 office visits per month, it costs you $32 for each visit. If you charge and collect $50, then you are actually making $18/visit, or about $9000/month, 500 visits x $18/visit. If you collect at 80%, $40/visit, you make $8/visit, or $4000/month, 500 visits x $8/visit.

Notice that if you spend $16,000/month on your office and you see 800 office visits, it costs you only $20/visit, and that means the same $50 fee makes your profit $30/visit instead of $18, a higher level of profitability because you see more people in the same amount of time. In this case, you would be earning $24,000/month, 800 visits x $30/visit.

Also notice that if it costs you $16,000 to run your office and you see 400 visits, it costs you $40/visit, so at a $50 ova you make only $10/visit, or about $4000/month, 400 visits x $10.

Learning to do this kind of analysis will help you comprehend and measure your profitability. You want to maximize not only the number of new patients you can attract, but also their number of visits and dollars per visit.

This is why it's so important to look at the additional opportunities in profitability beyond your office visit. There are a dozen or more outstanding products and services that improve your patient's quality of life and put extra money in your pocket, which you earn by making a good recommendation for that patient's needs. Your expertise is worth something, and you are entitled to a reasonable profit on your care and your advice.

Remember, profitability is optimized through the interplay of three parameters in your practice – the number of new patients, the number of visits they stay, and the amount they spend each visit. By understanding how these measurements work together, you can develop the appropriate blend for you, based on your technique, philosophy and chosen office procedures.

In this way, you design a practice that is the best fit with your identity and practice philosophy, and reflects the maximum return a practice like that and a doctor like you can expect.

Bob teaches us about dollar productive behavior – some of your time is major outcome activity (MOA) time, some is neutral time, and some is fun time. You want to pack your MOA time with as much profitable activity as possible, another way to maximize your profitability.

The more you study and pay attention into this critical aspect of business, the more you improve your return on your hard work. Use your coaches as resources to enhance your profitability – it will come back to you as more evidence of having served well.

Clarity   April 2013

There is a subtle but powerful resource that many overlook, though it is a significant part of every decision you make. I'm talking about clarity, the ability to see the landscape objectively and respond in a relevant and consistent fashion.

Dictionary.com tells us that clarity is "clearness or lucidity as to perception or understanding; freedom from indistinctness or ambiguity." In other words, clarity is when you develop certainty that you comprehend and can therefore react effectively to your current conditions, by being both present and proactive.

BJ taught that "conflicts clarify," and what I think he meant by this is that when we get into a compromised position, it's recognizing and gaining leverage from our ethics and core ideologies that surfaces and gets us through. Wayne Dyer said that when you squeeze an orange, what comes out is orange juice – what comes out when you get squeezed?

In times of adversity, the first kind of clarity you need is clarity about your vision. Wallowing in the current unpleasantness will only recycle the pain. Begin with the end in mind. Remember that Einstein said we can't solve our problems with the same level of thinking that caused them, we need to create a new reality where the problems don't exist.

Next, you'll need clarity about your own identity – who you are determines how well what you do works, so getting crystal clear on who you are and how you need to show up will light the way toward what to do.

Then you must get clarity about your purpose – when your purpose is clear your decision-making gets black and white. You must know why your vision is important to someone with your identity, and your purpose defines that – it's the reason you will do or not do what you will do or not do

To focus your attention and energy, now you must get clarity about your missions, the individual goals and objectives you feel compelled to accomplish.

Finally, you must get clarity about your plans and strategies, with a list of properly chunked action steps based on the beliefs, resources, materials and people you need to hit your immediate targets.

This system helps you focus from your most expansive intentions to your most precise ones, and filling in the details helps you gain the clarity you need about fulfilling your destiny and building the life you want, one piece at a time.

Having clarity helps you act congruently and without tolerations. If you can see how your behaviors are serving you, you can continue and amplify them, and if you can see how your behaviors are not serving you, you can vary and refine them until they do.

How can we increase our level of clarity? At the "do" level, you can improve your sensory acuity – be more aware, and stay in "up time" – this means keeping your attention directed outward. This gives you the environmental distinctions you need to inter-relate with your world.

Then, at the "be" level, you can build clarity with a resource builder, or practice visualizing your vision, identity, purpose, missions, strategies and action steps, so you have a solid internal representation of your desired outcomes.

This concept of developing clarity pervades all aspects of our lives. Get clear, get present, get focused and get into a mindset of crystal clarity – it will accelerate your movement toward your most cherished goals and dreams.

Ownership   May 2013

We frequently hear about "taking responsibility" or "holding yourself accountable" -- the buck stops somewhere, an essential principle of leadership and in all aspects of success.

But there is another level of this quality that I refer to as ownership. Ownership is responsibility and accountability… and then some. Ownership means that not only does the buck stop with you, it's your buck.

Ownership is closely related to mastery, only it adds a dimension of engagement. Masters are excellent within their field of mastery, but ownership is applied mastery, seeing and acting upon the relationship between mastery and the matters at hand. It's being a field leader, a ring general who seizes control of the situation and does whatever is necessary.

At a Tony Robbins Certification course twenty-two years ago, I had the privilege of meeting the late General Norman Schwartzkopf, who oversaw an army of up to 750,000 soldiers during Operation Desert Storm. His motto was, "When placed in command, take charge."

This is the essence of ownership – claiming the right to ultimate decision-making and following through by putting it all on the line when the chips are down.

As an entrepreneur, how can you develop a sense of ownership? We've heard Bob say that leadership is 20% earned and 80% assumed. With ownership, it's more like 100% earned and 100% assumed.

To earn 100% ownership, you must invest the time, effort and fully associated work to get the required distinctions into your cellular memory, so it becomes automatic, faster and more complete than a reflex, just a presence, a consciousness, like Malcolm Gladwell's blink.

Then, to assume 100% ownership, raise your standards, distill your beliefs and develop strategies of success that cannot fail. Find some way to prepare for any eventuality, whether affirmation, mental rehearsal, visualization, role-playing, or any tool or system you can learn or design to put yourself in the appropriate driver's seat. Establish outcome clarity through your vision and purpose, and systematically coordinate your missions. Show up in your practice and your life with this kind of authenticity, confidence and self esteem, and you'll be expressing ownership.

Ownership can also be claimed by your team – not literally, of course, but the way they show up will enhance or detract from the overall vibration of your practice, and their contribution is something they can indeed take ownership of.

I remember, from October 1, 1987, my first day of coaching at Markson Management, I acted as if it were my company. I worked very hard, took on as much responsibility as I could, and contributed as much as possible. Over a convoluted ten year period, I became a partner and then co-owner of what is now The Masters Circle, an accomplishment of which I am exceptionally proud. That's part of ownership, too.

To turbo-charge your practice, encourage your team to take ownership of their position. The role they play is that vital to the wellbeing of those you serve, and you want to empower them to make decisions up to the level of their experience, allowing that they may not get it right every time, but that they must experiment with this kind of leadership in order to grow into the best they can be.

You want teammates who are willing to be responsible for the part they play in the office's growth and success. This doesn't mean that they overstep their boundaries, but rather that they treat your practice as if it were their own. They need to play their position with skill, concentration, and love, just because that's the way it's done with people who take ownership.

Long time Wal-Mart executive Michael Bergdahl said, "Sam Walton instilled ownership of the products in the stores into the collective consciousness of every associate regardless of what job they did for the company."

Ownership means congruency, no ambiguity, complete and utter immersion with the highest integrity. Ownership means you are the one who answers for yourself, your creed, your tribe or group. Ownership means that you say what needs to be said and do what needs to be done, whether it feels good at the time or not. Ownership is absolute, unwavering, definite.

Ownership also insinuates owning up, admitting when you have made a mistake, and accepting the consequences.

Finally, you want to do your best to convey ownership of the chiropractic wellness lifestyle to your patients. They have experienced miracles, they have seen and heard amazing things happen in your office, and we need them to spread the word, with certainty, power and commitment.

Movie and sports mogul Peter Guber said, "Telling purposeful stories is interactive. It's not a monolog. Ultimately, purposeful tellers must surrender control of their stories, creating a gap for the listener(s) to willingly cross in order to take ownership. Only when the listener(s) own the tellers' story and make it theirs, will they virally market it."

This is a complex and fascinating topic, esoteric yet penetratingly practical. Give some thought to those places in your life where you already feel a sense of ownership, and those which require some shift on your part to do so. It's a great way to direct your personal and professional growth, and build resources to handle your most relevant weaker areas.

Tall Poppies   June 2013

You may have heard the story of the Turkish opium poppy farmers, who learned that when they harvested their crops too young, many of the poppies they reaped were immature, costing them money when the yield of opium was smaller than expected.

So, they learned to set their threshers a foot high instead of at ground level, thereby cutting down only the tall poppies, a sound strategy to maximize their return and allow the younger poppies to grow before being collected.

Tall poppy syndrome, then, came to mean that you should keep your head down, to keep from getting it cut off.

I wonder how many of us are in defense physiology, at the same time depriving our communities of the benefits of chiropractic care and ourselves and our families of the rewards of having served well? Marianne Williamson warned us about playing small – step up to your potential, make something big happen!

There is an Australian derivative of this tall poppy idea, where people disparage or vilify successful people, perceiving success to be a zero-sum game, an "if they have it I can't have it so I have to hate them for having it" kind of thing.

This "politics of envy" keeps people pinned in mediocrity and interferes with normal growth, which is the reason we need to understand it.

As chiropractors, we are at the cutting edge of healing and wellness, and if we keep our light under a basket, everyone involved suffers.

Elephant trainers know that if they tie the baby elephant to a stake, it will quickly learn that it cannot pull out that stake, and that memory carries over into adulthood, when the elephant could easily break free but does not because it is trained into the habit of captivity.

Similarly, many of us have learned to "keep our heads down" and not make trouble, flying below the radar but also achieving below our capabilities.

What would it take for you to realize that your shackles are imaginary and insufficient to restrain you, and that you can liberate yourself at any time? You have the power, you have the intellect, you have the opportunity, so what is holding you back?

Much like those elephants, if we have learned that we are restricted, we act as if we are restricted, even if really we're not. It's the newfound awareness of our own greatness that will trigger the ascent to our rightful place in health and wellness.

Bob says that leadership is 20% earned and 80% assumed, so bring some swagger back to your practice and your life! I'm not talking about cockiness or conceit, just a little self-assuredness to exploit your significance, and make yourself a bit more available to serve. Please stay humble, just be a little more willing to broadcast the benefits of working with you, and the consequences of missing out on chiropractic.

There is, of course, a right time to keep your head down – when the slings and arrows are coming at you, that's no time for bravado, duck and be safe. At any crossroads, we have three choices, lead, follow, or get out of the way, and sometimes, we need to get out of the way.

But as a general rule, you'll discover that standing tall among the other poppies, holding your head up high, being proud of yourself and of being a chiropractor, and presenting yourself front and center, to put yourself in position to do the most good possible, is a winning formula that will pay off for you as it has for so many others who are willing to take the risk.

Every one of you has something unique and special to offer. Be generous enough, courageous enough and resilient enough to speak your truth, and add your verse to the song of health and wellness!

Recognition July 2013

I turned sixty years of age a few days ago, and I thank all of those who acknowledged my special day – at this point in my life, when I wake up, look down and see the ground, I am deeply happy, because every day above ground is a great day.

I always do my best to recognize the good in all people and situations I come into contact with – I know that no matter how thin you slice it, there's always two sides, and I am only too aware of the philosophies based on the Shadow, about which I am reading a fascinating book I'll tell you about at a later date – but I can't help feeling that people are so battered and bruised by their interpretation of their own reality, I attempt to break the pattern by pointing out those things worth being optimistic about.

Hope springs eternal, and I do believe that the recognition of something special and valuable in someone builds them up in strong and noble thought, and facilitates their development of their self esteem, an important secret to success that is often overlooked.

If we truly believe that who you are determines how well you show up, it's essential to show up as the best you possible to get the best results possible.

Some opinions vary on this. Carol Dweck, author of "Mindset," says that there are two kinds of mindsets, a fixed mindset and a growth mindset. Those who dial into a growth mindset are likely to see the opportunities in their environment, while those who are more fixed are likely to overlook or ignore them.

Dweck goes on to say that if we reward people for conditions that are beyond their control, like their intelligence or beauty, it could potentially throw them into a fixed mindset, since they don't perceive that they can grow and improve on things that seem God-given.

In this scenario, Dweck suggests recognizing the hard work and effort, rather than the raw ability – her research demonstrates that this is more relevant and effective reinforcement.

Still, I love complimenting people's natural talents, including reminding people that they are physically attractive, since most of us are so judgmental of ourselves and others in this regard.

As a bit of homespun research, please let me know if, at any point when I am recognizing something positive that I perceive you were responsible for, if I step over this line Dweck defines. It will be useful for me to know if my efforts to enhance your self image actually work or not.

The act of recognition falls on your shoulders as well – recognizing your staff for fine performance, your children for genuine accomplishments and courage in seeking new experiences, your spouse in standing by you through tough times and helping you celebrate your victories – recognition is an often overlooked aspect of our communication, and done well, it can shape a relationship, add emotional charge and skyrocket the love, appreciation and respect, leading to more connection, higher achievement, and more happiness.

How do people prefer to be recognized? In your intimate relationships, please consider deriving your formula from the Five Love Languages material Bob taught us about, from the book by Gary Chapman – you can use words of affirmation and encouragement; you can spend quality time with him or her; you can buy gifts and material representations of your devotion; you can provide acts of service, doing things that feel valued and worthwhile; or, you can offer physical touching which enhances connection and demonstrates sensitivity and vulnerability.

With your friends, colleagues and staff, explore if they are visual, auditory, or kinesthetic – you can match your recognition to the ways that the other prefers and enjoys being recognized. Nothing has any meaning but the meaning we give it, and we can never know the meanings someone else chooses without asking.

This willingness to calibrate, define and apply can get you more impact when you recognize someone, so spend the extra effort.

Socrates says that the unexamined life is not worth living, meaning that we should look inside to be sure our actions match up with our values. A derivative of this thought is that anything worth doing is worth measuring, and you can extrapolate this to include your recognition of others. If you measure that someone does something good, let them know it in as close to their own language as possible – it can brighten their day, give them positive reference experiences, and inspire them to pay it forward, your contribution to making this world just a little bit happier.

Love Bomb   August 2013

As most of you know, I had the privilege of speaking at The WAVE, Life West's homecoming, elegantly and artfully produced by Brian Kelly, a rising star in chiropractic.

He brought in top shelf talent like Marianne Williamson and Patch Adams, along with dozens of others from within and beyond the profession, like consulting icons Chuck Gibson and Charlie Ward whose chiropractic brand recognition spans over four decades; environmental activists like Jeff Smith blowing the whistle on genetically modified foods and those responsible for instigating genetic mayhem on our planet; and cutting edge chiropractic philosophy, science and art from Dan Murphy, Christopher Kent, and Gerry Clum – it was a smorgasbord of chiropractic thought, word and deed.

But one of my favorite moments in the program was a young chiropractor recently in practice in northern California, who conceived of and decided to drop… a love bomb. She explains it best with these excerpts from her website, promoting her documentary movie of her mission trip to Peru:

Love Bomb" is a story about transforming trauma and fear into love and service. While living in New York City, Rhea Zimmerman experienced the emotional shock of the events on 9/11… (which) ultimately moves her into action where she decides to do something that would begin her own healing process and assist her to express her hope for humanity. She finds this through chiropractic.

Rhea joins forces with boyfriend, Dr. Austin Komarek and teammate Dr. Alejandra Robles Arizmendi, to set out on a chiropractic service trip to The Sacred Valley, Peru. What happens when good intentions to be of service meet high altitude, a lost passport, and physical exhaustion? How does the team come together to support one another to break through their own barriers and find out what they are capable of in order to give their best care to thousands of people in five days? Do their efforts make a difference?

How does the "Love Bomb" impact the hearts of the team members, the people that they are serving, and those who observe their actions?

Themes of living love, connection to self and others, transformation from trauma, and individual purpose are woven throughout the story through the action of the service team and supported by the voices of featured experts in the fields of human development, consciousness studies, mind/matter science, epigenetics, social anthropology, chiropractic, yoga, and personal development.

Ultimately this story reveals "what we are capable of" as human beings. From the tragic to the awe inspiring acts of loving service, now known as, "Love Bombs", to our innate capacity to heal, transform and connect. It demonstrates that with daily intention, we are capable of choosing to let go of our fear to find out what awaits us on the other side.

This is advanced citizenry at its finest, a selfless journey through suffering to hope and healing, with no apologies for tireless optimism and random acts of kindness. It's a modern day mission to spread love, chiropractic style, throughout the communities that make up our world, and slowly but surely the health of our planet will shift.

And maybe not so slowly, if it's a big enough love bomb.

Many of you have gone on mission trips, introducing a lot of people to chiropractic and offering them live-giving adjustments. But theoretically, you can go on a chiropractic mission without leaving your immediate vicinity – by volunteering one day a month, in cooperation with a few colleagues, you could be turning on life in people who are less fortunate, and perhaps providing the boost they need to get healthier and improve the quality of their lives.

In this way, you can drop your own "love bomb" on your community, and leave an indelible impression of caring, wellness and good will.

Imagine what would happen if, slowly or quickly, incrementally and then in an explosion of mutual admiration and support, a love bomb were to be detonated in communities around the world – project for a moment the impact of an epidemic of caring and sharing, each of us taking responsibility to do some good – the results would be widespread positivity, cross-cultural growth and camaraderie, and would surely make this world a better place. How can you participate in this movement? How can we all? Or better stated, how can we not?

Troubleshooting With the
PFQ   September 2013

As Winners Circle members, you have been exposed for a while to the basic concepts of troubleshooting your practice issues – more often than not, the easy stuff you just figure out a way to deal with it, and the more complex issues are handled with coaching support.

One of the most useful tools for problem-solving and practice evaluation is the Practice Fulfillment Quotient, the PFQ, described in great detail in your Masters Guide. This five-part model of practice being and doing is worth a bit of discussion, so you can refine your application of it.

The Practice Fulfillment Quotient (PFQ)

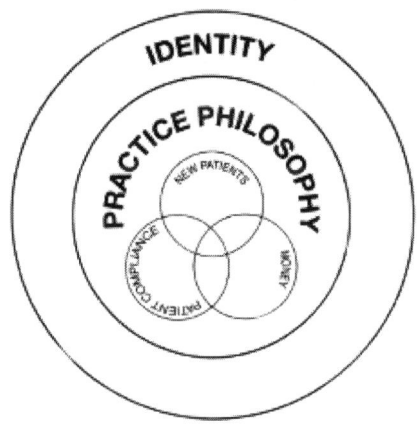

If you look at the three inner circles, you get a snapshot of the operations or mechanics of your practice. Most who study Capacity Technology™ recognize that the size of the inner circles must approach your ideal, but remember that the fit, the distance from the center, is also a factor – twenty new patients, for example, is not twenty new patients – twenty seniors is a lot different from five young families of four. One is not better or worse than the other, but they are different, and if you want to serve families, twenty seniors may make you more successful, but not necessarily more fulfilled.

This refinement is represented as the inner circles moving closer to the center – notice that while the center area, representing the degree of fulfillment, gets bigger when the circle grow in size, it grows even faster in response to the circles moving toward the center, since improving the fit is a more direct route to fulfillment.

This is obvious with new patients, but it is also true about patient compliance and money management. For example, a PI practice that partners with attorneys for optimal settlements for their mutual clients has a very different take on a program of care from a subluxation-based wellness office. In the PI practice, the intent is to document the disability, and then to walk a fine line between providing relief and maximizing the reportable impact of the injury for the attorneys to substantiate their case and support the patient's position. So, a practice like that tends toward a lower PVA.

On the other hand, the wellness doctor wants a long term relationship with the patient, so a higher PVA is a better fit. Notice, there is no correct or incorrect number – it's based on the intention and fit.

Same thing with money management. You can make more money by serving, charging and collecting more, or you can make more money by refining your money management systems, reducing overhead and optimizing your return on investment. Ideally, you'd do both, and how you do in this area will decide the size and position of the money management circle.

The outer circles will define how far the inner circles can take you. The inner circles cannot outgrow the boundaries set by the outer circles. So, you must learn to enlarge your sense of self and carefully adjust your practice philosophy so that your degree of congruency intensifies and your practice expression matches your practice intention. Only then can your inner circles be provided more room to increase.

To grow your identity, eliminate capacity limitations – at the "do" level, you could add hands, add days, add hours, add speed, add systems or technology, or add attitude and energy. At the be level, you could affirm and visualize, or set goals, or build resources – you could shift your beliefs, reprioritize your values, reorganize your organizing principles, or develop habits of excellence. These tools can help you build more capacity to fill, and when you get to the point that you are using optimal habits with optimal attitude and energy, you'll fill your increased capacity with more attraction.

To refine your practice philosophy, notice your personal blend of musculoskeletal patients, traditional subluxation-based patients, and wellness patients. Compare your findings to your ideal, and proceed accordingly – if it's a good fit, turn your attention elsewhere, and if not, work toward establishing more consistency between your intentions and your actions and behaviors.

This kind of troubleshooting will save you hours of head-banging and earn you piles of money. Bob says proper planning prevents poor performance – explore your practice with the PFQ, and make your office more efficient and more profitable.

Goal Setting   October 2013

I was surprised to discover out how many of you are dragging your feet on getting your 2014 goals in place – in fact, some of you may even resist the whole idea of goal setting, and if you can find satisfaction without it, more power to you – but for most of us, setting goals and making plans to pursue them is a cornerstone of success and accountability.

What is a goal in the first place? It's an aim or objective considered worth achieving, a definition of victory to focus on.

Is setting goals essential? Well, no, not in the most technical sense, but they are a tremendous asset, both in having a way to measure how you are doing, and also to calibrate if the effort involved is worth the end product you are attempting to create. The mind is target-oriented, so giving yourself a bull's eye to point yourself toward increases your odds of fulfillment.

There are several fundamentals supporting your goal setting. First, you must be aware of the balance between believability and motivation, one of the most common pitfalls in contemporary goal setting. Set the goal too far out in the distance, and it will seem very motivating, but not as believable. Set the goal too close to yourself, and you'll think it's very believable, but not that motivating. Establish a goal that is just far away enough to be motivating, but close enough to be believable.

Next, you must have a system of goal setting that covers the bases the way you want them covered. You can use the Six P's, which suggests that you chunk your goals into your purpose, personal goals, professional goals, people goals, prosperity goals, and play goals. Or, you can simplify it into just personal and professional goals. Or, you can simply construct a wish list.

None of these techniques are correct or incorrect – find a system that works for you, and commit to applying the principles of that system consistently. It is this commitment that is the x-factor in goal setting – it's challenging enough to write the goals in the first place, but raising your standards and following through on what you have written, well, that separates the pretty good achievers from the outstanding world class performers who make the biggest difference.

I find that my preliminary plans are often incomplete, until I begin to visualize the end product, and then some of the missing pieces begin to come into view and fall into place. Add this extra dimension to your goal setting, as championship athletes and master entertainers do, and you will be amazed at the advantage it gives you.

I also find it useful to read my goals frequently – when I'm in an intense creative period, I may read them daily or even a few times a day, but usually a weekly review is sufficient for me – how does it work for you? Check in as often as you need to, in order to keep your desired outcomes in mind.

One more distinction about goal setting – I don't know about you, but I don't achieve all of my goals on my first attempt. Sometimes I have to troubleshoot the process to see where the glitch is, and for that kind of assessment I use the Results Quinary, which defines the five steps of goal setting, going from Idea to Goal to Plan to Action and finally to a Result, and then cycling back through the process when necessary, refining as you go to relentlessly pursue your objective.

Each step requires both leverage, a reason to push onward, and strategy, a path to push onward upon, and reviewing this foundational goal-setting material will sharpen your approach and yield better results overall.

Mark Victor Hansen says to set too many goals, and it's hard to argue with his level of success. For me, I try to stick with Bob's three-to-eight concept – we can handle somewhere between three and eight goals at a time, so regardless of which goal setting system you choose, pick a few key goals to work on and accomplish them before you spread yourself over many goals at once. You'll find your own natural rhythm on this, once you engage the process.

The world's great leaders and entrepreneurs agree that goal setting is a key part of their success – be sure you are applying this global truth effectively in your own experience, and you'll do more good and have more to show for it.

Seven (Plus Two) Kinds Of Smart   November 2013

I became interested many years ago in the work of Harvard Professor Howard Gardner on the multiple forms of intelligence. It was apparent to me that the way I was rewarded in school for being good at math and science and also having some fluency in the written and spoken word positioned me for an outstanding college education and a sure entry into professional school.

It was equally obvious to me that many of my friends who were not similarly gifted were also intelligent, just in different ways – but it wasn't until I became aware of Gardner's research that the pieces of this puzzle started to fit together for me.

You see, it seems that there are at least seven basic forms of intelligence, and the latest philosophy suggests at least two more – by understanding how people's talents and tendencies vary, we can stop overlooking the magnificent contributions of individuals who are not skillful with words and numbers, but rather in some other meaningful way.

Gardner's groundbreaking book, "Frames of Mind: The Theory of Multiple Intelligences" was rendered more accessible and public-friendly by psychologist and learning expert Thomas Armstrong in "Seven Kinds of Smart." Let's look at this foundational information and see how we can apply it in our practices and our lives.

In our schools, the students who are generally most-rewarded are the ones who are good at English and the ones who are good at math and science, since those abilities are reasonably easy to quantify and measure -- I mean, words are either spelled correctly or not, the solution to the math problem is either correct or it isn't.

Look at these two statements:

1. "In a right triangle, the square of the hypotenuse is equal to the sum of the squares of the other two sides."

2. "The whole is greater than the sum of the parts."

While both remarks consider the concept of a "sum," in the first statement, only linear thinking is required, leading to a measurable, quantifiable meaning, while the second demands a more abstract viewpoint, not measurable in typical units. In the first, the sum is the result of a precise mathematical equation, in the second, the sum appears inexact, something less than the whole. Looking at the world through different filters gives you a different sense of reality, and this gives rise to the many forms of intelligence and creativity, not only words and numbers, but also others that can be grouped into these categories.

What I first learned as "Verbal/Linguistic" intelligence, Armstrong calls "Word Smart"– being able to write, speak, and comprehend what you read are cherished and highly rewarded skills.

What I first learned as "Mathematical/Logical" intelligence, Armstrong calls "Logic Smart" – being able to reason logically, apply math concepts, calculate and extrapolate are qualities well-suited to many prominent professions, including doctors of all kinds, engineers, accountants, and teachers in those fields.

Yet I know people who can't add or put two words together, but put a guitar in their hands, and magic springs from their melodic mind. These people have "Musical" intelligence, they're "Music Smart."

And then there are those who are able to draw, take great photographs, interpret the space around them with uncanny accuracy, and visualize with their mind's eye – these people have "Visual/Spatial" intelligence, they're "Spatial Smart."

How about Michael Jordan or Tiger Woods, who have specialized talents in their physical bodies? They have "Physical" intelligence, they're "Body Smart."

You probably know people who are expert at connecting socially with others, networkers extraordinaire, terrific husbands and wives and committed parents and friends – they are demonstrating "Interpersonal" intelligence, they're "People Smart."

The seventh type of smart describes someone who has great self-awareness and self-knowledge – they have "Intra-personal" intelligence, they're "Self Smart."

The eight and ninth forms of intelligence are of special interest to chiropractors – not that the others aren't, but these are especially relevant.

When someone relates to, studies, interprets and develops a deeper understanding of Nature, they are expressing "Naturalistic" intelligence – they are "Nature Smart." Chiropractic, as we all know, is the science, philosophy and art of things natural, so those who connect with that message are showing their "Naturalistic" intelligence.

And finally, someone who is able to detect, comprehend, evaluate and discuss the ultimate issues of life has "Existential" intelligence – they are "Existence Smart." Acknowledging Universal and Innate Intelligence, grasping the essence of vitalism, and recognizing the need to reconnect "man the spiritual and man the physical," even assimilating the idea of wellness, it all falls under "existential" intelligence.

It may seem perplexing as to why patients or even some colleagues struggle to understand our message – they are not dumb, they just may have a blend of intelligence that doesn't emphasize this way of thinking. Think about your own gifts, and those of the significant people in your life – appreciating them for who they are, instead of comparing them to some arbitrary ideal based on cultural bias, will reduce your stress, reframe your judgment, make you more loving and accepting, and probably improve your sense of humor, too.

Determination   December 2013

There is a subtle but essential quality that is shared by the most successful people on earth. It can be called by many names – persistence, perseverance, stick-to-it-iveness – but I call it… determination.

Determination is a magical x-factor that separates those who get close to victory from those who actually get to experience standing gloriously in the winner's circle.

I've collected some great thinking on this topic – see which of these remarks you resonate best with: (from brainyquote.com)

"Nothing in this world can take the place of persistence. Talent will not: nothing is more common than unsuccessful men with talent. Genius will not; unrewarded genius is almost a proverb. Education will not: the world is full of educated derelicts. Persistence and determination alone are omnipotent."
-- Calvin Coolidge

"A dream doesn't become reality through magic; it takes sweat, determination and hard work."
-- Colin Powell

"The price of success is hard work, dedication to the job at hand, and the determination that whether we win or lose, we have applied the best of ourselves to the task."
-- Vince Lombardi

"I long to accomplish great and noble tasks, but it is my chief duty to accomplish humble tasks as though they were great and noble. The world is moved along, not only by the mighty shoves of its heroes, but also by the aggregate of the tiny pushes of each honest worker." -- Helen Keller

"I never could have done what I have done without the habits of punctuality, order, and diligence, without the determination to concentrate myself on one subject at a time."
-- Charles Dickens

"Desire is the key to motivation, but it's determination and commitment to an unrelenting pursuit of your goal - a commitment to excellence - that will enable you to attain the success you seek." -- Mario Andretti

"When we first begin fighting for our dreams, we have no experience and make many mistakes. The secret of life, though, is to fall seven times and get up eight times."
– Paulo Coelho, The Alchemist

These are variations on a theme, one that we will all need to draw upon at some time during our lives and practices. Even the most blessed of us have adversities and challenges to deal with, and the relentless pursuit of excellence and of breaking through limitations is one of the most cherished habits in our culture, often rewarded with fame, power and financial return, often in extreme proportions, not to mention the personal satisfaction for a job well done.

Another way to think of determination is as extended motivation – in other words, if you take motivation and stretch it over a longer period of time, it becomes determination. This anecdote may illustrate this better for you:

When I was working as a Master Trainer for Anthony Robbins, I was charged with the responsibility of standing at the front of fire lanes and getting the participants into a resourceful state before they safely walked on fire. The entry level was about a twelve foot walk, and beginning firewalkers would get into a very intense state, and storm across the coals, exclaiming ":Cool moss! Cool moss!" all the way across.

But at the certification course, it was a forty–five foot firewalk, almost four times the distance. This is typically a more poised, slower and more conscious firewalk. It would be difficult to maintain the intensity of a short firewalk for four times as long, so a different resource state is necessary, similarly present but extended over a longer period of time, as assertive but not necessarily as aggressive.

This is like the relationship between motivation and determination – the short, intense firewalk is like motivation, and the longer, more centered and balanced but still powerful long firewalk is like determination. It's like taking the pattern of motivation and continuing it until it blends into every moment and becomes second nature.

Think of some area in your practice or your life where you have been doggedly determined to solve a problem, follow through on a goal or plan, or address a weaker area to increase capacity. Notice how you do that – you probably have characteristic mind and body details you use in that scenario, which you can choose when you are aware of them.

For example, is there a typical facial expression, posture or rate of breathing you might use when you are feeling determined to do something? Think about it, what are you doing with your body when you are feeling persistent?

Now, notice the details of your mental processing – do you make pictures, hear sounds, talk to yourself, get feelings or remember reference experiences? Again, recognize the common patterns of your thoughts and feelings, and catalog those that take you toward feeling more motivated, resilient, and perseverant right now. These are clues to harnessing this resource for you to apply as you wish.

You can't go wrong working on yourself. Every day, you are asked to raise your standards and hold yourself to a higher degree of execution. It takes character to walk the road less traveled – never, never quit, and remember that nothing has any meaning but the meaning you give it, so choose empowering ways to look at and respond to your world, and you can create the life and practice you really want.

Integrity   January 2014

One of the greatest compliments you can pay to someone is to say that they have integrity – but what does that really mean, and how does it help us to move forward?

Dictionary.com gives us three important meanings for this essential trait.

1. adherence to moral and ethical principles; soundness of moral character; honesty; as in "BJ Palmer epitomized chiropractic integrity."

2. the state of being whole, entire, or undiminished; as in "chiropractic enhances neural integrity."

3. a sound, unimpaired, or perfect condition; as in "the integrity of the spine."

I collected some pithy remarks from some of our great thinkers on this multi-faceted quality. I find these kinds of inspirational quotations at goodreads.com, brainy-quotes.com, and from googling other websites designed to supply such ideas. Notice each of these shades of difference in definition in the following observations by these philosophers – the way they express themselves can give you clues about refining your own communication style, one-on-one and to groups.

"Whoever is careless with the truth in small matters cannot be trusted with important matters"
– Albert Einstein

"When you are content to be simply yourself and don't compare or compete, everyone will respect you." – Lao Tzu

"Real integrity is doing the right thing, knowing that nobody's going to know whether you did it or not." – Oprah Winfrey

"I am not bound to win, but I am bound to be true. I am not bound to succeed, but I am bound to live up to what light I have." – Abraham Lincoln

"Nothing is at last sacred but the integrity of your own mind." – Ralph Waldo Emerson

"When will our consciences grow so tender that we will act to prevent human misery rather than avenge it?" – Eleanor Roosevelt

"Somebody once said that in looking for people to hire, you look for three qualities: integrity, intelligence, and energy. And if you don't have the first, the other two will kill you. You think about it; it's true. If you hire somebody without [integrity], you really want them to be dumb and lazy." – Warren Buffett

"Every man must decide whether he will walk in the light of creative altruism or in the darkness of destructive selfishness." – Martin Luther King Jr.

"Achievement of your happiness is the only moral purpose of your life, and that happiness, not pain or mindless self-indulgence, is the proof of your moral integrity, since it is the proof and the result of your loyalty to the achievement of your values." -- Ayn Rand

"Integrity has no need of rules." – Albert Camus

"Before speaking, consult your inner-truth barometer, and resist the temptation to tell people only what they want to hear." – Wayne Dyer

"Find the courage to ask questions and to express what you really want. Communicate with others as clearly as you can to avoid misunderstandings, sadness and drama." -- Don Miguel Ruiz

"The foundation stones for a balanced success are honesty, character, integrity, faith, love and loyalty." -- Zig Ziglar

"Live with integrity, respect the rights of other people, and follow your own bliss." -- Nathaniel Branden

"Integrity is the ability to stand by an idea." – Ayn Rand

There are many others, but I think you get the point – as diverse influencers as Ayn Rand, Martin Luther King Jr. and Warren Buffett come to about the same conclusion – that devoid of integrity, humans are little more than intelligent beasts, and with it, we can transcend the mundane and exemplify the finest virtues of being human.

How do we chiropractors demonstrate our integrity? Every day, we are called upon to serve our patients with the best we have – to offer them less is out of integrity. We often operate behind closed doors, whether in the adjusting room or the collections office – holding yourself to the highest possible standard is a necessary precondition to consider yourself a person of integrity.

Perfection may elude us, but at every conceivable juncture, we have choices, and the optimal choices will always reflect our best selves. Connect with your truth before you make such decisions – you will err on the side of your higher nature, and while this may not guarantee that your preferred outcome will manifest immediately, there's reason to believe that your congruency invites an ultimate success, regardless of any speed bumps along the way.

For most, being out of integrity is nothing more than a toleration, since all of us are good at the core, behavior to the contrary notwithstanding – if you need to, clean up your act.

And if you feel like you've been doing well along these lines, bravo to you, and keep it up – as doctors of chiropractic, we must be above reproach, role models of excellence for our families, our colleagues, our teams and for those we serve. There is an energy field to that kind of authenticity that will make you stand out in the marketplace and amplify your joy and passion.

Don't settle – raise the bar, act consistently with your higher self, and be a person of integrity.

Mindfulness   February 2014

Those of us who had the extraordinary pleasure of going to Miraval for our first Transformational Weekend of 2014 got exposed to a word that we may have heard before, but only now are we starting to see how relevant and powerful it is – that word is mindfulness.

Mindfulness is presence and then some. It suggests that we are putting our attention in the optimal place it belongs, given the current circumstances.

Let's look at how Miraval defines mindfulness:

"Mindfulness is a state of active, open attention in the present moment. When you're mindful, you observe your thoughts and feelings without judgment. Mindfulness means living in the moment and awakening to experience.

Our focus is on healthy and sustainable living. The Miraval experience is fresh locally sourced ingredients to make flavorful food, growth and development activities that make the heart pump and the head re-think, fabulous spa services that make the senses ignite, and an unrivaled team of wellbeing specialists to help you make positive and lasting change in your life. Lest we forget the natural splendor and year round warmth.

Mindfulness is the core of the Miraval philosophy. In everything we do, we encourage our guests to live in the present moment, conscious of the unique intersection of mind, body, and spirit. Miraval can be your catalyst for a healthy lifestyle change; your escape and support through challenging times; or simply somewhere to rest, reflect and re-energize as you begin the next chapter in your life story. For most of our guests, the Miraval experience is nothing less than a life-changing and life re-affirming moment."

And I think it's fair to say that those of us who engaged the Miraval process saw what they meant. It was a full immersion, from the food to the smoothies to the beds to the first rate facilities to the team teachers and everything in between.

I found a discussion of mindfulness at Helpguide.org, in collaboration with Harvard Medical School, adapted from "Positive Psychology: Harnessing the Power of Happiness, Personal Strength, and Mindfulness," a special health report published by Harvard Health Publications.

They declare that mindfulness improves your health, both physical and mental. They also state, "Mindfulness is the practice of purposely focusing your attention on the present moment — and accepting it without judgment. Mindfulness is now being examined scientifically and has been found to be a key element in happiness."

It was Dr. Jon Kabat-Zinn, founder and former director of the Stress Reduction Clinic at the University of Massachusetts Medical Center, who helped to integrate the practice of mindfulness meditation into mainstream medicine, advising that mindfulness can improve physical symptoms as well as change health attitudes and behaviors for the better.

Mindfulness practices can be used to reduce stress, treat heart disease and lower blood pressure, relieve pain, enhance sleep patterns and ease gastrointestinal disorders.

Such habits are also used to deal with depression, substance abuse, eating problems, relationship issues, anxiety and obsessive compulsive disorder.

Experts theorize that this works because it helps people to accept their experiences instead of denying or avoiding them.

Mindfulness meditation requires concentration, and here are a few pointers on generating that kind of focus:

1. Go with the flow
2. Pay attention
3. Stay with it
4. Practice acceptance
5. If your mind wanders, redirect it
6. Stay at it

Here are the mechanics for you to model:

1. Sit comfortably, forward on your chair or cross-legged on a cushion.

2. Concentrate on your breathing, making it even and steady.

3. Once you have a rhythm established, broaden your focus, noticing ideas, sensations, and sounds.

4. Consider your experience without judging it. If your mind races, return to your breathing, then expand your focus again when you are ready.

To connect with and engage the present moment, consider this strategy:

1. Bring your attention to the sensations you experience in your body.

2. Breathe in through your nose, drawing the air down into your belly, allowing your abdomen to expand.

3. Breathe out either through your mouth (more energizing) or nose (more relaxing).

4. Connect with the sensations of breathing.

5. Turn your attention to the task at hand, while maintaining your presence.

6. Fully engage your senses, and if your mind wanders, bring your attention back to the present moment.

We are generally in such a hurry to achieve at the highest level possible, we too often forget to take care of ourselves properly. Something as simple as adopting some of these mindfulness practices can go a long way toward optimizing our results and reaching our potential.

Hope   March 2014

We find ourselves in a perplexing dichotomy – as chiropractors, Masters Circle Members, Winners Circle Members, we find ourselves compelled to embrace a particular worldview, where all things are possible, there is a direct relationship between working hard and getting results, and where higher purpose trumps pleasure and pain.

So, if we're really going to be objective about it we don't really know for a fact if any of that stuff is actually true – we just know it has played itself out favorably at times, and it beats the alternative, a dour and tepid reality where success is random and efforts often go unrewarded. I believe most of us would prefer to believe that we live in a friendly universe.

But the challenge is unmistakable – why do our best intentions sometimes go unfulfilled, and why do we see some people succeed while others do not, unrelated to the goodness of their souls?

If you study the philosophy of Robert Scheinfeld, you discover that his take on this phenomenon is spiritual in nature – that we write our own scripts at the soul level, and then play them out as actors in the movie of our lives, at first unaware of our preconceived life-drama, and then increasingly supportive of it as we unfold our experience.

For most of us, though, it is a matter of hope – positive expectancy lights our path and directs our attention, and then the optimistic perspective encourages us to plunge forward.

Some success philosophers see hope as a copout – I heard Tony Robbins say that hope and certainty can't simultaneously co-exist, because if you are hoping something will happen, you would have to make two pictures, one of what you hope will happen and one of the opposite, and your attention divides between those two mental images.

I can't claim that this is completely inaccurate, since I have tested it and it does seem to hold at times, but the question is, what meaning do we assign to those two pictures? If you believe that only one is possible or likely, then it doesn't seem to be hope, just contrast.

But hope turns on sensations inside of us that are not bound by logic and reason. A close cousin to faith, hope unlocks the trapdoor of emotion to our subconscious, and reveals to us a world of possibility that may not yet exist but is palpably achievable.

Let's look at what some other notable philosophers said about hope.

"You may say I'm a dreamer, but I'm not the only one. I hope someday you'll join us. And the world will live as one." – John Lennon

"Learn from yesterday, live for today, hope for tomorrow. The important thing is not to stop questioning." -- Albert Einstein

"We must accept finite disappointment, but never lose infinite hope. Only in the darkness can you see the stars." -- Martin Luther King Jr.

"Optimism is the faith that leads to achievement. Nothing can be done without hope and confidence."
– Helen Keller

"I believe that imagination is stronger than knowledge... that myth is more potent than history... that dreams are more powerful than facts... that hope always triumphs over experience... that laughter is the only cure for grief... and I believe that love is stronger than death." -- Robert Fulghum

Hope gives fantasy that touch of credibility that breathes reality into it. Hope can sustain you through adverse times, and keep your creativity flowing. Hope is a constant resource, a reminder to maintain an outlook of optimism.

And after all, one of your primary objectives as a healer is to give people hope. Chiropractic helps people in a way nothing else can – turn on life in people, and more often than not, their hopes will be realized, which will help you to realize yours.

Enthusiasm   April 2014

I just reviewed a YouTube video by a member I've known for quite a while. He doesn't have the biggest practice in the world, nor is he the greatest speaker I've seen, but there were two main reasons this video works – first, he reeks competence, and is very confidence-inspiring – and second, he is enthusiastic, passionate and excited about his subject matter, and that translates beautifully to the viewer.

Not all of us can be physically beautiful, or powerfully eloquent, or massively persuasive, but all of us can learn to use the power of enthusiasm to add an x-factor to our communication and put it over the top.

You probably know that the word enthusiasm stems from the root words "en theos," meaning "god within." This is more than just a convenient coincidence – when we are expressing that joyful, upbeat energy, it's almost as if a divine presence is speaking through us, a buoyant, effervescent vibration that lifts our audience to a new level of appreciation.

We may each have shades of style difference, but we would all benefit from observing ourselves, and seeing where we naturally express enthusiasm, so we can learn to tap into it as a regular resource.

Here are some comments by great thinkers and leaders on the subject:

"Enthusiasm is one of the most powerful engines of success. When you do a thing, do it with all your might. Put your whole soul into it. Stamp it with your own personality. Be active, be energetic, be enthusiastic and faithful, and you will accomplish your object. Nothing great was ever achieved without enthusiasm." – Ralph Waldo Emerson

"Success consists of going from failure to failure without loss of enthusiasm."
-- Winston Churchill

"Enthusiasm is the yeast that makes your hopes shine to the stars. Enthusiasm is the sparkle in your eyes, the swing in your gait, the grip of your hand, the irresistible surge of will and energy to execute your ideas." -- Henry Ford

"I know of no single formula for success. But over the years I have observed that some attributes of leadership are universal and are often about finding ways of encouraging people to combine their efforts, their talents, their insights, their enthusiasm and their inspiration to work together." -- Queen Elizabeth II

"There is a real magic in enthusiasm. It spells the difference between mediocrity and accomplishment."
-- Norman Vincent Peale

"If you aren't fired with enthusiasm, you will be fired with enthusiasm." -- Vince Lombardi

"The secret of genius is to carry the spirit of the child into old age, which means never losing your enthusiasm." -- Aldous Huxley

"I play to win, whether during practice or a real game. And I will not let anything get in the way of me and my competitive enthusiasm to win." -- Michael Jordan

"A mediocre idea that generates enthusiasm will go further than a great idea that inspires no one."
-- Mary Kay Ash

"How do you go from where you are to where you wanna be? And I think you have to have an enthusiasm for life. You have to have a dream, a goal. And you have to be willing to work for it." -- Jim Valvano

Where in your life and your practice could you invest more enthusiasm? Whether you are asking for referrals, presenting health care class or delivering a report of findings, the extra energy you bring could be the difference that makes the difference for those you touch and serve.

Making A Difference   May 2014

It may seem like a hackneyed phrase, but in the final analysis, it turns out that we do what we do for one reason – to make a difference. Sometimes this is interpreted as making a difference in many other people's lives, but it can also refer to making a difference in your own life, or in the lives of people near and dear to you.

No matter what your target, making a difference is the foundation of our work – to help people discover wellness, to relieve the horrible consequences of brain stress, and to reshape the group consciousness from one that passively waits for some heroic intervention to solve their health riddles to one that actively participates in, even spearheads a movement toward better health, more personal responsibility, better data to draw from and decide upon, and committed professionals who put their patients' best interests before profit and greed.

Sure, easy for me to say – but if you've noticed, there are subtle signs everywhere we look that the public is beginning to move away from drug solutions for every little malady, and toward a more natural approach that may not yet resemble what we do, but is moving in that direction. We must double our efforts if we truly want to make the most significant difference possible.

No doubt you remember the story Guy Riekeman tells about the starfish – a young man was walking along the beach, and saw in the distance a young lady performing an odd dance along the shore, where she would bend down, seem to pick something up, and then fling it into the surf.

As he got closer, he could make out what was transpiring – she was bending down to pick up starfish that had been washed up on the beach to die, and was rescuing them by throwing them back into the water.

The young man approached her, and in a burst of cynicism, proclaimed, "Why are you wasting your time? They're just going to be washed back up onto the sand again. Can't you see that what you are doing just doesn't matter?"

The young lady smiled sweetly, calmly bent down to pick up a starfish, and as she tossed it back into the life-giving ocean, she said, "It matters to that one."

This is the big frame around our service – yes, we know that everyone is ultimately going to die, and that many people will get sick and suffer along the way. We see it in our families, in our friends, in the newspapers and on TV – it's unavoidable, people will die.

But can we make a difference in any of those lives? I contend that we can, and it will surely matter to that one.

You make a difference every day when you put your loving hands on a patient in need. You make a difference when you lead your team, and show them a better way of life and how to be role models for your patients and for their own sphere of influence. You make a difference when you guide your family to better decisions about health and wellness. You make a difference when you share what you know with other professionals, to wake them up to a new way of thinking.

You make a difference when you add your energy to the groundswell of change that is manifesting in our world. Many of you will recall the scene from the movie "Dead Poets Society," now brought back by Apple in a poignant and meaningful ad, narrated by Robin Williams:

"We don't read and write poetry because it's cute. We read and write poetry because we are members of the human race. And the human race is filled with passion. And medicine, law, business, engineering – these are noble pursuits and necessary to sustain life. But poetry, beauty, romance, love – these are what we stay alive for."

To quote from Whitman,

"O me, O life of the questions of these recurring. Of the endless trains of the faithless. Of cities filled with the foolish. What good amid these, O me, O life? Answer: that you are here. That life exists and identity. That the powerful play goes on, and you may contribute a verse."

That the powerful play goes on, and you may contribute a verse.

What will your verse be?

This, then, is the essence of making a difference – we know we can, but the question is, how will we exercise this sacred option? When you have a pocketful of cash, you can spend it on trivial self-indulgences or food for the needy – but where will you spend your pocketful of intentions?

The powerful play goes on…

Balancing Tradition and Innovation   June 2014

I was talking with a member not long ago, and she confessed to me: "I hate brain based wellness. It used to be so easy to talk to my patients, and now it's so complicated, like learning a whole new language. I wish I could go back to the way things were."

After soothing her jangled nerves, and reassuring her that we would find the right way to integrate these advanced concepts into her work without disrupting her intentions, I started thinking about the great responsibility we have as visionaries and trendsetters.

History is important – you've heard it said that "those who ignore history are doomed to repeat it," but this is actually a mis-quote of George Santayana (1863-1952), who, in his "Reason in Common Sense, The Life of Reason, Vol.1," wrote "Those who cannot remember the past are condemned to repeat it."

These words from Santayana are actually derived from Edmund Burke (1729-1797), a British statesman who is regarded as the philosophical founder of modern political conservatism, who said "Those who don't know history are destined to repeat it." So these thoughts from hundreds of years ago have stood the test of time, and illustrate why we should be at least somewhat interested in from whence we've come.

Whether Santayana and Burke are right or not in any given situation, we do need to look backward at times to confirm our certainty about fundamental principles, but you can't drive looking in your rear-view mirror – you need to direct your attention to where you are headed. Know where you've been, but look where you're going.

This ushers in the concept of innovation, which by definition is not history. The past doesn't equal the future, Anthony Robbins tells us, and rightly so – without innovation, there could be no forward movement.

In fact, in his 1954 classic "The Practice of Management," Peter Drucker said "There is only one valid definition of business purpose: to create a customer. .... Therefore, any business enterprise has two -- and only two -- basic functions: marketing and innovation."

So our foray into brain based wellness has two important assets behind it – first, it is fresh and new, and appealing to those who are interested in the philosophy, science and art of things natural – what could be more relevant in chiropractic care than brain function?

The second asset is the ease of discussion and patient education compared to the standard chiropractic rap – it just seems simpler for people to wrap their minds around brain stress than it is to consider spinal nerve root radiculopathy and vertebral subluxation.

And there are other places in practice that require inspection to see if updating is appropriate. Many of our fee policies and methods of payment are antiquated and based on a dysfunctional third party pay system or old beliefs and values about health and health care payment options. The integration of wellness practices and the constructive side of medical practice are infiltrating traditional chiropractic practices and the beliefs of traditional chiropractors. There are many new techniques to study. And marketing has shifted to include and in many cases rely on social media, rather than the well-established talks and screenings, which can now be updated, automated and even delegated.

Again, there is nothing contrary to chiropractic reasoning in brain based wellness – in fact, it may be the clearest expression of chiropractic yet, enhancing the meaning of the phrase "above down, inside out.".

But if it isn't what we are used to, it is uncomfortable, and people tend to avoid what feels uncomfortable, even when pushing through the discomfort leads to a better outcome. It's a resistance that, however natural, is counterproductive and anti-progress.

So, it's up to each of us to determine where we are in this continuum of tradition and innovation – there is no correct or incorrect balance, except in the eyes of the beholder, but there is a more or less effective way to demonstrate that balance. If the pendulum has swung too far in either direction, it's fairly easy to tell – if you've dragged your feet, you'll spill patients toward more modern practices. If you're too aggressive in change, more established patients will give you feedback that it's "not what they expected."

Note that you have no obligation to reformat what you do based on such input, but it is always on you to fill your practice with people who are a good fit – hence Drucker's assessment that in addition to innovation, you must also focus on marketing.

It may be helpful for you to make a list of all the aspects of your practice (and your life, for that matter) that are leaning toward the traditional, and others that lean toward the innovative. It's a simple way to locate yourself on this curve, so you can be sure that your actions match up with your intentions. Change is hard, but it is essential to keep pace with our world – observe, evaluate, and adjust yourself to make sure you're on target to achieve the outcomes that are most important to you.

How Talent Becomes Command   July 2014

Everyone reading this has considerable talent. You could not have made it this far in life without it.

But talent, in my estimation, is overrated. The most talented people are not necessarily the most successful, nor are the most successful people necessarily the most talented. It just doesn't work that way.

Just having the raw ability to do something does not get it done – it takes more than just competence to move a process forward toward its ultimate completion and fulfillment.

Those of you who read Malcolm Gladwell probably remember that in "Outliers," he declared that in order to achieve mastery, one would need to invest 10,000 hours. That translates to 40 hours a week for five years – or 20 hours a week for ten years – I think it's safe to say that many or most of us are either well beyond that marker or not far from it. But do you feel like masters?

Some people may have ten years invested, but in the absence of learning from the distinctions made along the way, it isn't ten years of know-how, it's more like one year's know-how ten years in a row. The necessary precondition of mastery is observing, growing and benefitting from each of the 10,000 hours, so there is constructive movement and the gathering of new thoughts and opinions based on that invested time.

Of course, while Gladwell may state this "10,000 hour" requirement as a product of his research, we all know that mastery is at least somewhat subjective – a master compared to whom and based on what? For the purposes of this discussion, I'd rather talk about command – the ability to produce a given result in a given environment.

So, to me, the command formula starts with something like this:

talent x experience → command

Yes, each of us has abundant raw materials, some more than others, perhaps, but all of us have more than enough to pursue excellence. It's the calibration of our experiences, and the meanings that we assign, that move talent toward command.

Notice that at the outer edges of this formula, where someone has very little talent or very little experience, the degree of command would be limited accordingly. But once you have reasonable talent to develop into effective behavior, how you apply what you learn from your experiences will determine the rate and magnitude of your ascent.

How quickly this happens is based more on intense desire than on the underlying talent – how else would we gain experience, if not by putting ourselves in position to get it? And how can we capitalize on experiences if we don't look for and engage them?

The quality that instigates this pursuit is drive – the forward thrust generated when a passion is expressed in reality.

So, more completely stated, the command formula looks like this:

$$\textbf{(drive)}$$
$$\textbf{talent x experience} \rightarrow \quad \rightarrow \quad \rightarrow \textbf{command}$$

In other words, if you want to accomplish at the highest level possible, apply your talent as often and as thoroughly as you can, with relentless intentionality.

How can we use this formula?

Let's say you know you have good raw ability as a presenter, but you don't yet have your talk refined enough, nor do you have that many positive reference experiences as a speaker. Each time you deliver a talk, notice where you improved, even a few percentage points. Those positive reference experiences create a foundation of confidence and certainty which provide a platform to push upward from. This leads to a sense of command on stage. The compulsion to stay on the path to mastery is a function of the drive manifested.

Every time you express your talent, you gain experience, and with drive you can keep this formula in motion.

Simplicity   August 2014

With all the complexities of life whirling around us, it's reassuring to re-connect with a basic organizing principle to help us regain our balance – simplicity is elegance.

Ninety-nine per cent of all living matter is composed of only six elements – carbon, hydrogen, oxygen, nitrogen, sulfur and phosphorus. Carbon, hydrogen and oxygen are the basic building blocks of organic compounds; nitrogen, sulfur and phosphorus are components of amino acids, DNA and RNA. The majority of life function depends on only those six atoms.

The fact that six elements can be synthesized into the myriad life forms is mind-boggling.

There are a total of 12 unique musical tones – A, A#, B, C, C#, D, D#, E, F, F#, G, and G#. Each is reproducible through a range of frequencies, but it's the same notes that are recycled, and through their application, all music is constructed, from the classics to heavy metal.

And how about color? All there is to work with is red, blue and yellow, but from those three fundamentals, all color is created, an infinite rainbow array.

I pulled this passage out of Wikipedia:

"In the philosophy of science, simplicity is a meta-scientific criterion by which to evaluate competing theories. In this field, a distinction is often made between two senses of simplicity: syntactic simplicity (the number and complexity of hypotheses), and ontological simplicity (the number and complexity of things postulated). These two aspects of simplicity are often referred to as elegance and parsimony respectively."

This made me laugh, of course, because it surely doesn't seem very simple – but what they are saying is that fewer chunks means greater simplicity, whether you're talking about the containers you keep stuff in or what you keep in them. If you really want to get your brain tied up in knots with philosophy like this, try reading some Ken Wilber. I've never been able to make much sense of it, maybe you can explain it to me.

Here are some thoughts from great thinkers about simplicity.

"If you can't explain it to a six year old, you don't understand it yourself." -- *Albert Einstein*

"Life is really simple, but we insist on making it complicated." -- *Confucius*

"Simplicity is the ultimate sophistication." -- *Leonardo da Vinci*

"Our life is frittered away by detail. Simplify, simplify." – *Henry David Thoreau*

"Manifest plainness, embrace simplicity, reduce selfishness, have few desires." -- *Lao Tzu*

"The more you have, the more you are occupied. The less you have, the more free you are." -- *Mother Teresa*

"There is no greatness where there is not simplicity, goodness, and truth." -- *Leo Tolstoy*

"It is not a daily increase, but a daily decrease. Hack away at the inessentials." -- *Bruce Lee*

"Nature is pleased with simplicity. And nature is no dummy." -- *Isaac Newton*

"That's been one of my mantras - focus and simplicity. Simple can be harder than complex: You have to work hard to get your thinking clean to make it simple. But it's worth it in the end because once you get there, you can move mountains." -- *Steve Jobs*

"Simplicity and sexiness, that's what people want. At a price that's not outrageous." -- *Diane von Furstenberg*

"I don't need a lot of money. Simplicity is the answer for me." -- *Linda McCartney*

"Simplicity is the final achievement. After one has played a vast quantity of notes and more notes, it is simplicity that emerges as the crowning reward of art." -- *Frederic Chopin*

Ultimately, your office will respond to wherever you can keep things simple. Look at every aspect of your practice – your technique, your office procedures and policies, your staff training and delegation, your money management – the simpler the better.

And this extrapolates to your life – keep your personal habits simple and meaning-ful. Simplifying your relationships will come back to reward you many times over. And simplifying your wealth accumulation, not to mention your playtime, will add dividends that go far beyond face value.

You've heard me say before that "the antidote to overwhelm is proper chunking." This is the essence of simplicity – just enough chunks of the right type and size, not too many or too few, not too big or too small – this is the way simplicity works, and how you can consistently manifest it.

Questions   September 2014

If you've ever done any roleplaying with me in coaching sessions, you know I am a stickler for asking questions – I learned early on from Tony Robbins that the one who asks the questions controls the communication, and this technique can be developed and improved upon with a little perspective and legwork.

First, let's start with self-communication. There are three questions that guide all internal processing – What do I focus on? What does it mean? What do I do?

These questions are essential for you to take any action whatsoever. If there's a patient on your table, you could focus on the patient, on being a sensitive and committed healer. That means you are in position to help that patient as much as possible, and you can go forward and deliver an excellent adjustment.

Now compare this scenario -- there's a patient on your table, and instead of focusing on the patient, you're focused on being tired, on the ball game, or on your upcoming vacation or child's wedding. Can you see how you'll create different, less supportive meanings for that moment and that encounter, which will lead to a distracted, diminished or substandard adjustment?

How about if you meet someone new? If you focus on what you like, you'll assign pleasant meanings and initiate a constructive, satisfying relationship. If you focus on what you don't like, you'll assign distasteful meanings and avoid the person.

The questions you use in communicating with others are equally important. As always, you need to know your outcome – knowing where you are headed facilitates a linguistic flow that points you in that direction. Once you have gained rapport, just think, what am I trying to accomplish here, and the language will start to happen organically.

For example, in your consultation, when the patient tells you of a painful problem, is your outcome to make the patient feel better? If so, you'll develop a particular line of questioning – where does it hurt? How long has it been that way? What makes it better? What makes it worse? These questions focus you and the patient on the pain.

But what if your outcome is to find the underlying cause? Can you see how your line of questioning would be different? What do you think is causing that? Why do you think your body hasn't healed that already, as it does with most of your illnesses? What do you think your body is trying to tell you? These questions focus you and the patient on the cause of the problem, not the symptoms of the problem.

Is your report of findings a long lecture that your patient drifts in and out of, or are you interspersing questions to maintain connection and evoke discovery? Simply asking, are you with me, do you understand, is that clear, are you following me, will enhance the patient's experience multifold, because instead of zoning out on your new information and terminology, they stay awake and dialed into your message. It can make all the difference in the world.

Is your patient education a drone of data and dogma, or are you engaging your patient with compelling questions? What do you think your pain is there for? What do you think happens to people with long-term nerve interference? Why do you think some people get colds and others don't when they've both been exposed to the same germs? Before you had symptoms, were you sick? How common is brain stress? The interactions that are spurred by such inquiry can inform your patients better than an intellectual spew, and spark not only better patients, but future chiropractors.

Some of you may remember playing the game of questions, an acting game I pilfered from the hit show "Whose Line Is It Anyway?" The rules are simple – two players initiate a conversation which must consist of questions only. If one is tricked into responding with an answer, he or she is "out," another player steps into the game and the next round begins. As such, you can easily play the game at staff meetings, or if there are only two of you, just go back and forth to increase your skill.

It might go something like this –

CA: "Is that a new tie?"

DC: "Do you like it?"

CA: "Why did you pick that color?"

DC: "Don't you think it matches my eyes?"

CA: "Actually it does – oh, uh...uh..." (you're out!)

You can turn it toward office lingo, so you gain experience at asking good questions – for example, if one player assumes the role of the doctor and one of the patient, it might go like this:

Doctor: "Aren't you happy to get your subluxations corrected?"

Patient: "What really happens when I get adjusted?"

Doctor: "Do you realize it's literally turning life on in your body?"

Patient: "I never knew that – oh, wait, questions..." (you're out, but you can see how the patient's education is amplified when you use good questions to guide their thinking.)

Jousting like this will sharpen your wits and refine your communication, de-stressing your dialogue and streamlining and systematizing the entire process.

This is a never-ending opportunity to attract people to you, to your story and to chiropractic care. Don't talk at people, talk with them by piquing their interest and causing them to be part of the conversation, not just a receptacle for it. The quality of your questions dictates the quality of your life – it's worth it to become masterful at this vital art and science.

Contrast   October 2014

If you attended the Winners Circle Personal Growth Weekend in New York City, you may remember the format of the debrief on Friday evening -- much like Derek Jeter was commemorated by his peers with a single word, we asked participants to summarize their experience at the 9/11 Memorial and Ellis Island with one word, and then to elaborate on why they chose that word.

We heard many poignant and relevant remarks from the group, as would be expected, but one of the highlights was when Erin Collins was called upon, the word she chose to describe her experience was... juxtaposition.

At first, the room seemed surprised to hear this response, but as Erin continued to explain, it became clear that she was tapping into one of our most important linguistic observations, the concept of contrast. The horror of 9/11 served as a point of contrast which made the raw optimism and welcoming tone of opportunity that permeates Ellis Island that much more compelling.

No doubt you have seen some derivative of this experiment, a prime example of the concept of contrast, right out of a grade school science class.

Set out three bowls of water – one cold, one lukewarm, and one hot. If you put your hand into the cold water, and then into the lukewarm water, it feels hot. If you put your hand into the hot water, and then into the lukewarm water, it feels cold. You can actually put your left hand into the cold, your right hand into the hot, and then plunge both hands into the lukewarm for a remarkable sensation, where one hand feels hot and one cold in the very same bowl of water!

That's how powerful perceptual contrast can be, and you can learn to use it throughout your practice.

For example, when presenting a financial report, you can soften the impact of your offer by exploiting the extreme expense of a medical approach to the same problem:

"You know, Mr. Patient, if you were to go the surgical route with this problem, it could cost $100,000 or more, and your out of pocket expense could be five or ten thousand – for considerably less than that, you can get six months of conservative care, which should help you as much or more without the risks of surgery and medication."

Or, you can compare your package price to the patient purchasing services a la carte.

"Mrs. Patient, the fee for a regular office visit is sixty dollars, but when you accept the program of four dozen visits I'm recommending, the price comes down to fifty, saving you almost five hundred dollars."

And contrast doesn't only help with money discussions, but also in comparing risk:

"Mr. Patient, to ease your concern about chiropractic care, which is new to you, you may be surprised to learn that orthopedists who deal with the same kinds of cases we do pay as much as $100,000 in annual malpractice premiums, while chiropractors pay less than 10% of that. The insurance companies have to know who is hurting people and who is not, that drugs and surgery are far more dangerous than natural care – that's why our insurance is so inexpensive, 90% less than orthopedists, because it's rare that anyone is hurt with all-natural chiropractic care."

Chances are you've had a real estate agent or car salesperson work a contrast-related tactic on you – either they show you an overpriced fixer-upper before they show you what you are looking for, to make it seem like a better deal, or they show you something over your head, to make what you have asked for seem pale by comparison, making it more likely you will stretch to the next level of purchase. Skillful sales professionals know all about using contrast to inspire clients to buy – caveat emptor, let the buyer beware.

You can also put this in your front desk CA's toolbox when answering questions about money on the phone.

Q: Do you take my insurance?

A: Our fees are so reasonable, many patients tell us it's cheaper to pay us directly because often our fee is the same or less than your co-payment. Please bring all your insurance information to your visit and we'll get all the details for you.

If you want to see more examples of how tools like these are applied in persuasion, read "Influence," by Robert Cialdini.

For another angle on contrast, consider Anthony Robbins' discussion of the mechanism for creating lasting change.

Tony's original format was six steps – identify where you are and where you'd like to be, gain leverage to create change, break the limiting pattern, establish a new resource, condition that resource, and check for ecology to make sure the implementation of the new pattern truly serves the individual.

But he found that for some people, the changes did not last as expected. Further research demonstrated that those people were going back to the original environments where the faulty patterns were played out, and this triggered old responses and interfered with the conditioning of the new pattern.

In this case, the lack of contrast set up a previous faulty pattern, whereas a different environment was less likely to bring back the old sensations. Here, the contrast works in your favor, by allowing the new pattern to proceed and condition unencumbered by memory, and so was born the seventh step to lasting change, the power of environment.

One of the reasons we don't spend a lot of time at Winners Circle events talking about practice statistics is because of our tendency to compare our results to the results of others. That contrast is not especially helpful in establishing a level playing field where all Winners Circle members are treated with equivalent respect and love. The naturally right emphasis on statistical success arises organically, and therefore helps us without hurting us.

And finally, we should surely avoid answering this obvious land mine question with a contrast-driven response, such as:

Q: Does my butt look big in this dress?

A: Compared to what?

Contrast is one of the most potent of all linguistic constructs. Sensitize yourself to see it in the communications around you, and you'll be amazed how prevalent it is. Learn to use it effectively, and you'll increase your mastery as a communicator and create an atmosphere that is conducive to full engagement.

The Enneagram   November 2014

The best way to communicate with someone is to know who you're dealing with – in other words, to understand his or her behavior patterns, values, beliefs and standards. Self-knowledge and self-communication is no different – you have your own set of characteristics and qualities that make you… well, you, and the better you comprehend such tendencies, the more effective the communication and the better the results.

There are many ways of categorizing personalities – the four personality styles we call driver, expressive, analytical and amiable, for example, or the sixteen Myers Briggs types based on introversion/extraversion, sensing or intuiting, thinking or feeling and judging or perceiving.

But the most profound and useful personality system I know of is the enneagram, which offers a system of psycho-spiritual pathways to growth, integration and evolution based on nine personality types.

To determine your type, first decide if, most of your life, you've been more assertive, more compliant, or more withdrawn. These distinctions are derived from the "theory of neurosis" as described by German psychoanalyst Karen Horney.

Within each of these three categories are three sub-categories, one driven by fear, one by anger, and one by image, the way they are perceived. This can be illustrated by this chart:

	Assertive	**Compliant**	**Withdrawn**
Fear	Assertive-Fear (AF) Type 7	Compliant-Fear (CF) Type 6	Withdrawn-Fear (WF) Type 5
Anger	Assertive-Anger (AA) Type 8	Compliant-Anger (CA) Type 1	Withdrawn-Anger (WA) Type 9
Image	Assertive-Image (AI) Type 3	Compliant-Image (CI) Type 2	Withdrawn-Image (WI) Type 4

These types can be organized around a nine-pointed figure, the geometric diagram that people associate with the enneagram (Greek for nine-pointed diagram.)

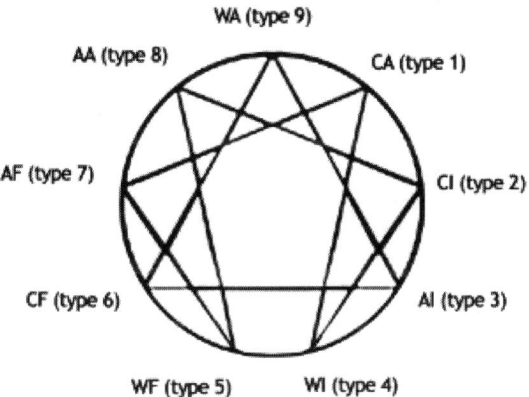

Why is this important? Most personality typing systems put you in a box with a label on it – the enneagram shows you the box you've been living in and how to get out of it. Here are a few simple guidelines, to whet your appetite to learn more.

The three fear types are head-centered, thinking types, which makes sense, since fear is a mental construct. The assertive fear type, Type 7, is passionate, adventurous, and enthusiastic, a good starter but not as good a finisher. The compliant fear type, Type 6, is competent, responsible and loyal, but is insecure and doubtful, constantly overanalyzing. The withdrawn fear type is Type 5, intelligent and wise, but arrogant and hiding behind their intellect. You could say that Sixes express their fear, Fives repress their fear, and Sevens suppress their fear.

The three anger types are body-centered, instinctual types, which makes sense because anger is a gut reaction. The assertive anger type, Type 8, is strong, dominant and direct, but can be controlling and manipulative. The compliant anger type, Type 1, is ethical, organized, neat and timely, but can be perfectionistic and rigid. The withdrawn anger type, Type 9, is peaceful, pleasant, and comforting, but is non-confrontational, stubborn and overly habitual. You could say that Eights express their anger, Ones repress their anger, and Nines suppress their anger.

The three image types are heart-centered, feeling types, which makes sense because image is about perceptions and emotions. The assertive image type, Type 3, is driven and achievement oriented, but can be ruthless, hostile and self-deceptive. The compliant image type, Type 2, is giving, loving and service-oriented, but can be co-dependent and needy. The withdrawn image type, Type 4, is artistic, sensitive, and appreciative of nature and beauty, but can be afflicted, melancholy, and self-absorbed. You could say that Fours express their feelings, Twos repress their feelings, and Threes suppress their feelings.

If it seems to you like none of the types are especially appealing, you're right. These are not really descriptions of who you are – they're descriptions of where you're stuck. By observing these patterns, you can move yourself in an integrative direction and facilitate your own evolution.

Needless to say, when you get skillful at this, you can not only move yourself along your own path of growth, you can help others to do the same. In over thirty years of studying behavior and personal development, this is the most penetrating and potent field of study I have found.

If you want to learn more about this fascinating topic, including my own personal research into the impact of these types on sexuality and relationships, it's my pleasure to share my ideas with you.

Generosity   December 2014

I saw a remarkable article, published by the Cleveland Clinic Wellness Team, which brought the essence of the season to focus. It's called "Why Giving Is Good For Your Health," and it proposes that giving has not only emotional benefits, but physiological benefits as well.

It quotes a 2006 study from the "International Journal of Psychophysiology," which concluded that people who engaged in social support of others had lower blood pressure than those who did not.

The same study also found that people who gave their time to help others through community and organizational involvement had greater self-esteem, less depression and lower stress levels than those who didn't.

In a previous study, done in 1999 at the University of California at Berkeley, men and women 55 and older who volunteered for two or more charitable organizations had a 44% better five year survival rate than those who did not, even when factoring in age, exercise and general wellness characteristics, including negative health practices like smoking. Similar research in 2003 at the University of Michigan showed consistent positive results with elderly people who helped friends, neighbor and relatives.

Perhaps the most compelling discovery was uncovered at the National Institute of Health in 2006, where an MRI investigation of the brains of people who donated to charities demonstrated that the mesolimbic pathway, the reward center of the brain associated with pleasure, connection and trust, was stimulated to release endorphins in response to giving. This creates what is referred to as a "helper's high," which can be as addictive as any other cascade of metabolic pleasure.

In short, science is proving that generosity is good for you, lowering your blood pressure, decreasing your stress, reducing depression, and improving self esteem, leading to greater longevity and an overall increase in happiness. That sounds like a formula for success we should all be enthusiastic about exploring and integrating.

"There is overwhelming evidence that the higher the level of self-esteem, the more likely one will be to treat others with respect, kindness, and generosity." -- Nathaniel Branden

Why is this important to us as chiropractors? There are at least three levels of giving that we need to engage through our practices.

First, as public servants we need to have a generous attitude toward the people we serve – not to flood them with free services, but rather to generate a tone of givingness in the context of the practice, with opportunities for you as their doctor to instill them with quality information, offer outstanding service, and extend a helping hand to those who truly require it. Most of us have a few families whose hardship dictates some special consideration, and in addition to doing something nice for those impoverished families, it will produce constructive benefits for you and your team, as noted above.

"Generosity is giving more than you can, and pride is taking less than you need."
-- Khalil Gibran

Second, you can contribute to worthy causes, initiating a flow of support toward groups and organizations that depend on strangers to cover their expenses and allow them to do their work to make a difference for others.

But subtly, the most powerful thing you can do is to inspire a giving mentality in your patients, so they can reap the rewards of giving for themselves. Running promotions that empower the underprivileged, from mission trips to inner city health and wellness programs, can spread the "wealth" of happiness and generosity and invite your clientele to tap into this not-so-secret method of getting healthier and happier.

You could recruit volunteers who can help you with your marketing events. You can invite participation in patient appreciation days. You can build an army of committed, involved health warriors who can help you get your message out and they will also benefit. Put on your thinking cap and invent ways for your patients to give back, and they will be healthier for it.

"A wise woman recognizes when her life is out of balance and summons the courage to act to correct it. She knows the meaning of true generosity -- happiness is the reward for a life lived in harmony, with a courage and grace." -- Suze Orman

Generosity is a missing link to health and wellness – it used to be more fashionable to help others, but it fell out of favor as the world got tougher to handle. We have an opportunity to make a big difference, when we redirect people's attention toward the value of being there for someone in need. Keep it in mind, and you'll dial into the real underlying meaning of the holiday season.

On Writing A Book   January 2015

One of the best ways for you to leave your mark and enhance the greater good is to capture your thoughts in writing. As you know, Bob started the ball rolling for us with his breakthrough collaboration with Jason Deitch, "Discover Wellness: How Staying Healthy Can Make You Rich." Tens of thousands of copies of this best-seller have influenced a wide spectrum of people and made the world a healthier place. I got to contribute an essay on the psychology of wellness, and I feel blessed to be able to reach so many people.

Bob has authored and published several books, the latest being "Awaken Your Flourishing Brain," co-written with Patrick and Cynthia Porter. It's destined to revolutionize patient education, as it is the first brain-based wellness book truly designed for the lay public. If I were in practice, every patient would get a copy, and I'd reshape my health care class and my patient education system around the important information found therein.

I have watched Bob up close and personal through this process, and he invariably does exhaustive research, reads books and magazines and scientific studies, inter-views people and carefully constructs his viewpoint, to be sure his content is as cutting edge and as relevant as possible. It's a spectacle to behold, and whether he is putting together a boot camp, a seminar or a book, he conscientiously does his due diligence and includes every critical point he can find.

I am also releasing my own new book this week, a three year project on the psychol-ogy of sexuality, and frankly, my book-writing process is a radical departure from the Hoffman method. While I do include the distinctions of twenty-seven years and over 35,000 hours of coaching and consulting, not to mention countless semi-nars, books and conversations on the subject matter, when it came to assembling the ideas, I built on a framework of practical knowledge and experience, and the rest of it I basically made up.

This is not to besmirch the words I've chosen to express these concepts, nor is it intended to demean the final product, of which I am completely proud. It's just a different approach, more stream of consciousness perhaps, but no less thoughtful.

"You Can Have Great Sex!" is a compendium of sexual perspective, giving structure to one of the most amorphous and incomprehensible aspects of our society. Sexuality has been a mystery for most, and my intention is to help people establish a brand new way to look at sex, through filters than explain why we feel the way we do, and what we can do about it to create great sex in our lives, regardless of our current status in relationship, experience or self esteem.

I know that many of you have also delved into writing, especially with the advent of the "Totally Booked Practice" advantage, which of course we support without reservation. In my opinion, Gary Trupo and Rob Hanopole are doing a tremendous service to our profession and our world, by creating a turnkey approach to writing that is flexible enough to allow for personal creativity without depending entirely on it.

But even if you have never considered writing a book, you would be amazed how the body of knowledge you have accumulated over the years can be assembled into a meaningful display that can inspire those in your sphere of influence to improve the quality of their lives.

Having spent so long working on my own book, I understand how intimidating it can be to go down that rabbit hole. But if you have something to say, why not say it in print and expand the likelihood that people will respond to your message?

There are ghost writers who are specialists in assisting those who need the support – but you can start by simply deciding the major thrust of your work, getting the big rocks in place, and sculpting the language from there. Create a brain-storming session where you just write down all the ideas you think should go into a book on that particular topic, and before you know it, you'll have the beginnings of an outline and a table of contents.

Or, you can run a recording device while you talk about your thoughts, ideas and philosophies, and then get the recording transcribed, to be edited for useful passages, sound bites and hooks. You gotta be in it to win it – find a way into the process and see where it takes you.

Personally, knowing my tendency to get off target in large projects like this, I hired writing and publicity coaches to keep me on point, and to teach me what I didn't know, which was a lot. You can work with our TMC coaches for general guidance, and if you need something more, we can mastermind to develop a strategy based on your intent and how far along you are on your project.

But even if you simply personalize some templates from Totally Booked Practice and use mostly their materials, a book is a deluxe calling card that positions you in your community and your marketplace as a thought leader. I believe it is worth your time, energy and capital to memorialize your purpose, vision and mission – think about how you could make more of a difference if you were to be so bold as to capture your essence in writing.

I know how good I feel about it – try it on, see what you think.

Continuing Dedication   February 2015

At our recent seminar at Parker, I was not surprised to discover that many of the hundreds of doctors I spoke to were there primarily to fulfill their continuing education requirements. They did sit in on some classes they were really interested in, but their schedules were shaped around classes they could get credit for.

At an extravaganza like Parker Vegas, there are enough classes that are both certified for CE and also worthwhile, so that attendees mostly aren't squandering their time on trivial material they'll never use. But to me, the whole purpose of education is in self-development – so my concept of "continuing education" is more like "continuing dedication."

The ongoing evolution of our worldview should be something we are dedicated to, and continuing that dedication throughout our careers is part classroom education, part experiential, and part esoteric and immeasurable. Just the maturation process itself brings about inside-out change, and that movement is more likely to be constructive when you guide yourself by your never-ending commitment to self-improvement.

Some of this is in the form of formal study – seminars, courses, books, systems and so on. Some of this is about enriching your internal map – why do you think we choose seminar destinations in exotic and intriguing places you might not otherwise go? Taking you to Barcelona, or New York City, or Miraval, or Aruba, all of these experiences make you a deeper, better version of yourself. Your Winners Circle membership is a form of continuing dedication – no one gives you CEUs for it, but you become a better you.

Some of this is based on feeding your essence, expanding upon the vibrational aspects of your life, through personal habits and behaviors that move you along your chosen path. Sometimes these take the most dedication of all, and often have the greatest payoff, too – the most important elements of your life are lived inside out. Happiness, love, health and success all come from you, not to you. Whatever you can do to generate mindfulness, congruency, self esteem and coherence will contribute greatly to your satisfaction, as well as amplifying any impact you can have on those around you.

When you stop to think about it, everything you do either moves you closer to your dream, or moves you away from it. This is why it's so critical to have a clear vision, with quantifiable goals along the way to measure your progress and self-correct when necessary. The willingness to even set goals in the first place takes focus and discipline, and establishing a ritual where you set goals each year and gain momentum behind the process is continuing dedication at its finest and most productive.

How do you initiate and maintain continuing dedication in your staff and patients? Get clarity about your practice philosophy, and reinforce your message consistently, blending authority and wisdom with charisma and edu-tainment in your own individualized way. You are selling yourself as well as chiropractic, if you want the patient to commit and your staff to remain loyal and enthusiastic.

This doesn't mean you have to be something you're not – there's a wide spectrum of styles that work, some more reserved and quiet, some more animated and overt. It's the integrity and believability that sells your position, which explains why you need to be certain about your vision and direction before you try to promote it.

Whether you see continuing education standards in your state as an uninspiring, wasteful burden or an opportunity to enhance your skill sets determines the ultimate benefit you reap. And when you add experiences that may not get you state credit but shape your identity and build capacity and attraction, that continuing dedication will come back to reward you many times over.

Progress   March 2015

I remember a motivational speaker who used to ask from the front of the room, "Do you want more money?"

When everyone shouted yes, he held up a dollar bill and asked, "Who wants it?"

His point was simple – just desiring more does not identify what you have in mind. You must be definite in your intention, and precise enough so you can attract the best possible response.

This brings up an important distinction in the process of success – the concept of progress. When used as a verb, it means to move forward. When used as a noun, it described the degree to which you have moved forward. But above all, it defines your direction of movement, without being encumbered by the magnitude – and that can be very important in manifesting sufficient drive to overcome the friction and obstacles that may interfere with your success, especially in the early stages of any endeavor.

Making progress may not be as glamorous as the moment of achievement, but it is essential in order to have that experience. Remember the tortoise and the hare, where the hare was clearly faster, but the tortoise's relentless, inexorable progress won the day.

So, the key is to establish targets that reflect the kind of movement and forward thrust you desire. This brings new specificity to goals, and a temporal component, how long does it take to hit this level, how long to get to that level, etc., which is essential to good goal-setting.

This idea of making consistent progress can be applied to every aspect of your personal and professional growth. No one loses fifty pounds in a month, it has to be done sensibly and intelligently over time, hitting milestones along the way to your anticipated end point. No one goes from a hundred visits a week to three hundred in a few months – again, it has to ramp up over a period of months and/or years, and it's the feelings of making progress that keep us from getting impatient and sabotaging our accomplishments with a sour or frustrated attitude.

How do we measure our progress in practice? On the surface it seems obvious, higher statistics. But really, you can grow your PVA by attracting fewer new lives to serve – and you can grow your office visits per day by working fewer days and consolidating your schedule. These look like progress at first, but are just another configuration of the same results, unless your outcome was to see fewer people or work fewer days.

No, real progress must hold whichever angle you look at it from. That's why you must understand how the three primary office operations, attracting new patients, generating patient compliance, and creating a fair exchange must work in harmony so your progress isn't eaten up by faltering in some other related area.

This can be tricky – remember, if you have a 50 PVA, it may take an average patient six months to come in that many times, and therefore, if you have a big influx of new people, it will temporarily deflate your PVA. Either you'd have to grow the new patient flow more gently to preserve PVA, or, more likely, when you push on bringing in more new lives, you must follow your protocols to the letter to make sure that every person gets the "A" experience.

It will still take time to see the PVA equilibrate at the established level, but it must be preserved or at least approximated in order for it to be real progress. If the PVA drops significantly, even if the volume grows, you've changed a fundamental measurement in the practice, making it somewhat of a different practice. Of course, it's up to you to decide on those tradeoffs – but it's all capacity related, as you already know.

If you attract more new people, and your PVA drops enough to keep your volume about where it was, then you found another way to get to the same place, the opposite of progress, which requires positive motion. So, don't be deluded into misinterpreting a "lateral move" as progress – you must see a parameter grow while the other averages at least hold their own, to truly progress.

You've heard me use the metaphor of rock climbing before – getting to the top is important, but squeezing all the juice out of the climb itself adds dimension and detail to the journey. That's the frame around progress – by celebrating intermediary goals, you can spark additional enthusiasm, extra forward thrust and even an enhanced vision.

So this concept of progress gives us an opportunity to frame our growth in the most positive way possible – without pretending things are better than they really are, we can measure our achievements and compare them to our expectations, being careful to avoid the trap of false progress that feels good but doesn't create the intended result. Taking responsibility for this is the pinnacle of success and prosperity, and bodes well for those who commit to this deeper understanding.

Planning   April 2015

I believe Bob when he says "proper planning prevents poor performance." – in fact, proper planning is an essential component of success, and the better you plan and follow through on your plan, the better your probability of achieving your goal.

When most people hear the word "plan," their minds go immediately to action steps, and this is understandable – the most popular view of success philosophy is based primarily on "doing" things.

But in an identity-based environment, we also consider the "being" aspects of the process of success, and therefore, planning takes on a somewhat different flavor.

In classical Capacity Technology™, the planning system is referred to as **exploding and layering**. This may seem like a radical departure from the commonly accepted methodology, and it's not for the faint of heart, but it is a more complete and thorough technology for developing your pathways to your best possible results, and is therefore worthy of consideration.

"Exploding" was derived from the instructions you might get with something you have to build, like a piece of furniture, toy or model airplane. On the front page of such instructions, you'd typically see an "exploded view" – the thing you want to build, fully assembled with the parts in context and alignment, but with space between them so you can see how they all fit together.

Using the exploding process is a lot like that – the idea is to get all the parts of the system on one page so you can see how they all fit together. This makes your plan more bulletproof and easier to implement and adjust.

There are five parts to the exploding process, the first two parts at the "be" level and the last three at the "do" level.

The first part is **beliefs**. You must have or adopt empowering beliefs before you take physical action toward your goal. If your beliefs don't support your objective, there will likely be some self-sabotage. But with constructive beliefs, there's less friction in the system and more likelihood of connecting with your vision.

Break down limiting beliefs with counter-examples where the belief isn't true; or, identify what you could or improve upon to make the belief fail, or get values leverage by asking, what does it cost me to believe this, and what would I gain by believing otherwise? Build positive beliefs through affirmation, empowering self-talk, anchoring or developing values leverage, what you'd gain or lose if you change to this new and better belief.

The second part of exploding is **resources**. You will need the relevant resources to accomplish your intended result, resources like confidence, motivation, resilience, determination, self esteem, confrontational tolerance, and a host of other qualities, based on the particular plan you are designing. Use anchoring, resource building, visualization and roleplaying to develop the resources you need.

The third part of the exploding process is **people**. You may need other people for teamwork, support, as specialty vendors, or mastermind partners. Select the people you'll need to carry out your plan, from among your team and the other people you know who can help.

The fourth part is **materials**. Do you need business cards or brochures? Do you need a sign in sheet, a pad to collect email addresses, an easel for your posters? How about envelopes for your mailing, ink for your printer, decorations for your holiday promotion, or welcome packets for the expected influx of new patients? List the materials you need to achieve this particular goal.

Finally, the fifth part of the exploding process is **action steps**. Trace back through the first four sections – do you need to dismantle or erect any beliefs? Do you need to manifest some resources? Do you need to enlist the aid of anyone? Do you have to procure any materials? These become your action steps, now based not only on mechanical operations, but also on personal growth and self-development, as any identity-based technology should be.

Complete your plan by playing out the accomplishment of each action step in succession, and seeing if your visualization takes you to an appropriate completion. This helps you refine in advance and make your best and most direct strategy for creating that result.

If you really want to maximize your efficiency and you're willing to think and act differently and push the envelope, you can study the layering process.

Layering is a reshaping of your action steps to gang similar steps across different goals and plans to streamline the entire process. For example, make all your phone calls in one sitting, run all your errands in one trip, do all your writing or accounting in one session, and so on.

While it may seem counterintuitive to work on many goals at once, the time and energy you save back makes this extreme new approach appealing – it's based on the same theory that led to the assembly line.

Evaluate your own planning tools and techniques, and see if your strategizing could use some updating or reconfiguration. Or, if your planning process works well, check in with yourself to be sure you are working it to generate optimal results.

Bob is right – plan well, and you'll accelerate your success.

Loss   May 2015

As most of you know, I lost my dad on May 4. He went in the way he wanted to go, quickly and with minimal discomfort, so I am sad to lose him, but happy that he left on his terms.

Each of us will face this kind of experience at one time or another – and how we process and assimilate loss will determine how well we come through such challenging times, and in many ways is a predictor of how successful we will be in the game of life, handling all setbacks gracefully.

In "Who Will Cry When You Die," Robin Sharma tells of a significant turning point for him, when his father said to him, "Son, when you were born, you cried while the world rejoiced. Live your life in such a way that when you die the world cries while you rejoice."

This whole idea of loss can be misleading and confusing, because it suggests that we "need" something to be okay, and that if we lose that something, we are no longer okay. In "Communion With God," Neale Donald Walsch talks about the Ten Illusions, starting with the illusion of need – he says "You may imagine that you need something to live happily – that you can be happy only under certain conditions. That is not true, but you have believed it to be true. And because belief produces experience, you have experienced life in this way... now here is a great secret: Happiness is not created as a result of certain conditions. Certain conditions are created as a result of happiness."

He goes on to say that love, compassion, abundance, all states of being, are part of this pattern of creation. "Need does not exist," he continues. "It is a fiction. In reality, you need nothing to be happy. Happiness is a state of mind."

This reframes loss – what have we actually lost? A game? Our keys? Our money? A friend? Our way? It's easy to see that with the right viewpoint, need does not exist, loss does not exist, because those things only occur in a distortion of reality that pretends that they exist. You can opt out of that by recognizing that nothing has any meaning but the meaning you give it, as Tony Robbins tells us, and apply more empowering meanings to the circumstances of your life.

Many of us find ourselves saying that things happen for a reason – what does that actually mean? If it insinuates a grand design, then we must acknowledge that it ALL happens for a reason, and it all serves us in some way, even the stuff that seems unpleasant at the time.

Like the caterpillar who seems to "die" when it is really metamorphosing within the cocoon into a new shape with powers and abilities that far transcend its previous form, so too do we transform and are compelled to relinquish the past in favor of the present and future – but if we frame it that we have "lost" the past, then we have irreconcilable pain. If, rather, we accept that we have moved into a new place where new conditions exist, then we safeguard our feelings and still stay present to experience whatever life has in store for us now.

John Demartini addresses this when he talks about "the center line," which is a confluence of neutrality and balance. When something deviates off that center line, it may be perceived as "good" or "bad" but it will always be mirrored with an opposite and equal reaction, which, again, we may classify as good or bad. The point is, everything remains in a cosmic equilibrium – as Einstein tells us with his theory of relativity, nothing can be created or destroyed, but merely changes shape.

So it is with our perception of loss – that which we feel we have lost is actually transformed into another vibrational incarnation, different perhaps but not necessarily less valuable, even if it seems less accessible in some ways.

So, we need to reframe loss – if you believe things happen for a reason, it can't only be when it feels good, it's either all or nothing

Different circumstances may have different emotional charge on the gradient of loss, but those intensities only compound the illusion. The trick is to match up the appropriate response with the level of loss suffered – choose words to describe your experience that match the appropriate emotional tone. Robbins calls this "transformational vocabulary" – picking the right language to properly express what you are feeling, either without inadvertently amplifying the pain unnecessarily, or choosing to amplify the pleasures accordingly.

For example, try on these language constructions:
Where are my flipping keys?
I lost my darn keys.
I misplaced my keys.
I'm looking for my keys.
I know my keys are somewhere.
I'm about to find my keys.

While these sentences express a similar sentiment, they have varying emotional charge, which you can use to moderate or enhance your emotions around your experiences.

Learning to express yourself in times of adversity is a fine art, but it is a worthy objective for most of us, as we do suffer periodic indignities along the path of our lives. Consider your worldview and perspective when you experience a loss – it can save you needless suffering, and set you up to process the situation as healthfully and expediently as possible.

Self-Indulgence   June 2015

I remember seeing Neale Donald Walsch speak a number of years ago – you may recall his profound book series called "Conversations With God." In this particular talk, he quoted Jean Houston, originally known as a psychic healer but now considered one of the grandmothers of the human potentials movement.

Houston said, "Our weaknesses are often our strengths turned up a little too high." So it is true for those who believe than self discipline must resemble austerity, or that working hard is an excuse for excessive partying.

I confess I have been consumed by my work for a few years, often sixty, seventy hours a week or more, and Regina works me under the table every day, always has. So when it occurred to us that we could visit our son Daniel at Life West and also vacation in northern California, we said duh, hit our heads in the "I should have had a V8" tradition, and we trekked across the continent to partake in a bit of self indulgence.

We arrived in San Francisco and checked into the Intercontinental Hotel, heading up to the 24th floor with a view of the skyline and the fog rolling in over the bay. We dropped our bags, grabbed a quick veggie sushi lunch at a local eatery (one of the tastiest rolls ever, cucumber and avocado inside out, dressed with a slice of sweet potato, crisped in tempura style and drizzled with a sweet brown sauce -- mmmmmm.)

We sped back to our room to get ready for the concert. None other than Marty Balin, founding member of the Jefferson Airplane and Starship and writer of some of the most recognizable and memorable songs in rock history was playing at the tiny Throckmorton Theater in Mill Valley the night we arrived. We sat dead-center in the third row, and three hundred or so of us were treated to his acoustic trio performing a fifty year retrospective, sung in one of the purest and most angelic voices in music.

The next morning, we headed to Palo Alto to visit Ananda, a multi-faceted spiritual community, to participate in their "Fire Ceremony" and enjoy their Sunday morning service. We even went to tour their residences, and our guide plucked a delicious juicy sun-ripened apricot off the branch and proudly presented it to us to enjoy.

That was Father's Day, and we had the delight of spending the rest of it with Dan. We had a lovely dinner, and made plans to visit him in the clinic on Monday for our examinations. He did a terrific job with his exam and bedside manner – he had great command, especially for someone at the very beginning of his career. His mom and I were bursting with pride, he was so professional.

Monday, we checked out of the high rise and signed into a quaint bed-and-breakfast in Sonoma, and began our winery adventure with a tasting at Phelps, best known for their Cabernet called "Insignia." We started to get the lay of the land as we drove through the scenic mountains between our charming accommodations in Sonoma and the wineries in Napa and St. Helena.

We were so happy with the food – as hard-to-please vegetarian foodies, we are picky, but also very appreciative of excellence. Standout dining establishments included FarmShop in Larkspur in Marin County, where we had the most lip-smacking burrata, a form of mozzarella cheese with a chewy exterior and a softer center, served with grilled peaches and apricots, in a hazelnut-pistachio sauce. I had a yummy raviolo with a runny egg in sage brown butter at Michael Chiarello's Bottega in Yountsville. Julia and Kevin Keiser recommended Club Le Haye in Sonoma, which featured organic haut cuisine, exotic dishes like a glowing purple beet risotto, wild mushrooms and polenta in white wine sauce, and Gruyere bread pudding. We loved Farm at the Carneros Inn, a Michelin star restaurant whose vegetarian menu included a corn velouté, a thick chowder with a sprinkle of parmesan and micro-greens on top, and a cheesy risotto with a generous layer of white truffle covering the surface.

But the best meal of the week was at La Toque at the Napa Westin on McKinstry Street. Chef Ken Frank, another Michelin star winner, offers a vegetarian tasting menu with a wine pairing that builds and amplifies the dining experience to new levels of sensory exhilaration. We're talking asparagus foam with fresh radish and watercress with a delicately floral Viognier. We're talking ricotta and sun-dried tomato ravioli with cabbage with a substantial layer of black winter truffle shaved on top, coupled with an '07 Barolo. We're talking cheese soufflé with stinging nettle pesto, with a robust Cabernet Franc from Pride Mountain. We've eaten at some of the world's finest restaurants, and we can't recall a better all-around showing.

Did I mention that we hit five more wineries? At the Keisers' suggestion, we took an informative Mondavi tour, and we picked another at Sequoia Grove, both of which gave us great information about wine tasting and wine pairing with food, invaluable for us because we love to cook (and eat) together. We found our best wine of the trip at Heitz Cellar, with Opus One and Cakebread rounding out the tour.

But the highlight was not food or wine, but a different kind of self indulgence – we went back to the clinic to get adjusted by our son. That closes the loop on three generations of Perman chiropractors. You know, we came home by way of Florida, where we paid our last respects to my dad, Dr. Bill Perman, at his memorial ceremony. There was a graceful cosmic symmetry to my father leaving the profession and my son coming into it. He gave us each a marvelous adjustment, far advanced from where we expected he would be – he's been studying with an outstanding mentor, Dr. Rebecca Nystrom of San Rafael, and had done a mission trip to India as well as a seminar journey to Japan to study with a little known master, Fujibushi, who developed an innovative upper cervical technique.

The last two nights we spent in a creekside cottage at the Candlelight Inn in Napa, furnished in elegant heavy French mahogany and cherry wood and offering a delightful balcony overlooking the stream in the woods. Each morning on that private porch, our personal server brought us a delectable three course breakfast, dishes like banana-nut pancakes with fresh berries and vegetable frittata, scrumptious.

With so much emotion and excitement, Regina and I found our communication and our mutual love and support at an all-time high. And that's a strength it's hard to turn up too high. But we feel that this amount of self indulgence enriches our internal map, and is well worth the expense and the saw-sharpening reprioritization of our time and resources.

Take a look at your own balance – are you planning enough self indulgence? No need to over-indulge, but there's also no need to live too small, either. In "The Power of Full Engagement," Loehr and Schwartz tell us that we go through cycles of stress and recovery, physically, mentally, emotionally and spiritually. Find your best formula, and you never have to worry about going over the line – though it feels great to walk right up to it.

The Innate Practice   July 2015

When I graduated from New York Chiropractic College in December of 1977, I truly believed I had the flame of life in my pisiforms. My worldview revolved around knowing that I had the greatest ally any healer could ever ask for, and that if I could only figure out how to get the interference out of the way, the body's natural recuperative ability would take over and the person would experience the proverbial chiropractic miracle.

Not surprisingly, this did play out more often than not in my office, but it reminds me of the story of the city slicker who moved to a country town, and saw a farmer out toiling in the fields. He beckoned to him to take a break and come over for a chat.

"What a beautiful farm God has blessed you with," the newcomer declared.

The farmer scratched his chin, thought for a moment, and responded, "Ayuh, but you should have seen it when He had it all to Himself."

We live in an abundant, friendly universe, of that I am forever convinced. But that doesn't necessarily mean that everything feels good all the time. There is a natural tide, a cosmic ebb and flow that transcends our human intellect, inhale/exhale, stress/recovery, storm/calm, sympathetic/parasympathetic, and tapping into that enormous rhythmic power is a secret key to chiropractic healing.

But there's a trap there, one we can sidestep when we think about the astute farmer's comments. Yes, innate intelligence is always on the job, and yes, its contribution is always at 100%, based on the underpinnings of chiropractic philosophy, Dr. Morter's perfect response.

But the full expression of innate presupposes that you have done your part in solving the riddle the patient brought to you, the elusive cause of their problem, the reason they are not automatically healing this condition at this time. Fortunately the patient also brought the solution, and your role is clear – discover why innate is not being expressed at 100% and eliminate those impediments.

The beauty of the brain-based wellness approach is that every technique adds a flavor or shade to the overall mix. All adjustments seem to reduce brain stress, but you can custom-tailor your strategy for each patient's best interests.

This is what Dr. Barwell was talking about – we are all accustomed to making recommendations based on frequency and duration, how many visits over what time frame. Barwell's contribution is the consideration of intensity, in other words, how aggressive or subtle should your program of care be, based on the type of brain stress the patient is suffering.

The BioChart concept provides some guidelines on how to manage your care plan – is the patient over-aroused, stuck too much of the time in sympathetic stress? This kind of patient, which makes up a large piece of your practice, probably would benefit from lesser frequency over greater duration, with more intensity the first adjustment and then varying the intensity based on your interpretation of the level of arousal of the nerve system throughout the program of care.

For those patients who are under-aroused, you may need to use a more assertive technique to wake up their nerve system, and if they are unstable, going back and forth, you'll need to interpret your findings carefully each visit, dancing with innate. Those very sick patients whose brains are exhausted need inspiration and kid gloves, steel wrapped in cotton. They need a strong, emotionally supportive approach delivered gently but with certainty and hope.

Ideally you'd have technology like a Neuroinfiniti or an Insight to make some of these physiological distinctions, not to mention bilateral blood pressure calibration, hand temperature devices, a balance apparatus and the like. But if not, feeling hand temperature and moisture, or noticing muscle tension, eye movement, breathing or any number of easily accessible signs will direct your attention. An innate style of practice invites this dialogue where you ask the body what it needs and it gives you clear feedback in a language that you learn through recognizing patterns, openness and positive expectancy.

Whether you have moved toward brain-based wellness practice or you are enjoying a more traditional style, knowing you are acting in conjunction with innate intelligence generates an alignment that goes beyond the spinal bones. No matter what your clinical vehicle, all healing is about energy and vibration at its core, whether it is neurological, structural, or esoteric, and you play a major role in facilitating the fine work of the body's inner wisdom.

Progress at your own pace – we chiropractors have a tendency to study the stuff we like, and that of course is human nature. But getting yourself to learn and apply some of these breakthrough distinctions, mysterious as they may seem at first, will pay dividends in the form of a healthier clientele and greater attraction, as people discover that something unique and wonderful is happening in your practice.

After all, Vern Pierce, co-creator of Pierce-Stillwagon Technique, seminal influence on chiropractic instrumentation and instrument adjusting, may he rest in peace, used to say "Hell, bang 'em in the backside with a bull fiddle, they'll get well!" as the ultimate reflection of his confidence in Innate.

My observation is, if you add your own intentionality and a dash of expertise, the farm looks better than if you left it alone, and you reap the myriad rewards of an innate practice, presented with your own personalized flourish.

Kindness   August 2015

"Would you rather be right or be kind?" asks Wayne Dyer.

We live in an information-based, fact-checking, google-obsessed culture. The lust for the latest research, the most recent breakthroughs and the slightest winner's edge is a driving force in most businesses, and it's easy for us as entrepreneurs to slip down that slope – to be absorbed by statistics and balance sheets, and by the details, stresses and challenges that come along with everyday practice.

We put a high value on being right – on being able to prove, protect and defend our position, to make our point and to move forward. It seems like so much of the structure of achievement depends upon being right about things.

But leadership is tricky. Sometimes just being right can only get you so far, because often our experience is defined not merely by facts but also in emotions, and emotions follow a different set of rules.

It's like a Ben Franklin Close – that's when you persuade yourself or someone else by making a logical case, with a line down the center of the page, pro's on one side, con's on the other, and whichever has a longer list wins the decision. But many times it doesn't turn out to work that way – after the logical process is completed, if we lean emotionally toward the non-logical choice, the feelings may prevail.

You can't solve emotional problems with logic, and vice versa. So, while Dyer's question invites us to be more compassionate, it also asks us to explore the equilibrium of the current moment, to calibrate the optimal blend of objectivity and consideration.

We have many opportunities every day to exercise this emotional muscle -- patients who don't yet understand our message and need extra support, teammates with difficult personal issues who may need guidance to focus their minds on their work, keeping the patients at the forefront, and so on. Instead of digging in to prove how right you are, either inside your head or in spirited debate, conserve your resources to invest in being as loving as possible toward yourself and anyone else involved, so you can start at a higher vibration, and go from there.

If you do need to be right, it will be expressed better at that higher, more loving, kinder vibration. You still may find yourself needing to take an assertive posture at times – that's normal in business and in life, especially for leaders, parents and doctors who manage teams and take care of patients. But if you apply a cold, matter-of-fact, logical approach without the flavor of kindness, it can come across as shallow, officious, arrogant or condescending. Coming from a place of love causes every communication to be received better.

Here are some thoughts from great thinkers on kindness:

"Be kind, because everyone is having a really hard time." – Plato

"Do your little bit of good where you are; it's those little bits of good put together that overwhelm the world." – Desmond Tutu

"No one has ever become poor by giving." – Anne Frank

"Tenderness and kindness are not signs of weakness and despair, but manifestations of strength and resolution." – Kahlil Gibran

"You cannot do a kindness too soon, for you never know how soon it will be too late." – Ralph Waldo Emerson

"Kindness in words creates confidence. Kindness in thinking creates profoundness. Kindness in giving creates love." – Lao Tzu

"Love only grows by sharing. You can only have more for yourself by giving it away to others."
– Brian Tracy

"I prefer you to make mistakes in kindness than work miracles in unkindness."
– Mother Teresa

"The smallest act of kindness is worth more than the grandest intention." – Oscar Wilde

I heard this story many years ago from a prominent chiropractor, who was just closing up after a busy, tiring day in his office when the doorbell rang. It was a big heavy construction worker type, smelly and greasy after work and looking for an adjustment to help his sore back. With one foot out the door, the doctor instructed the patient to go home and take a hot bath, and come back the next morning. He was halfway home before he realized that his service consciousness had been tested and he had fallen short. He vowed not to make that mistake again.

Circumstances that call us to be kind are always all around us. Adjust your senses, raise your antennae to pick up when, where and how to do good – it will come back to you personally, to be sure, but the real reward is in creating as much positive change as you can. When more of us commit to that, paying it forward with random and non-random acts of kindness, the world will become a much better place.

Loyalty   September 2015

As I sit and collect my thoughts to share with you, I am watching a breathtaking spectacle the likes of which most of us have never witnessed.

The Pope, perhaps the most influential person on Earth, the spiritual leader of one-sixth of the world's population, is visiting the US, to hordes of adoring worshippers and spectators cutting across all persuasions. They took planes, trains and automobiles and traveled hours or days to be in his presence, hoping for a blessing, a smile, a wave, a selfie or some other souvenir to take forward with them. The meaning of such a memento is of course quite individual, but there is an underlying personal quality that drives people to such extreme actions.

In this time of great social and political upheaval, role models like the consistently gentle and humble but still commanding and supremely powerful authority of Pope Francis light the way to resolving and growing through our differences. We are reminded that we must live a life of love, mutual respect, honesty, compassion, gratitude, and a list of other necessary characteristics, not the least of which is… loyalty.

Loyalty is more than a blind acceptance and vacuous following of a doctrine or philosophy. Dictionary.com says loyalty is a "faithful adherence to a sovereign, government, leader or cause," and that faith is the fuel that drives loyalty – the unshakable belief that your cause is the right one for you to engage and represent.

It wouldn't be inaccurate to say that in our own ways, we are loyal to, in varying degrees, our God, our religion, our nation, our alma mater, our community, our family, our spouse or significant other, our children, our profession, and a list of causes we hold dear.

The question is, how do we construct the priorities? It's obvious that these entities are not equal in everyone's values hierarchy – how do we orchestrate these commitments so they remain consistent with our worldview?

In microcosm, this is what happens in the mind of virtually every chiropractic patient. They come to your office with a high value on whatever it is they are hoping you will deliver for them – relief, answers, quality of life, and everything in between.

But notice, as they get closer to accomplishing their intention, their priorities may shift, and then their loyalty may ebb and flow accordingly. When they are suffering through a flaming sciatica, they may still love golf, but your visit is more important to them than going out to play, since they can't swing a club anyway.

As soon as they feel better, their loyalty to their golf game starts to overtake their loyalty to your program of care, and barring relapses, you can only compete with that to the extent that you can demonstrate that loyalty to you gains them more value than whatever they have shifted their attention toward.

It would be pointless to deny this, as each of us does this, again, to varying degrees, but we all do it – we're all expert at rationalizing a position, based on our perceptions of our current reality.

So, be patient when your people opt out, but also do what it takes to create loyalty – let them disengage gracefully with an eye toward future re-engagement. Recall them, be good to them, keep trying to get them back in, and many times it will pay off.

For students of the enneagram, each personality type has a slightly different relationship with loyalty. Ones are loyal because it's the right thing to do. Twos are loyal through service, loving those people and causes to which they are loyal. Threes want to appear loyal, but limit their loyalties to those who return the favor and help them get ahead.

Fours are loyal to their emotions, and Fives are loyal to their ideas. Sixes are loyal to causes and leaders that offer them certainty. Sevens are loyal at first, but are more loyal to adventure and variety than any current configuration of their experience.

Eights demand loyalty in their entourage, returning the compliment only when they choose, my rules for you, no rules for me. Nines are loyal because they don't want to confront the consequences of disloyalty, and once they develop a habit of supporting a position or thought leader, their commitment is strong because the familiarity makes them comfortable with it.

These perspectives, oversimplified though they may seem, can be useful in leadership – when you know who you're dealing with, you can communicate better and generate better teamwork.

If you want more distinctions on each of these personality types, read "The Wisdom Of The Enneagram," by Don Richard Riso and Russ Hudson, or get the album "The Enneagram" by yours truly. Or just ask me.

Loyalty turns out to be the secret glue that holds people together. Being able to count on someone is a precious gift indeed – and giving it to someone can have a profound impact on their sense of self. Loyal support is that important.

So, I would be remiss if I didn't take this opportunity to thank you, beloved Winners Circle members, for your loyalty to our cause, and to each other. Surely you recognize how committed we are to you and your success and fulfillment, and you can rely on us to preserve and maintain that, to the best of our abilities.

"Success is the result of perfection, hard work, learning from failure, loyalty, and persistence."
-- Colin Powell

"The foundation stones for a balanced success are honesty, character, integrity, faith, love and loyalty."
-- Zig Ziglar

"Achievement of your happiness is the only moral purpose of your life, and that happiness, not pain or mindless self-indulgence, is the proof of your moral integrity, since it is the proof and the result of your loyalty to the achievement of your values." -- Ayn Rand

"Loyalty and devotion lead to bravery. Bravery leads to the spirit of self-sacrifice. The spirit of self-sacrifice creates trust in the power of love." -- Morihei Ueshiba

The best loyalty goes both ways – keep that in mind as you consider your organizing principles. Your spouse or significant other, your family, your friends, your team, your patients, your colleagues, your community, and the world are looking to you for leadership – show them how engaging your causes serves their best interests, and the result will be the highest degree of loyalty.

Looking For A Miracle   October 2015

I have a lovely little mastermind on Thursday mornings, during my open consulting session. Dear friends and longtime Masters Circle members Myles Starkman of Miami and Michael Bennett of Crystal River, FL are a constant source of intellectual and philosophical stimulation, and I look forward to engaging them, as well as others who often patch in, like Winners Circle members Tom Salmon, Jeff Cumro and Jimmy Leonette.

Last week, we were talking about what brings people to chiropractic offices, and the discussion ranged from pain relief to better quality of life and everything in between.

But then it occurred to me that, really, these were the tangible results of what they came to us for. Actually, they came to us looking for a miracle.

If a patient goes to a doctor of any other kind, they are typically looking for help, for relief, for answers, for treatment – but not so when a patient chooses to go to a chiropractor. Between the reputation chiropractors enjoy, and the desperation of many patients once they finally find their way to us, treatment and relief no longer measure up to their expectations. They are looking for a miracle.

If a patient goes to a provider of any other kind, and it isn't a successful experience by their standard, they choose another provider and see if they have better luck – but not so with a chiropractor. When a patient goes to a chiropractor the entire profession is riding on that experience, since a typical patient who isn't happy with the chiropractor they go to either never goes back to another chiropractor, or only after all other options have been exhausted – you see, they were looking for a miracle, and they didn't get one, so the profession is punished en masse for the shortcomings of that one doctor with that one patient in that one situation. That's what happens when a patient comes in looking for a miracle.

But there's a bright side to this – when you think about it, the huge majority of chiropractic patients are very happy with chiropractic. The approval numbers are off the charts compared to most other professionals – and that is a comment on how frequently we chiropractors deliver on that seemingly impossible promise – of witnessing miracle after miracle after miracle in our offices.

Too often we reduce or overlook the amazing things that happen daily in chiropractic offices, either because we are keeping our light under a basket, or we just simply expect patients to have extraordinary responses to our care, rendering those responses "ordinary," or rather, commonplace.

But what happens in someone's body when the brain is re-connected and interference is removed is nothing short of magical – I personally saw a blind woman regain her sight, many tumors remiss, and numerous infertile couples become able to conceive – in fact, I recently had a family stop me in a restaurant, confirm that I was indeed Dr. Dennis, and report that the handsome strapping young man seated with them was birthed as a manifestation of my chiropractic intervention, one of the last success cases I remember before my retirement in 1987 – twenty-seven years later, they got a chance to thank me, a sweet and meaningful moment, to be sure.

It's no less miraculous to take care of someone who avoids serious illness with chiropractic, or experiences a greater sense of well-being, though it may be a bit less dramatic. But the miracle of chiropractic care is not in the effect, but the cause – that chiropractors have tapped into the essence of wellness by seeing the body as an integrated whole, to a greater degree than any other healers on earth. We care for the body by seeking to act consistently with its innate needs, and the miracle is not what we do, but that the body knows exactly what to do with our subtle concussion of forces, to transform it into a healing trend.

What are some of your favorite chiropractic miracles? Trace back through your patient base, and notice how many lives have been improved because of your guidance and service. Pick out your three or four most astounding patient responses to your care, and after reflection and connecting with your humility, compare notes with your Winners Circle buddies, and prepare to be inspired – we have incredible stories to tell, and we need to tell them, for the betterment of our profession and the people we serve.

Resilience   November 2015

After our Winners Circle event in New Orleans, the key theme that emerged was the resilience we witnessed in the committed townspeople of The Big Easy. Many of us have faced hardships of assorted magnitude, but most have not been wiped out and forced to start over, or been among dozens or hundreds of neighbors who had to deal with that type of adversity.

I wonder what I might have done under the circumstances – would I leave and begin again elsewhere? Would I stick around but play small to avoid another catastrophic loss? Or would I be one of those hardy souls who buckled down and rebuilt a life better than before, one brick and board at a time?

It's tough to speculate on your response to unforeseen disaster, but it's useful to imagine being under that kind of demanding pressure to try on the qualities of resilience, determination, focus and self-discipline. For example, when you use the Two Questions, the foundational exercise of Capacity Technology™, the Dream exercise asks you to consider, if there were no rules and you couldn't fail, what would your practice be like, while the second exercise, the Identity Profile, asks, who you would need to be or become to have that practice.

But there's an adaptation of this exercise that asks, if there were no rules and you couldn't fail, what extreme conditions could you endure, and then the identity profile defines the qualities you'd need to handle that massive stress and come through stronger, more confident and better on the other side?

I can make an argument that prosperity is harder to manage than adversity, since moving forward in prosperity can seem optional, while tough times tend to demand your attention, like it or not. But usually we draw from a familiar palette of resources, so exploring the underbelly of success to discover what qualities you'd need to handle things going badly can be immensely valuable. And when you add up those qualities, what you get is resilience.

Morihei Ueshiba is credited with discovering aikido, a gentle and dignified martial arts practice that uses balance and leverage to incapacitate attackers without harming them. A student once asked him, "Sensei, how come you never get knocked off center?" Ueshiba smiled and said, "I do get knocked off center – I just recover so quickly no one can tell." That's resilience.

One of the best measures of overall health is adaptability, whether you quantize it by speed of recovery, history of avoiding or withstanding health problems, or epigenetic and physiological responsiveness, like through serum thiol testing, heart rate variability or bio feedback. In this context, adaptability, the ability to respond, and resilience, the ability to bounce back are two sides of the same coin.

It's important to recognize that resilience is not only having a great attitude and being persistent, while that is surely part of it. You can be as optimistic as you like, but it won't overcome a faulty strategy. You have to be resilient at both the be and the do level, and that's when your struggle gives way to effortless ease. Resilience is supposed to be an outgrowth of natural rightness, not an ordeal. A master prefers what occurs.

Give yourself credit for your breakthroughs and accomplishments, and forgive your frailties – as long as you pick yourself up one more time than you get knocked down, you're still in the game with a shot to win – and that's how you stay resilient.

Givingness   December 2015

When we think of giving, we often imagine tangible gifts, like money, jewelry, clothing, or hobby equipment. Sometimes, we make gifts of experiences, like dinners, show tickets or travel.

But what's behind these material displays of affection and appreciation? It's givingness, the essence of giving, of which gifts are a manifestation. It's an energy field that is generated from the sensation of plenty, of not needing – in fact, a feeling of neediness may interfere with the feeling of freedom to give.

This creates an odd paradox – some people have plenty, but because of the feeling of need, they are less inclined to give. Others may not have near as much, but the feeling of need is not as pronounced for them, so they are more likely to be comfortable giving.

Deepak Chopra articulates this beautifully in discussing his Second Spiritual Law of Success, The Law Of Giving.

He says, "This law could also be called the Law of Giving and Receiving, because the universe operates through dynamic exchange. The flow of life is nothing other than the harmonious interaction of all the elements and forces that structure the field of existence. Because your body and your mind and the universe are in constant and dynamic change, stopping the circulation of energy is like stopping the flow of blood.

Whenever blood stops flowing, it begins to clot, to stagnate. That is why you must give and receive in order to keep wealth and affluence--or anything you want--circulating in your life. If our only intention is to hold on to our money and hoard it--since it's life energy, we will stop its circulation back into our lives as well. In order to keep that energy coming to us, we have to keep the energy circulating. Thus, the more you give, the more you will receive."

He goes on to say, "In fact, the most powerful forms of giving are non-material. The gifts of caring, attention, affection, appreciation and love are some of the most precious gifts you can give, and they don't cost you anything."

But givingness is hardly a New Age concept – John Wesley, who founded the Protestant Methodist movement in the Eighteenth Century, wrote this ode to giving:

"Do all the good you can
By all the means you can,
In all the ways you can,
In all the places you can,
At all the times you can,
To all the people you can,
As long as ever you can."

Gandhi moved to a new neighborhood, and went out to help the townspeople. A friend complimented his humanitarian actions, but he responded, "I am here to serve no one but myself, to find my own self-realization through the service of these village folk."

Gandhi shows us that by helping others, we are working on ourselves. Every time we demonstrate compassion, we feed our own hearts, too. When we serve others, they heal; and when we serve generously with an open heart, we heal.

The point is, we are truly fortunate to be in the position to give and serve every day, but the attitude and tone of our giving is an important component to be considered. When we acknowledge what's in it for us, and go as far as we can to do good for the people we touch, everyone wins – this is the secret to giving.

Some of us give to children, or parents, or other friends or relatives who need us. Some of us take on community projects where we get to give to our neighbors. Some participate in charities, giving to people whom you will probably never meet, but who are grateful for your willingness to support them anonymously. It almost doesn't matter how you decide to give of yourself, but rather that you see the importance of doing so.

Many spiritual traditions talk about tithing, or dedicating a tenth of your income as a donation to those who may need it more. The amount is not really the most important aspect of tithing, but rather the commitment to regularly offer a spiritual gift.

This can be a gift of time where you volunteer, a gift of money where you flow financial resources to those who need it, or you can come up with something creative, but giving is a necessary part of our personal growth, and a necessary trigger for the giving-receiving cycle. What goes around comes around – keep it in mind as you sketch out your goals and strategies for the coming year. It's one way to make it your best year yet.

Target Orientation   January 2016

One of the core ideologies of The Masters Circle is that "the mind is target-oriented." This is the reason for identifying your goals, values, beliefs and standards – you can't hit a target if you don't aim at it, and you can't aim at a target if you don't know what it is.

For this reason, it is highly recommended that you experiment with the assortment of different goal-setting and planning systems, and find the combination that gives you the best target orientation – in other words, the one that makes it most obvious to you what you're trying to accomplish, and who you have to be and what you have to do to accomplish it.

For many years, I have used and recommended the Six P's – first, write your Purpose, and then select your Personal goals, your Professional goals, your People goals, your Prosperity goals, and your Play goals. I suggest writing them by October First, reviewing them Thanksgiving Eve, and finalizing them on New Year's Eve. Write as many as you like, but I find it best to consider only up to three at a time in each category, to stay focused and generate enough forward thrust to create impact.

You may do it that way, or some completely different way, or similar but different in some ways – no problem. The idea is to develop targets to aim at, not to default to any particular methodology. Do what works for you. I propose these ideas because they have worked well for me and others, but feel free to research your own technique and style, because what's important is the target orientation, not the way you get there.

One of the trickiest parts to target orientation is recognizing whether your target is an outcome or a process. Outcome goals are milestones, accomplishments that are completed and done. For example, if your goal is to save $100,000, and you save $100,000, that is an outcome you have achieved.

But what if your goal is to meditate every morning? Or to maintain your weight at 180 pounds? Or to collect $40,000 each month? These goals can be participated in and continued, but they will never be complete, because they are processes, not outcomes, unless you want to get to 180 pounds or $40,000 a month once, to be able to say you did it. If you want to remain at those levels at least, that would be a process goal.

So, for a process goal, your target is to be fully engaged in the process, to exercise five days a week or eat more vegetables and less meat or whatever. It's another angle on target orientation.

Choosing the right targets is one of the fine arts of goal-setting. That's one of the reasons to keep your focus on only three goals in each category, instead of keeping all of your objectives in front of you at the same time. You will need to focus on your priorities, to avoid overwhelm or confusion.

That's why your Purpose is the first P – your purpose will clarify this system for you. The goals you select either are consistent with your purpose or they are not, and the actions you take will either move you toward those goals or they won't. It streamlines the system to know that your goal structure supports your purpose without reservation, so you can get leverage on yourself, fully engage and congruently commit.

Once your goals are established, in reality each action step is a target in and of itself. If you plan your action steps in a realistic, efficient and productive sequence, you create the shortest distance to your goal, which is of course another target.

If you take action and you get your outcome, you can move on to the next set of targets. If not, then you have to refine your plan before you take more action, again, to be sure you have a proper target to aim at.

Usually, setting Personal and Professional goals flows smoothly, and Play goals tend to take shape rather easily as well. Here are a few words about your People and your Prosperity goals.

People goals are about relationships. They are not goals you set for other people, they are goals you set for yourself within the context of that particular relationship. You can goal to support someone in a certain way, to lead someone to a different conclusion, or to resolve issues or forgive someone, but these goals are goals for yourself, not the other person.

For your Prosperity goals, most people choose a target for their income, but many still need to aim at a savings number, a debt reduction number, or a donation standard – these figures grow out of having a current Financial Master Plan, which includes at least six areas – office or work overhead, home and personal expenses, taxes, savings, debt reduction and fun or entertainment.

Compute these monthly targets, do what it takes to earn that amount, and then allocate or distribute the money to those six buckets without deviation. If you earn more than that amount, pay the additional tax and then invest it, save it or spend it as you wish, since your needs are fulfilled by fully funding each of these six objectives.

Each day, you should be taking strides toward achieving those major goals, as part of an overall system of productivity, so you can apply your resources to create the best results possible.

Generating effective target orientation is one of the critical keys to success. Raise your standards, and hold yourself to a higher level of execution, and you will be delighted with your forward movement.

Compassion   February 2016

We live in a harshly judgmental society, where people take sides based on their own personal agenda, often in utter disregard for the greater good. We as chiropractors exert our strongest possible influence to represent our viewpoint effectively, and to varying degrees this has a positive effect, but nowhere near the sea change we are hoping for.

I recall an old study from the New England Journal of Medicine, I think around 1975, where the researchers analyzed chiropractic care to discover why it is so effective.

Their conclusion? They couldn't understand any clinical value, but they observed that chiropractors were mostly very nice to their patients, and that if there was anything to learn from chiropractors, it would be for medical doctors to be nicer to their patients, and they would get better results.

After you stop laughing at the absurdity and condescension of such a conclusion, look deeper at the compliment they are paying us as a profession – even through their veil of prejudice, they could tell that we got good results, and the only thing we did that they could wrap their minds around was that we understand the healing power of compassion, and our very caring for the people we serve helps them to get well faster and better.

A few minutes of googling turned up a treasure trove of profound comments on compassion from the world's greatest thought leaders, some dating back thousands of years.

"Be kind, for everyone you meet is fighting a harder battle." – *Plato*

"Compassion is the basis of morality." – *Arthur Schopenhauer*

"If we have no peace, it is because we have forgotten that we belong to each other." – *Mother Teresa*

"If you want others to be happy, practice compassion. If you want to be happy, practice compassion… Love and compassion are necessities, not luxuries. Without them, humanity cannot survive."
– Dalai Lama XIV

"Too often we underestimate the power of a touch, a smile, a kind word, a listening ear, an honest compliment, or the smallest act of caring, all of which have the potential to turn a life around."
– Leo Buscaglia

"Finally, all of you, live in harmony with one another; be sympathetic, love as brothers, be compassionate and humble." -- First Peter 3:8

"To change the world we must be good to those who cannot repay us." – Pope Francis

"No act of kindness, no matter how small, is ever wasted." – Aesop

"I have no idea what's awaiting me, or what will happen when this all ends. For the moment I know this: there are sick people and they need curing." – Albert Camus

"Compassion hurts. When you feel connected to everything, you also feel responsible for everything. And you cannot turn away. Your destiny is bound with the destinies of others. You must either learn to carry the Universe or be crushed by it. You must grow strong enough to love the world, yet empty enough to sit down at the same table with its worst horrors." – Andrew Boyd

"When we give cheerfully and accept gratefully, everyone is blessed." – Maya Angelou

"Until he extends the circle of his compassion to all living things, man will not himself find peace." – Albert Schweitzer

"If your compassion does not include yourself, it is incomplete." – Gautama Buddha

"Our task must be to free ourselves… by widening our circle of compassion to embrace all living creatures and the whole of nature and its beauty." – Albert Einstein

"True compassion is more than flinging a coin to a beggar; it comes to see that an edifice which produces beggars needs restructuring. " – Martin Luther King Jr

"Compassion is a verb." – Thích Nhất Hạnh

"Compassion is the signature of Higher Consciousness. Non-violence is the tool to evolve into the Higher Consciousness." – Amit Ray

These ideas help us to comprehend the immense power we wield when we engage someone in the healing arena. By congruently demonstrating genuine compassion, we turn on universal forces that dwarf our intellect, that outperform our wildest expectations. By turning on hope and optimism, we facilitate the healing process and play our role in moving the world toward wellness.

Thanks for taking this so seriously – as BJ says, I love you because you love what I love.

Optimization   March 2016

With the rousing success of the Winners Circle Practice Success Day in Chicago, the foundational concepts of our office operations shone through – the optimization formula we learned from Jay Abraham was revisited from many perspectives, so let's review the optimization process so we can easily catalog what we learned into the categories that serve our best interests.

Abraham says that there are three ways to increase your profitability – more new business, more repeat business, and a higher unit sale. To translate these concepts into the language of chiropractic practice, new business is called new patients (NPs), repeat business is the number of visits a patient returns, known as Patient Visit Average (PVA), and unit sale is the amount you collect per office visit, known as Office Visit Average (OVA.)

So, you can increase your profitability by attracting more new patients, by building a higher PVA with patients coming in more visits on average, or by increasing your OVA, the amount of money you collect per office visit.

Another way to say this is NPs x PVA x OVA = Income – so,

Increase in NPs x Increase in PVA x Increase in OVA = Increased Income.

You may find it challenging to grow all of these three factors at the same time – this suggests a limitation of capacity. To grow, you would usually need to increase one while you hold the other two steady, then grow another while you hold the other two steady, to the best of your ability.

For example, if you usually attract 20 NPs at a 40 PVA, you see 800 OVs. If you collect 50/OV, you collect 40,000.

20 NPs x 40 PVA x 50 OVA = 40K

If you increase by 5 NPs, and hold the PVA and OVA even:

25NPs x 40 PVA x 50 OVA = 50K

If you then raise your OVA to 60, and hold the NPs and PVA even:

25 NPs x 40 PVA x 60 OVA = 60K

If you then raise your PVA to 50, and hold your NPs and OVA even:

25 NPs x 48 PVA x 60 OVA = 72K

As you can see, these numbers compound quickly when you grow in more than one of these three areas. Or, you can power out on one area – the growth is not as rapid, but over time you can ramp up one area enough to make a big difference:

20 NPs x 40 PVA x 75 OVA = 60K
30 NPs x 40 PVA x 50 OVA = 60K
20 NPs x 60 PVA x 50 OVA = 60K

But of course:

30 NPs x 60 PVA x 75 OVA = 135K

Be aware if you increase new patients and the office visit volume does not respond accordingly. That tells you that you have a capacity limitation preventing you from growing. Look for evidence of where you are leaking, so you can build resources to handle those weaker areas, at the "be" level, the "do" level or both.

Analyze your statistics each month, quarter, half and year. Seek support from your coaches, who have analyzed thousands of these. Notice trends, and focus your energy on areas that call for it.

With a structured game plan, you can boost your profitability significantly. You work hard to deliver an outstanding service to your community – why not maximize your return? With a scientific approach to optimization, your path is clear, and the rewards are great.

Transcendence   April 2016

Most of us have seen Gerry Clum speak before, many of us numerous times, but he never fails to share perspectives that can only manifest after four decades of serving the profession worldwide. His remarks on Maslow's hierarchy of needs, suggesting that transcendence through compassion leads to the highest level of fulfillment, fit magnificently into the worldview of the Masters Circle and Winners Circle

Just look at the roots of our philosophy – Larry was groomed by Jim Parker, Bob by Sid Williams, myself by Tony Robbins. Parker said, "Loving Service My First Technique." Sid said, "Give for the sake of giving, love for the sake of loving, serve for the sake of serving." Tony said, "Success is evidence of having served well."

So, these foundational tenets are cornerstones for us, and serving others is clearly the way to happiness and self-esteem.

You may remember that I started my "Happiness Factor" class from the last seminar with a story about French monk Matthieu Ricard, named the "world's happiest man." He participated in a twelve-year neurological study of the brain characteristics of happy people, and he came out by far the most developed in this area.

And why is he the world's happiest man? He says it's because he meditates on compassion every day, and has been doing so for fifty years. He says an investment of as little as twenty minutes each day in meditation will decrease stress and increase joy.

So this is very lofty thinking, but how can we apply it in daily life? How can we show up transcendent and compassionate? What do those words even mean?

Let's look at some definitions, from dictionary.com.

Transcendent:
1.   going beyond ordinary limits; surpassing; exceeding.

2. superior or supreme.

3. *Theology.* (of the Deity) transcending the universe, time, etc.

4. *Philosophy.*

   a. *Scholasticism.* above all possible modes of the infinite.

   b. *Kantianism.* transcending experience; not realizable in humanexperience.

5. (in modern realism) referred to, but beyond, direct apprehension; outside consciousness.

Compassionate:
feeling deep sympathy and sorrow for another who is stricken by misfortune, accompanied by a strong desire to alleviate the suffering.
commiseration, mercy, tenderness, heart, clemency

So what Maslow was saying and what Gerry was referring to is that genuine caring, not as an action but as a primary filter of emotion, leads to moving beyond normal perception and to approaching bliss, the ultimate happiness.

This is in perfect alignment with our vision of a well world, our purpose of helping people be happy, satisfied and fulfilled, and our mission of expressing this end through chiropractic and wellness practice.

Other than adopting the habit of regular meditation, what else can we do to become more transcendent?

We can be trapped by thinking transcendence is less than a present experience, envisioning it as something off in the distance, but transcendence is actually an advanced form of presence, present not only to the present moment, but to all of time and space simultaneously.

Spiritualists may refer to this as "God-consciousness," a global feeling of both connection and freedom where we are both a cell in the organism of life, and the entire organism at the same time. While this is tough for the logical mind to comprehend, we have all glimpsed it at times – up on a mountain top, walking in the forest, scuba diving or making love, as examples where time stood still and we peered through a wormhole at our own immortality.

The irony of transcendence is that not only is no action required to experience it, but action may interfere with it. It's the stillness, the silence, the fully engaged disengagement that manifests this elusive quality. There's nothing for you to do, and there's nothing for you to not do. It's the closest thing to pure being we know of, and oddly it primes us for the most monumental and significant actions we could ever take.

Our greatest artists, sports heroes, and thought leaders demonstrate it – students aspire to it, and all of us have access to it. It takes a willingness to not think, but be thought through, as Bob says – it's neither active nor passive, but occurs as an energy field when the conditions are right.

So, my best advice to you is to not seek transcendence, just pay attention to your world, and notice examples of it, and opportunities to engage it. Be present, and keep bringing yourself back to the present moment – transcending it is a gift you are given when you get yourself out of the way.

Perfection and Excellence   May 2016

I was talking with Jimmy Leonette last week, and he complained to me about not being able to accomplish the level of perfection he desired. I laughed and pointed out that it was a trap of his personality type – Type Seven, known for enthusiasm, passion and adventurousness, stresses by acting more like Type One – more particular, more rules-y, rigid, critical, nitpicky and perfectionistic.

Jimmy explained that when he was working for the government, he was rewarded for such behaviors – the more detail-oriented his reports, the more he was acclaimed in his position, so it drove those patterns of perfectionism deep into his work ethic.

The problem is, for someone wired like him, it's a source of ongoing stress to be constantly pulled toward errorless, idealized results, when his natural tendency would be to be more flexible -- and the fact is, give or take our personality fixation, this is difficult for many or even most of us.

I learned from Tony Robbins over twenty years ago that contrary to the typical interpretation, perfectionists actually have lower standards than others – knowing that perfection will elude them, they aim for it but always feel like they will fall short, and since they know inside that they will fail, they adjust their expectations subconsciously, so they don't have to suffer repeatedly.

On the other hand, shouldn't we try to get it right, the best we can?

Absolutely, but that's not called perfection – it's called excellence.

The scientific landscape is dotted with "accidental" discoveries, from penicillin to X-rays to safety glass – no amount of planning and execution could account for the mystery of cosmic manifestation and divine coincidence. That's one of the pitfalls of perfectionism – when you are aiming for what you perceive to be a "perfect" outcome, it can create tunnel vision and shut down side benefits and unexpected gains, or at least cause them to be overlooked.

It takes a form of genius to be able to see an unanticipated result in the proper light – Robbins helped me to better understand this phenomenon. He said that most of us hold one mental picture in our minds at a time. The genius can hold two or more pictures in mind simultaneously, offering a sense of scientific comparison that is automatic and immensely powerful.

For example, imagine DD Palmer palpating Harvey Lillard's neck and visualizing his cervical spine with the axis out of position, with a picture right next to it with the alignment restored, giving him the original idea of adjusting. He had to invent concepts like line of drive, depth of thrust and patient positioning right there in the moment – it had never been done before. But while seeking a method to restore hearing, he discovered chiropractic, and the implications far surpass a remedy for deafness. He couldn't have planned for that without juxtaposing the problem and the solution, and interpreting his observations creatively.

Malcolm Gladwell talked about it in "Blink" – it's not so much a thinking process as a creativity and assessment reflex. It's a response that masters can produce at will, and it's clear that aiming at "perfection" would disrupt or even prevent this creative process.

So, the alternative to being imprisoned by the misconception of "only one right answer" is to strive for excellence – to generate an ongoing pursuit of the very best achievements, guided by goals but not limited by them.

So then, how can we recognize when we are caught in the clutches of chronic perfectionism, and how can we shift our attention toward excellence?

Watch out for "diminishing returns" – up to a certain point, efforts to improve reflect positive, measurable movement towards the intended objective. Once the investment no longer leads to growth or substantial refinement, you may have moved past the point of "excellence" and defaulted to a futile course toward the perfection that can rarely if ever be achieved.

Please don't misinterpret this as settling for less than the best you can do – it's actually the opposite, knowing when you have gotten to or near that level of achievement, and reassigning resources to address the next set of challenges instead of fruitlessly covering the same ground over and over.

Be careful of reinforcing this perspective with sloshy self-talk – dismissing your wastefulness by affirming, "well, I'm just a perfectionist" is toxic and distracting, and as stated above, takes you down a primrose path of squandered time and energy.

This requires careful navigation around the "good enough is good enough" deception – standards are critically important to any process leading to achievement, so be aware of corner-cutting, usually inconsistent with the best possible results.

Rather, establish meaningful, thorough goals that ask something reasonable of you and your team, and acknowledge when you have achieved them or something close, to avoid missing opportunities that arise that could be lost in the fog of perfectionism. And keep your peripheral vision activated, in case side benefits materialize.

Perfection is an arbitrary rule, where excellence is a state of mind that yields great results – get certain about the difference, and act accordingly.

Stress   June 2016

There has been a subtle and not-so-subtle shift in the way we at The Masters Circle are looking at our profession's service to humanity. We have been focused on the vertebral subluxation complex for all of my forty years in chiropractic, and well before that.

The net impact has been a spotty but meaningful utilization of chiropractic for painful disorders, and by the best estimates I have been able to track down, about 10-12% of the public has tried chiropractic, and about 1-2% of our neighbors are engaged in regular chiropractic care, either for prevention or wellness.

Part of this, of course, is due to our capacity as a profession – the ACA says there are about 60,000 DCs in the US, and the Bureau of Labor Statistics says about 45,000 are in active practice, about a third of them part-time.

If there are 300+ million citizens, then even with all 60,000 DCs practicing, each would have to be responsible for 5000 lives, meaning that if everyone came in once a month, each doctor would have to see two hundred visits a day six days a week, not a reasonable expectation for the average chiropractor. And that doesn't even count the many people who may need extensive care.

Most chiropractors don't have anywhere near that capacity, so two things are true – first, we need a lot more chiropractors. Second, and perhaps more immediately important, we need to make sure our message is coming across, and to concentrate our power on growing at the grass roots level. The ACA says chiropractors take care of about 30,000,000 people yearly – we couldn't reasonably expect the average doctor to multiply tenfold.

But that doesn't mean things aren't looking up. The Bureau of Labor Statistics also says the job outlook for chiropractors is excellent. They state, "Employment of chiropractors is projected to grow 17 percent from 2014 to 2024, much faster than the average for all occupations. People across all age groups are increasingly becoming interested in alternative or complementary healthcare. Chiropractic care is appealing to patients because chiropractors use nonsurgical methods of treatment and do not prescribe drugs."

Our opportunity has never been greater – but if we have the same strategy as always, why expect a different outcome? Some bold action is called for, to produce new and better results.

The concept of vertebral subluxation is vital to the preservation of chiropractic, and in no way would I ever advocate to move away from the term. The problem is, it's such a dense and incomprehensible phrase for most patients, we confound them when we open the conversation with it. There must be a way to educate people about the effects of subluxation and why it's important to fix subluxations without talking about subluxations.

And that's why we have shifted the tone of our recommended patient education toward talking about stress. If you ask a hundred people if they have a subluxation, a few will say yes. But if you ask those same people if they have stress, it will be near unanimous.

If we can show people how we help them cope better with stress, and avoid the wear and tear that comes along with stress, they have a reason to not only get relief from painful conditions, but also to tune their bodies to cope with the stresses of daily life.

Physical stress, chemical stress, mental/emotional stress, electromagnetic stress, they are bathed in it constantly, and when you position yourself as a stress-reducer, you'll have plenty of time to discuss and educate them on subluxation, because they have a reason to participate beyond relief.

Everyone acknowledges that they have stress, and often for good reason – but the issue is not avoiding stress, that's unlikely, it's everywhere and constant.

It reminds me of the story of Morihei Ueshiba, renowned martial artist who was reputed to have the best balance of anyone on earth. A student asked him, "Sensei, how come you never get knocked off center?" And Ueshiba smiled and said "I do get knocked off center, I just recover so quickly no one can tell."

It's more a matter of recovering quickly – stress, recovery, stress, recovery, as we learned about in "The Power Of Full Engagement." When you're in stress too much and recovery too little, that diminishes the expression of your potential. When patients understand that and come to you on that basis, they don't need to be convinced to make their visits, to pay or to refer those they care about.

I do believe that brain-based wellness is the long-awaited missing link in educating the public about chiropractic. The academic community is starting to wake up – Dr. Carrick was named researcher of the year at Harvard, and has a horde of MDs and neuro post-docs following him around to learn what he knows.

Convincing people that they have subluxations? It hasn't been all that productive. But alerting people to the epidemic of brain stress? Now you're talking. That's something everyone can understand, and as you learn to talk about chiropractic in terms of brain stress, your message will clarify, your impact will expand, and your fulfillment will skyrocket.

Fear and Faith   July 2016

We live in crazy and uncertain times. In the last few weeks, there have been several shootings, slaughters, really -- cops killing citizens, citizens killing cops, citizens killing citizens, brother and sister killing brother and sister. A lunatic drove a truck through a crowd in Nice, France, slaying and maiming hundreds. Night clubs and social gathering places have become fair game for violence. Terrorism lurks around every corner, the masses are arming in preparation for whatever wars they may be called upon to fight – there's no other way to describe it, fear is muscling its way into our emotional storage, a deep fear that is unlike any we have ever felt before.

As a four-decade student of philosophy, there are few things I am totally sure of, but I do believe fervently that things happen for a reason – what possible reason could there be for all the carnage and murder?

Tony Robbins taught me almost thirty years ago that fear is our mind's way of telling us we need to prepare for something, and that other than performing the necessary preparation to the best of our ability, there's only one other thing we can do – have faith.

Faith is the antidote to fear, and I sense that this is part of the opportunity hidden in all this pain. Faith is non-judgmental, faith is pure, faith is a doorway to the divine we experience based on our level of engagement.

So, in trying to sort through this morass of convoluted feelings, I am arriving at an unshakable conclusion -- if we live our lives in fear, we are not living at all, and the way to feel courageous in the face of such adversity is to develop and express faith, not only a spiritual faith, but a faith in the natural, innate goodness of humanity, and faith in ourselves to come through it better than ever.

Many of you have seen John Demartini talk about the center line, his model that describes the balance that is ever-present at the macro level of reality. That center line, which represents love and light, acts as an anchoring point, and any movement off the line must be countered with a balancing energy to the other side. By that reasoning, when there is such violence and grief, it must be counteracted with peace and happiness. When there is selfishness, there must be service. When there is hate, there must be compassion.

As Neale Donald Walsch tells us, in the world of the relative where we reside, is-not-ness is required to experience is-ness.

So, fear comes from an inability or unwillingness to see past our own immediate sphere of influence. Things happen the way they happen, and those who are more skillful at the art of living recognize it as such – it's not what happens, but how you respond to what happens that seems to make the biggest difference.

Which brings us to the tremendous responsibility we have – being charged with spreading the chiropractic message.

Some of us may fear being a spokesperson. Effective preparation usually takes care of that. If you sense or demonstrate resistance to speaking your truth, get support from your coaches.

Some of us may lapse into fear in our explanation to our patients and prospects -- some approaches are quite heavy-handed, painting a dismal picture of the future of the under-committed. I'll be the first to say that people are motivated either toward pleasure or away from pain, so it stands to reason that using a little well-placed fear will get some people's attention and generate a shift in them.

But we must remember Demartini's center line – what the world is calling for now is a balancing of the fear and unrest, which is done with a positive message of optimism, hope and the promise of a better quality of life.

You can move people away from consequences without overdoing the fear – remember, their brains are mostly overloaded already, so it doesn't take much to push them over the edge. The majority of them are in sympathetic stress, so of course they will react to fear, they're hardwired to do so, but you can be more artful and elegant, and use their values for leverage, rather than the threat of horrible things happening to them if they don't do as you say.

Let the patient adjust the fear level by asking good questions – what do you think will happen if you don't get this taken care of? They'll tell you, you can be sure of that – they can comprehend that they have a problem without you making them feel terrified. You can always turn up the heat if someone is especially stuck, but so much of what we do is based on patterns, it is unnecessary to freak people out – just take a stand, help them see the relevance of your message, and you'll be delighted with the results.

In such challenging times, we have an opportunity to step up as thought leaders, and develop a vision of a healthy and prosperous future – tune the emotional charge of your communication to the proper intensity, and remember who we really are, and what our work is really about. Your community is hungry for it, and they'll embrace it and thank you for it.

Empathy   August 2016

I was masterminding with Winners Circle alumnus Dr. Manuel Mazzini from Milan, Italy, about expanding his impact by training more doctors and opening more offices that use his methods. Manuel is an advanced healer and a tireless learner, and as such he has amassed a considerable arsenal of useful tools to heal the nerve system and produce miraculous results.

I asked him to go through some of his basic concepts, and the first one stopped me in my tracks. Rather than launching into a detailed explanation of the clinical approach, he told me that the first part of any healing technique is empathy – putting yourself in the patient's position so you can see the world through his or her eyes, to gather perspective and fully engage with the patient's situation.

This is the product of great talent and ability, and also being immersed in the identity-based and service-oriented culture of The Masters Circle and The Winners Circle for many years, I'm sure Dr. Mazzini would confirm. The great successes we strive to generate can be measured accurately in the numbers of lives that improve because of something we did or represented.

Empathy is defined as "the psychological identification with or vicarious experiencing of the feelings, thoughts, or attitudes of another." This is another way of saying that you walk a mile in someone's moccasins, that you are willing to adopt their viewpoint to connect with what they are sensing. This draws you closer, but also gives you information on how to communicate most effectively.

The more compassion, the more love, the more connection we feel with someone, the more likely we are to go the extra mile to serve them well. That patient is someone's mom or dad, sister or brother, someone's best friend – you have no obligation to feel what they feel, but it is constructive if you have supportive feelings for them.

I remember a study published in the mid-70's in the New England Journal of Medicine, even at that point one of the more progressive medical journals, about the effectiveness of chiropractic.

It turns out that they could make no sense at all of what chiropractors did clinically, and they utterly dismissed it – but they had to acknowledge that chiropractic patients did indeed get better, and here's the only explanation they could come up with – they said that because chiropractors were nice and really cared about their patients, the patients responded.

Breathe, breathe -- I get how insulting that is, but I want you to see the golden nugget buried in that pile of dung. It's near impossible for medical professionals, especially forty years ago, to see how chiropractic helps people, but they did get a glimpse into how kindness, love and optimism can be keys to healing.

They are trapped in a reductionist universe where little bugs invade the body and make it sick, which requires external agents to counteract the negative effects. But they actually made a valuable observation, though they were ill-equipped to apply it – caring about someone, and making an effort to put yourself in their position and feel what they feel, gives you an inside-the-skin inkling of their experience, and makes you want to help them more, which they can clearly feel.

Being nice does indeed initiate the healing process for many patients, and if it was that simple you'd think MDs would want to learn how to do it. In fact, I've seen articles about doctors taking acting classes so they could learn how to appear compassionate – you can't make this stuff up.

But chiropractors, right from the beginning with the Palmers and on down the line, had a special way to relate to and touch the sick and suffering, a message that caused closeness and engagement between doctors and patients, something difficult for medical professionals to grasp because they are trained in heroic intervention, not understanding that Innate does most of the heavy lifting. Respecting that foundational principle has to help.

If you're going to excel at the clinical side of your practice, empathize with your patient – the word will get around that there's a doctor in your neighborhood who really cares, and you couldn't ask for a better reputation.

Here are some great thoughts on empathy:

"When you show deep empathy toward others, their defensive energy goes down, and positive energy replaces it. That's when you can get more creative in solving problems."
-- Stephen Covey

"When people talk, listen completely. Most people never listen." – Ernest Hemingway

"No one cares how much you know, until they know how much you care."
-- Theodore Roosevelt

"There are two ways of spreading light: to be the candle or the mirror that reflects it."
-- Edith Wharton

"Leadership is about empathy. It is about having the ability to relate to and connect with people for the purpose of inspiring and empowering their lives." – Oprah Winfrey

"You can only understand people if you feel them in yourself." -- John Steinbeck

"Too often we underestimate the power of a touch, a smile, a kind word, a listening ear, an honest compliment, or the smallest act of caring, all of which have the potential to turn a life around."
– Leo Buscaglia

"Each one of us has lived through some devastation… when we look at each other we must say, I understand. I understand how you feel because I have been there myself. We must support each other and empathize… because each of us is more alike than we are unalike." -- Maya Angelou

*"This capacity for empathy leads to a genuine encounter – we have to progress toward this culture of encounter – in which heart speaks to heart…" -- Pope Francis*In practice, in business and throughout our lives, really relating to those you serve and work with is essential. Seeing as if you are looking through their eyes provides new insight into how you can help.

Develop your sense of empathy – it's compassion from the other's point of view.

Common Sense   September 2016

We live at a time where spin dominates our communications pathways. Between the social media, the special interests and the intense polarization of our citizens, I thought it might be helpful to re-connect with a value that is currently at a premium, common sense.

What is common sense? Ralph Waldo Emerson says that "common sense is success in working clothes." It is the distilled wisdom of everyday life, expressed in plain language, usually by people who speak with their actions, not only their words.

The phrase common sense, from the Latin "sensus communis," was first coined in 1525. Dictionary.com defines it as "sound practical judgment that is independent of specialized knowledge, training, or the like; normal native intelligence."

So you can easily see how common sense permeates our philosophy, science and art, and how devoid of it the allopathic approach often seems to be. Let's be grateful that when we find a way to properly explain what we do to people who need our services, the most frequent response is, "that makes sense."

Let's look at some other remarks about common sense, from some of our great thought leaders. Some are pithy and philosophical, others may be sardonic or wistful, but all of them help to clarify this vital filter for best interpreting our experiences and our lives.

"The three great essentials to achieve anything worthwhile are: Hard work, Stick-to-itiveness, and Common sense." -- Thomas A. Edison

"Common Sense is that which judges the things given to it by other senses."
-- Leonardo da Vinci

"Common sense is instinct, and enough of it is genius." -- George Bernard Shaw

"If we don't plant the right things, we will reap the wrong things. It goes without saying. And you don't have to be, you know, a brilliant biochemist and you don't have to have an IQ of 150. Just common sense tells you to be kind, ninny, fool. Be kind." -- Maya Angelou

"Taste is the common sense of genius." -- Victor Hugo

"The best prophet is common sense, our native wit." -- Euripedes

"Common sense is merely the deposit of prejudice laid down in the human mind before the age of eighteen." -- Albert Einstein

"I can never fear that things will go far wrong where common sense has fair play."
-- Thomas Jefferson

"A lot of people think something is right, and so that thing becomes right." -- Paolo Coelho

"Common sense is the knack of seeing things as they are, and doing things as they ought to be done."
-- Harriet Beecher Stowe

"A handful of common sense is worth a bushel of learning." -- Proverb

"From the errors of other nations, let us learn wisdom," -- Thomas Paine

<u>Wikihow actually offers an eight step process for developing common sense:</u>
1. Familiarize yourself with the purpose and meaning of common sense.
2. Notice how the mind tends to default to previous understanding.
3. Disengage your current reality enough to transcend your brain's typical patterns.
4. Reflect on a bigger picture that allows a realistic assessment.
5. Focus your mind acutely so you are ready for action.
6. Learn and re-learn basic common sense, through practical knowledge and application.Put new common sense thinking habits into place. Use mental flexibility and clear, affirmative thinking, and value ideas above the status quo.
7. Running this process instead of just accepting others' worldviews will position you for common sense. You don't need education as much as

open-mindedness and curiosity. This theme is only one way to common sense. Analyze and refine it for your purposes – after all, that's only common sense. And look for situations that call for common sense rather than just an intellectual response – the more you use common sense, the wiser and more sensible you become.

Legacy   October 2016

"There are certain things that are fundamental to human fulfillment. The essence of those needs is captured in the phrase 'to live, to love, to learn, to leave a legacy.'"
-- Stephen R. Covey

There's a current ad running for Stella Artois beer, with the legend, "Be Legacy." It refers to the story of Sebastien and Isabella Artois, eighteenth century entrepreneurs who parlayed their belief in a small Belgian brewery into a worldwide brand. Their advertising campaign challenges the viewer to aim at leaving a representative mark, and if we were to be completely transparent, this thought has most likely crossed each of our minds, some more than others.

What will they say about you after you are gone? Does it matter? Why or why not? The more fatalistic among us concentrate more on the present moment at the exclusion of all else while those whose perspective encompasses a broader swath of time may be more sensitive to public image and the potential for great good and great harm.

In the final analysis, probably none of this does matter, but from our current vantage point, legacy is more important as a barometer of the good we've done than any self-importance or narcissism. But to be honest, while doing good is not driven by acknowledgment, I'd be lying if I didn't confess that part of my motivation is to leave behind ideas, perspectives and models that others can benefit from and build upon for generations to come. Maybe I'm inflating that in my own mind, and maybe not, but the point is, leaving a legacy is significant to me, and I bet it's significant to many of you as well.

Are you interested in an endowment for a school, organization or charity? Are you intent on capturing your words in written, audio or video form for posterity? Do you want your practice to survive you? Is your family your finest contribution to the world? Is your spiritual leadership? Your business savvy?

When you stop to think of it, you have many aspects of yourself you'd like to pay forward if given the opportunity, and with legacy, we never quite know what among our gifts will be accepted and retained. That's why, if legacy is important to you, you must facilitate the process by putting what you want to leave in a form that it can be found and applied.

"If you would not be forgotten as soon as you are dead, either write something worth reading or do something worth writing." -- Benjamin Franklin

For me, this has manifested as five books, four hundred hours of video of TMCtv including over 60 hours of myself, 168 editions of MasterTalk, almost 1000 issues of Message of the Week, about a hundred Advanced Citizens and Chiropractic Miracles newsletters, hundreds of recorded talks and interviews, and over 100,000 coaching experiences with thousands of members, which at least helped them to crystallize new thought, and at best reshaped their chiropractic destinies, touching millions of patients, staff and family members.

And at 63, I feel like I'm about halfway. You may feel the same or otherwise, but one thing is for sure – we're all working this hard for at least two reasons. First, we aim to do as much good as we can right now… and second, we desire to offer what we can to the next generations, so they can push up from the platform we've built, and add their two cents, standing on the shoulders of giants as we have.

I once saw an interviewer ask the late Wayne Dyer, "How would you like to be remembered?" He calmly and congruently said, "It doesn't matter," and I thought, yes, it doesn't matter to you, but the amazing influence you've had on positive psycho-spirituality is profound, and to me, that clearly does matter.

Each of you is capable of leaving such a legacy, where the good you do outlives you. I wouldn't go so far as to advise you to live your life based on that, but it is a factor that should be kept in mind – what you do now can make a big difference for those who come next. It's just something to think about.

"Come out into the world about you, be it either wide or limited. Sympathize, not in thought only, but in action, with all about you. Make yourself known and felt for something that would be loved and missed, in twenty thousand little ways, if you were to die; then your life will be a happy one, believe me." -- Charles Dickens

Imagination   November 2016

"Imagination is more important than knowledge. For knowledge is limited to all we now know and understand, while imagination embraces the entire world, and all there ever will be to know and understand." -- Albert Einstein

Brain-Based Wellness. Capacity Technology. UCCAFF. The PVA Skills. Sympathetic Stress Syndrome. The Practice Fulfillment Quotient. What do these phrases have in common?

These are all terms Bob and I invented, because we needed them to describe and encapsulate some idea, concept or notion that we had been thinking about and developing. You can argue whether they are based on truly original creative thought, or if they are derivative in some way, but one thing cannot be disputed – they came from our imagination.

I like the British Dictionary definitions of imagination: the faculty or action of producing ideas, especially mental images of what is not present or has not been experienced; mental creative ability; the ability to deal resourcefully with unexpected or unusual problems or circumstances.

We use our imagination, as described above, quite frequently. Every time you come up with a fresh marketing idea, a new tweak on an adjusting style, a metaphor to explain what you do to your patient, or an innovative payment plan, you are using your imagination.

Whenever you set a goal, consider a promotion, or visualize yourself doing a great talk or report of findings, you are using your imagination.

Whenever you solve a problem, overcome a challenge, or break through to a new level of contemplation that leads to action, you are using your imagination, and it is one of the most powerful of all the tools in your toolbox.

Wikipedia says, "Imagination is the ability to form new images and sensations in the mind that are not perceived through sight, hearing, or other senses. Imagination helps make knowledge applicable in solving problems and is fundamental to integrating experience and the learning process."

"You may think I'm small, but I have a universe inside my mind." – Yoko Ono

You can apply your imagination to the tiniest details of your life and practice, or to the grandest vision you can conceptualize.

You can think about a roleplay with a patient to address some finer point of compliance they need to integrate, or a request for a referral of some loved one or co-worker.

Or, you can picture a truly well world, where all babies get a spine, brain and nerve system exam by a doctor of chiropractic at birth, and all families have access to regular chiropractic services.

What if everyone adopted natural health principles and lived the chiropractic wellness lifestyle? What if people ate well, moved well and thought well? What if our tendency was to love, understand and accept each other? What if our world was cleaned up, our food supply untainted, our people well educated, our spirituality highly evolved and practically engaged?

The point is, while your experience of the world may seem limited, your imagination is boundless.

"Without leaps of imagination or dreaming, we lose the excitement of possibilities. Dreaming, after all, is a form of planning." – Gloria Steinem

So, when you are moved to set goals, to make plans, to take action, you are actually entering into the world of applied imagination. "Whatever the mind can conceive and believe, it can achieve," Napoleon Hill reminds us, and this is the foundational principle of imagination – think it and do it, as simple as that.

So then, what if someone has an "imagination block", where the creative resources seem temporarily out of reach? This is what happens with your patient who has been everywhere, done everything, and has not been able to find answers to a persistent health problem. This is an example of a fixed mindset, rather than a growth mindset.

Here, you have to supply or at least stoke the imagination, to inspire the patient to manifest the best healing possible.

This takes empathy, resilience, and determination. You must put yourself in their place to fully grasp their struggle, begin to reshape their experience with suggestion and support, and keep going until you outlast their inertia and get them into positive motion.

"Imagination is not only the uniquely human capacity to envision that which is not, and, therefore, the foundation of all invention and innovation. In its arguably most transformative and revelatory capacity, it is the power that enables us to empathize with humans whose experiences we have never shared."
– J.K. Rowling

Ultimately, imagination turns out to be a pathway to the ideal life, as well as a guidebook for dealing with adversity. Every issue you address, as well as every step forward, depends on being able to access this most versatile and attractive asset, the imagination.

"I believe that imagination is stronger than knowledge. That myth is more potent than history. That dreams are more powerful than facts. That hope always triumphs over experience. That laughter is the only cure for grief. And I believe that love is stronger than death." *– Robert Fulghum*

Grit   December 2016

"Above everything else I've done, I've always said I've had more guts than I've got talent."
– Dolly Parton

Few things really come easy to us. Yes, we've rehearsed skill sets that help us execute more expediently, but let's face it – we've put in thousands, in many cases tens of thousands of hours developing ourselves, overcoming obstacles, handling setbacks gracefully, setting and re-setting goals and formulating and reformulating plans – we are stubborn, determined, and driven to aim at our targets and keep firing until we hit them. In other words, we have grit.

Grit is resiliency and unwavering perseverance. Grit is intention and focus, filtered through self-discipline and relentlessness. Grit is refuse to lose, look out I'm coming through – it's damn the torpedoes, full speed ahead, shoot the wounded, eat the dead.

"It doesn't matter if people are playing jazz or writing poetry -- if they want to be successful, they need to learn how to persist and persevere, how to keep on working until the work is done. The vocational approach at NOCCA (New Orleans Center for the Creative Arts) helps build grit in students. It teaches them how to be single-minded in pursuit of a goal, to sacrifice for the sake of a passion. The teachers demand hard work from their kids because they know, from personal experience, that creative success requires nothing less." – Jonah Lehrer

There are examples of grit everywhere we look. The athlete who raises her standards above the expected, the bricklayer who regards his labor as a vehicle to leaving something strong and useful like a wall or fireplace as his legacy, the sick kid who overcomes the naysayers and gets well through your loving touch – we see it all around us.

"The future bears down upon each one of us with all the hazards of the unknown. The only way out is through." – Plutarch

For example, my dear niece and long-term TMC member Dr. Michelle Kobbe of East Northport NY is out on maternity leave, but in her coaching visit right before she went out, she asked if I had any pointers for her to help her prepare for or handle the delivery.

I told her the following story, which I heard from Tony Robbins a long time ago. It seems there was an American teenager who became a fan of Sumo wrestling, and decided to go to Japan to study with Sumo masters. Most Japanese wrestlers begin training as young children, so it didn't seem likely that he would succeed – but he did indeed become a Sumo wrestling champion.

When asked how he did it, he shared his secret weapon – he said, "I believe that when my energy is gone, I have ten times more energy." And when he competed, when his energy was gone, he believed he had ten times more energy and as his opponents ran out of gas, he picked up steam, outlasting bigger and more experienced competitors.

Michelle told me that when she was in labor, she was thinking about that story and credits that belief with helping her to a smooth delivery. That's grit.

"We must build dikes of courage to hold back the flood of fear." -- Martin Luther King Jr.

It isn't always about clenching your teeth – you can be relaxed and gritty at the same time, like a dancer, scuba diver or NBA player. It's more a matter of unwillingness to buckle, of sheer power and concentration of force, generating optimal performance and the best possible results. When you decide you will not settle for any less than that, you have grit.

"In plain words, you've got to make up your mind to study whatever you undertake, and concentrate your mind on it, and really work at it. This isn't wisdom. Any damned fool in the world knows it's true, whether it's a question of raising horses or writing plays. You simply have to face the prospect of starting at the bottom and spending years learning how to do it." – Eugene O'Neill

When the chips are down, and things may not seem to be going your way, you can succumb to the doubt of the runner-up, or you can assess the conditions and make your best movement forward. I always figured it made more sense to be a moving target than a sitting duck. Getting into action is grit in motion, a moving meditation of success that transcends time and space to give you a glimpse of what's possible.

"Do not lose hold of your dreams or aspirations. For if you do, you may still exist but you have ceased to live." -- Henry David Thoreau

As chiropractors, we have an unusual and challenging path to travel. Everywhere we look, there are people who need us, and also there are detractors, worried that we will somehow outshine them or supplant them. But that's not our intention – all we want is to do as much good as possible, and have a little something to show for it. It's not at their expense, but rather on behalf of the people we serve that we flex our muscles and insist on taking our rightful place in the healing professions. That, too, is grit.

"We must adjust to changing times and still hold to unchanging principles."
-- Jimmy Carter

Colors of the Rainbow   January 2017

I confess, I like things my way. In fact, pretty much everyone I know feels the same. We all like what we like, and we have good reason for liking it.

I remember David Simon, may he rest in peace, author of "The Ten Commitments" and longtime partner of Deepak Chopra, presenting at a SuperConference on consciousness and healing. He concluded that humans are simple creatures -- at our core, we're wired to experience our world in a binary fashion. Based on our interpretation of our contemporaneous reality, we default to one of two readings, "yum" or "yuk." We either resonate with something or we don't.

Yet, the deluge of information bombarding us every minute of every day risks overwhelming those crude and simple filters. Making sense of and responding to our immediate surroundings is a gradient, not an on-off switch, and requires hundreds or thousands of small yes/no decisions to meet our own standards and preferences.

In "The Long Tail," Chris Anderson talks about the shift in the music business, away from play lists, top ten hits and million-sellers, and toward myriad eclectic artists to match myriad eclectic tastes. Each song or album rarely sells as much as the megalithic hits of yesteryear, but in total they generate a huge market penetration by appealing to many kinds of consumers. The digital world changed everything

What we perceive as white light actually contains all the possible tones and hues – when you shine it through a prism, it disperses into its component colors. When something looks blue, or green, or red, it just means that all the other frequencies of the white light are being absorbed, and only those particular frequencies are being reflected. If that were not the case, we'd live in a black and white world, depending on whether the object we were viewing reflected or absorbed light.

You probably know that Regina and I like to cook, and last week she sent me to the store to get her some garlic pepper in a grinder, you know, peppercorns and dried garlic bits in a special bottle with a rotating crusher top, no doubt you've seen them.

As it turned out, I couldn't find plain garlic pepper, but in my quest I came across an organic mixture of black pepper, sea salt, garlic, dill, coriander, and chili pepper. The extra ingredients add some nuances and a pleasing perfume to the flavor, not to mention the bonus zippity-doo-dah, something we might never have known existed if I had been fixated on only one solution to my problem.

This translates to the adjusting room as well. How many ways do you know to move a bone? I can adjust your atlas while you are sitting, lying face up or face down, or on your side with a toggle recoil. I could use a DNFT sequence, a Logan contact, or a cervical stair step. And within each adjustment, there would be specific details that make that adjustment exactly right for that patient at that time – contact point, line of drive, traction, depth of thrust, speed, torque, placement of the indifferent hand and many others. You do a lot of it intuitively, but it still represents a point on the curve of infinite options in adjusting even a single vertebra, much less developing a plan for reconstructing a spine and de-stressing a brain and nerve system. We need to be able to juggle dozens of variables at once to make sense out of the data and come to any meaningful conclusion.

Even given the same set of signs and indicators, there may be numerous strategies to influence the brain, spine and nerve system that could lead to similar successes -- full spine or upper cervical, SOT or KST or CRA or CRT or whatever, all unique, all effective when properly applied.

These varied methods are just colors of the technique rainbow. How could you brighten your adjustment with some new shades of difference?

Enjoy the spectrum. Do something fresh. Dine someplace you've never eaten but heard good things about. See a movie you typically wouldn't see that got good reviews. Go somewhere for a long weekend you ordinarily wouldn't think of going but sounds cool. Stretch yourself – it's a big, complex and exciting world out there. Enrich your internal map by varying and intensifying your input – it makes you a more complete and more interesting version of yourself.

My dear friend and mentor Michael Gelb taught me that DaVinci's first principle of creative genius is curiosity, and it's in that spirit that I urge you to embark upon such forays into uncharted territory. The knee-jerk may be to seek familiarity, since it leads to comfort, certainty, and control. But to appreciate all the colors of the rainbow, we must be willing to broaden our perspective, to generate a wider range of acceptability, and accommodate that which may at first seem uncomfortable, so we can discover new frontiers and open new pathways of possibility.

Decisiveness   February 2017

Great leaders have many traits in common. They care passionately about their causes. They are willing to step up and represent their constituencies. They're strong and reliable. They're good communicators, and they love to learn.

But there is no quality more important to an evolving leader than decisiveness. The ability to size up a situation, compare the available options, and come to an appropriate conclusion is the difference that makes the difference for those willing to accept a position of command.

Some decisions are basic and structural – how often do we meet? What color should we make the walls and floors? What equipment do we need? When should we be open for business, and so on.

But while most decisions matter to some degree, some decisions are pivotal, and these are the decisions that tend to separate the great leaders from everyone else. For example, look at the decision-making for concentrating on a chief aim:

What is the vision? Why is it important? What are the key beliefs and resources necessary to get there? What players and allies will be recruited? What obstacles need to be planned for? How will I measure my progress?

And then, decisions on identity and how to show up:

Who am I? What are my organizing principles? What are my optimal resource states? Which habits should I be amplifying, and which should be refined, reduced or eliminated? Are my current beliefs consistent with my ultimate objectives? Am I clear on my priorities, and am I acting in harmony with them?

And then, decisions on team:

How can I maintain inspiration and morale and still move things forward as efficiently and powerfully as possible? What players are assigned to play which roles, and do I have people in the right seats on the bus? Do I have the right players, do I need to add or does someone need to be changed out? How can I get the most out of everyone on my team, including myself?

And then, decisions on daily operations:

Do I have systems in place that should logically take me toward my vision? Do I have the preferred balance as a technician, a manager and an entrepreneur? Where do I see weaker areas that require training, new policies or procedures, or a new strategy? Do I know the measurement parameters to evaluate daily productivity?

This, of course, is just a thumbnail sketch of the decisions we would demonstrate our decisiveness on. But how can we develop our decisiveness?

Decisiveness is a state – in other words, you make it with your mind and body. Obviously, you have been decisive somewhere along the line, even if it was just choosing dinner off a menu – we make decisions all the time, some bigger than others.

If you want to tap into your decisiveness resources, think about times when you were most decisive, and borrow that mindset and bodyset to prime the pump and get your decisiveness flowing. If you like, create an anchor or trigger that means decisiveness to you, and while you hold yourself in a decisive state, make the signal over and over until it becomes indelibly linked to the sensations of decisiveness. Then you can summon your decisiveness by hitting your signal to turn it on.

You can also become more decisive by making more decisions. The more decisive you are, the more proactive you can be – the opposite is procrastination, killer of dreams and a black hole of unfulfilled intentions.

So, create a rules structure to give yourself a more systematic approach. Adopt a one touch rule for any piece of paper – do it, delay it, delegate it or dump it. Statistics are complete by the fifth of the month. Marketing calendars and goals are prepared and planned a quarter or more in advance. A trustworthy team member is trained to submit a doctor's call list at the end of each day, complete with daily production, calls to be returned or made, prompts for tomorrow and anything else the doctor needs to know.

When you have all the information, you can make better decisions. Do your homework, and engage other teammates, strategic alliances, experts, mentors and the vast scope of the internet to gather the data you need to maneuver into the best possible decision-making position.

Napoleon Hill, author of the classic "Think and Grow Rich," said, "The way to develop decisiveness is to start right where you are, with the very next question you face." Your success will depend on the quality of your decision-making – raise your standards, hold yourself accountable, and take your best shot.

Positive Expectancy   March 2017

You probably remember the old story about the twins, one an optimist, the other a pessimist. In an effort to help them grow up as normal as possible, their parents took them to a famous psychiatrist to see if they could be cured.

The doctor explained that they needed an extreme emotional event to cancel out their current behaviors, and designed a special protocol just for them.

The pessimistic twin would be placed in a room with every possible amusement – computers, video games, television, toys, musical instruments, sports equipment, stuffed animals, literally anything a gloomy kid could need to cheer up.

The optimistic twin would be placed in a room filled with horse manure, likely to take the edge off even an unflagging great attitude.

The parents did not question the renowned doctor, and they proceeded with the treatment.

After one hour, they went to the pessimist's room, and opened the door to find the kid sitting in the middle of the floor crying. "What's wrong?" they exclaimed.

"Well," he sniffed, "I knew all these toys and stuff weren't mine, and I was afraid if I played with them, I'd break something, and then I'd be in real trouble!"

Flabbergasted, they walked next door to see what was going on in the other twin's room.

To their amazement, the optimist was diving into piles of horse manure, picking up handfuls and throwing them into the air, laughing hysterically. They cried out, "What are you doing, what are you doing?"

The optimist grinned and retorted, "With all this horse flop, I figure there must be a pony in here somewhere!"

Your mindset is an unforgiving filter that determines to a great extent your experience of your own reality. The lenses you look through define your world -- your resources, your beliefs, your values, your personality, your identity. Are you peering through rose-colored glasses, or are your dark shades blocking out the sun?

I remember like it was yesterday, though I was only about seven years old, standing on the corner in Brooklyn waiting for a bus with my little brother Steven and our Grandma Doria, one of my earliest and most influential mentors.

The bus pulled up and Grandma Doria enthused, "Oh boys, will you look at those bus tires – have you ever seen more beautiful bus tires?"

My little kid brain fried. Bus tires? What's beautiful about bus tires? It took many years before I understood what she was saying. Beauty is everywhere! Our rules may draw unnecessary boundaries for us, but there is beauty everywhere you look in everything you look at, if you look at it right.

Those of you who were on the ChiroMission with us probably recall Aura's story about the scientists who put some rats into a swimming pool. After fifteen minutes, the rats fatigued and drowned. Then they took more rats and put them in the water, but this time, they pulled them out after ten minutes. They then put those same rats back in the pool, and amazingly, they were now able to survive for 60 hours!

Why did their endurance increase 240 times over the first group? The difference was hope – rescued once, they kept swimming, anticipating being rescued again.

The power of positive expectancy is one of our most versatile and potent assets. Whether you're looking for a pony, seeing beauty in bus tires or swimming for your life, expressing a sense of hopefulness and faith will serve you greatly – at the very least, it helps you feel better while you're working to turn things around; and at best, it adds a subtle and not-so-subtle vibrational energy to your actions and behaviors, which serves as an x-factor that drives you to higher accomplishment and better results, no matter what path you choose.

In "The Psychology of Winning," Denis Waitley says, "There never was a winner who didn't expect to win in advance. Winners understand that life is a self-fulfilling prophecy. And they know that you usually get what you expect in the long run. So winners accept the belief that hope and a deep, unbreakable faith — forged into a fundamental attitude of positive self-expectancy — is the eternal spring from which all creative, motivating energy flows."

Positive expectancy – it lubricates times of friction, and facilitates your forward thrust. It makes lemons into lemonade. It exposes the silver lining held in every cloud. Just expect the best, prepare for the worst, and aim down the middle. Maintain an uplifting self-concept and invest in winning strategies – it will come back to reward you many times over.

Love and Precision   April 2017

Over the last nine years I've written over a hundred of these essays, and while I often have a theme or point in mind, I confess I don't always know what I'm going to write about until I sit down to create something.

This particular month, I arrived before my computer open to my Muse's input, and the words "love and precision" flashed across my field of vision.

Love and precision? What an odd juxtaposition of words, yet it immediately unfolded a world of meaning to me. I thought about the delivery of the right adjustment at the right time – love and precision. I thought about the enormous responsibility of raising a child – love and precision. And, I thought about the sculpting of the ideal inter- and intrapersonal relationship – no doubt, two more perfect examples of love and precision.

So, in keeping with Da Vinci's first principle of creative genius, I got curious. Who else has put these two ideas together? I polished up my Googler, and I was surprised by what I found.

In 2009, soon after I started writing the Advanced Citizen, we took The Masters Circle to London and founded our European base. Since we took the red-eye to Heathrow, we arrived mid-morning, and when we checked into the hotel, my room was not yet ready. As I was new to the UK, I asked the concierge if there was anything within walking distance that I would enjoy visiting. With a chuckle, he asked if I'd been to Harrod's.

Harrod's? The super-exclusive department store, offering designer everything at ultra-luxury prices? Harrod's, synonymous with class, style and extravagance? It turns out that it was just a few blocks from the hotel, so I walked over to kill an hour or two until I could get into my room.

I was astounded to discover that every top clothing brand had its own dedicated section, Gucci, Dolce and Gabbana, Givenchy and more, some occupying most of a floor – there were walls and counters of elegant jewelry, literally thousands of pairs of shoes, the best perfumes and cosmetics used daily by royalty, upscale dining on site, even complimentary champagne in some areas, all you would expect in a top-of-the-top-shelf shopping experience.

I was determined to bring Regina a souvenir of my British adventure, so I searched the racks and shelves for something, anything I felt I could afford and rationalize the expense to my more cost-conscious wife. I discovered the cutest little t-shirt, multi-colored and cut just how my sweetie likes it – and for only $90, I became its proud new owner.

So wasn't I surprised and entertained when I investigated who has chosen to combine these two disparate words into a single unique phrase, and my search took me to… Harrod's website, the page with the planet's finest custom watches.

The banner at the top of the page proclaims, "Made with Love and Precision" and continues with the following statement:

"We are delighted to celebrate our exceptional watch offering with the launch of 'Made with Love and Precision,' featuring special-edition watches created exclusively for Harrod's."

Then, they proceeded to display one eye-popping timepiece after another, made by Hublot and Breguet and Glashütte and Omega, as much as fifty thousand pounds and more for a watch – love and precision indeed!

The point is, love is priceless and precision quite rare, and so those who are able to assemble their lives and their worldview around these two concepts are destined to make a mark and enjoy the process. And even an object of great beauty like a $60,000 clock to wrap around your wrist pales in comparison to the magnificence of the human body, or the beautifully structured marriage, or the potential of the maturing child, or the delivery of a great new idea to the marketplace.

Which circles back to my first few examples. Your adjustment, one of your main contributions to the greater good, is best delivered precisely and lovingly. Your child-rearing asks of you both a nurturing environment and a rules structure that supports the family's values and best interests. And developing a relationship with someone important, or getting to know yourself and responding accordingly, will take as much love and precision as you can imagine implementing.

I urge you to consider these filters in your decision-making and planning – whatever you dedicate yourself to, it should be worthy of and imbued with your love, and it should also be important enough to you to perform with the requisite degree of care and excellence. It's like manufacturing a Swiss watch – you get to fuse love and precision into the optimal reflection of your talent and ability, where intention meets execution, a manifestation of the brilliance at the heart of who you are.

Alignment   May 2017

At the last show of our spring tour in London, I had the pleasure of meeting and learning from Dr. Krista Burns, co-founder of the American Posture Institute and expert in postural neurology. As an oversized kid with a lifetime of anterior head carriage and with every authority I've ever looked up to barking at me to stand up straight, I was especially moved by her comparison of the typical lean-forward Parkinsonian posture with the standard head-down position of a normal kid using his or her cell phone.

Poor alignment in our children is setting an unfortunate precedent, which will inevitably lead to health challenges – we must accept the responsibility to corral the attention of our youth and invite them to choose another, less stressful posture. In fact, we can start by noticing our own transgressions – I see friends and family succumbing to the same demons, defaulting to a habitual cervical kyphosis that can only cause harm in the long run.

It strikes me that the foundation of our chiropractic philosophy depends on alignment – alignment of the spine, alignment with universal forces, above-down, inside-out, and also alignment of our habits and behaviors with our desired outcomes. To optimize our lives, we'd better check ourselves for congruency, not only in our physical posture, but our vibrational posture as well.

I learned a long time ago that what goes around comes around, and that's where keeping a healthy spine and keeping a healthy character dovetail beautifully. Watch – if you do a good job keeping your spine in alignment, then the likelihood of chronic nerve disturbance reduces.

Likewise, if you maintain an ethical code you can be proud of, it increases your chances of the seeds of your integrity sprouting, growing and ultimately bearing fruit.

"Just as your car runs more smoothly and requires less energy to go faster and farther when the wheels are in perfect alignment, you perform better when your thoughts, feelings, emotions, goals, and values are in balance." -- Brian Tracy

So how can you evaluate your own alignment? Much like a spinal exam, you establish a sense of normal or ideal, and you contrast the current conditions against the model so you can detect deviations, glitches and idiosyncrasies. It is in this analysis that you begin the process of aligning – you can't hit a target if you don't aim at it, and you can't aim at a target if you don't know what it is.

Knowing your start point is critical – sometimes I ask, "How do you get to Grandma's house?" And the next logical question would have to be, "from where?"

That's right, from where? Your instructions only make sense when you have a context so you can interpret the action steps and take them. If you don't know your start point, it's tough to create a series of directions you can follow.

So when you sense misalignment, identify the current circumstances objectively – you'll be able to make changes to improve the situation, and remember, you can use the unpleasantness of the existing conditions to generate response potential to move away from them. Hiding from your present reality is not only delusional, it's counter-productive.

Yes, have the courage to know where you are, and then, as if you were adjusting a spine, begin to make corrections, major dysfunctions first, and then fine tuning to get closer to your best.

"Your life and work are made up of outcomes and actions. When your operational behavior is grooved to organize everything that comes your way, at all levels, based upon those dynamics, a deep alignment occurs, and wondrous things emerge. You become highly productive. You make things up, and you make them happen." – David Allen, "Getting Things Done: The Art of Stress-Free Productivity"

So whether you are talking about a spine or a mind, you want it aligned. And, if you expect your patients to respond to your recommendations, be sure you are walking your own talk and taking proper care of yourself.

Leading others, whether it's your family, your circle of friends, your practice or your community and beyond, calls upon you to act consistently with your best sense of self, which will reward you with a great reputation, devoted followers and inner peace you can't buy any other way.

Congruency, authenticity, honesty, humility, self-esteem, love, presence, gratitude – live in alignment with your highest virtues and it will light your way to your best life.

"It's not an accident that musicians become musicians and engineers become engineers: it's what they're born to do. If you can tune into your purpose and really align with it, setting goals so that your vision is an expression of that purpose, then life flows much more easily." -- Jack Canfield

Finally, examine the alignment between your head and your heart. We think in terms of aligning the body/mind, but alignment with a fitting heart-space is essential for complete self-actualization and coherence.

Assess your kindness, compassion, generosity, and service consciousness – your willingness to bring these key values into alignment will turbo-charge your practice, your family relationships, your love life and your status in your community. Let your heart-light shine, and do as much good as you can.

"When you are in alignment with the desires of your heart, things have a way of working out."
– Iyanla Vanzant

Self-Awareness   June 2017

"It takes courage...to endure the sharp pains of self-discovery rather than choose to take the dull pain of unconsciousness that would last the rest of our lives."
— Marianne Williamson

Between 1986 and 1998, my brother Steve, my wife Regina and I served as three of the first eight Master Trainers for Anthony Robbins, presenting his curriculum, developing creative techniques to train his trainers, and taking on fun and classic assignments like "Date with Destiny" in Cannes in 1991, or "Unleash the Power Within" in Milan in 1998.

We also led teams at the Hawaiian NLP/NAC certification courses where Tony would take over a resort on Maui or the Big Island with 1500 participants and a staff of a hundred or more, and build a "Robbins City" for a week or so, where we attended or taught classes fifteen to eighteen hours a day, climbed fifty-foot high poles and walked forty feet of hot coals, exercised daily and ate a wholesome vegetarian diet, with no whining, as examples of some of the organizing principles of the community.

One of Tony's foundational concepts is that awareness is the first key – you can't change or improve something unless you recognize that it needs to be changed or improved.

"The curious paradox is that when I accept myself just as I am, then I can change."
— Carl Rogers

You can't hit a target if you don't aim at it, and you can't aim at a target if you don't know what it is. So, awareness is essential to enter into any process of success, from self-preservation to typical function to peak performance.

Tony also taught me about four levels of leadership – first, to be able to lead yourself; then to be able to lead another; third to be able to lead a group, and the fourth and highest level of leadership is leading without being physically present – to have your ideas lead without you being there, through other people and through effective information distribution.

But most people are challenged enough by the first level of leadership, to be able to lead themselves. And I contend that if awareness is the first key, and the first level of leadership is to be able to lead yourself, then the first key to leading yourself is self-awareness.

Let's face it – for many of us, we can be tricky and elusive, and avoid confronting or addressing areas we know would help us move ahead. If we deny ourselves a conscious experience of our weaker areas, then we can pretend we don't know.

"Your visions will become clear only when you can look into your own heart. Who looks outside, dreams; who looks inside, awakes." – C.G. Jung

But of course, we do know. There isn't one of us who couldn't come up with a list of weaker areas that we could make better – we could probably go on stage and teach how to be everything we're not. Yet, for many of us, we under-respond to such introspection. If we don't cerebrate it into a thought or speak it into existence, we can make believe we don't have to do anything about it. We are infinitely skillful at this obfuscating self-hypnosis.

Whether it's laziness, sloppiness, poor time management and organization, majoring in minors, co-dependency, over-aggressiveness, lack of self-discipline or any of the myriad issues we could face, none of it comes into view to be acted upon without self-awareness. Being mindful of these opportunities to grow leads to another of Robbins' fundamental technologies.

Tony says if you want to achieve at a higher level, first you must raise your standards; second, you must build an empowering belief system; and finally, you must implement winning strategies.

Therefore, to grow, you must be willing to raise your standards, to expect more of yourself. But before you can expect more, you have to identify where you currently are, and which standards need to be raised, and that requires… self-awareness.

And to examine your beliefs so you can notice any flawed or limiting patterns also depends on self-awareness. And finally, calibrating your strategic approach so you can use that measurement to stay the course or re-direct your effort when necessary calls for... you guessed it, self-awareness.

"At the center of your being you have the answer; you know who you are and you know what you want." – Lao Tzu

In fact, when I share distinctions gathered from a Tony Robbins, or a Marianne Williamson, or a Carl Jung, that is an example of those significant and meaningful philosophers reaching that fourth level of leadership, leading without being physically present, because I've passed along their wisdom – you can be a thought leader and do the same, either by acting as a conduit for distributing what you know, or by generating innovative and worthwhile perspectives so others want to share what you've shared with them.

So, listen to that wee small voice inside, pay attention to your intuition, and practice looking more deeply into yourself – the pay-off is a more sure-footed execution on your path to making your life a masterpiece.

"As you become more clear about who you really are, you'll be better able to decide what is best for you - the first time around." – Oprah Winfrey

Grace   July 2017

It's the few words of appreciation you say before your meal. It's the unusual balance and elegance athletes and dancers express. It's the pardon of a prisoner, or a little extra time from the bill collector to straighten up.

These are the beautiful shades of meaning of grace -- whether you invoke it with gratitude, demonstrate it with beautiful movement, or receive it as a benefit of divine intervention, you are experiencing the gift of grace.

"All the natural movements of the soul are controlled by laws analogous to those of physical gravity. Grace is the only exception. Grace fills empty spaces, but it can only enter where there is a void to receive it, and it is grace itself which makes this void. The imagination is continually at work filling up all the fissures through which grace might pass." – Simone Weil

What is luck actually made of? It's tempting to dismiss the occurrences that make up our reality as random, but are they really? Either things happen for a reason or they don't. And if you believe that things happen for a reason, then it can't be denied that all things must happen for a reason.

It's clear that there are universal laws that transcend our comprehension, but as with a windmill, they can be harnessed and applied for the betterment of all. Our very philosophy as chiropractors invites the perspective of the interconnectedness of all things – above down, inside out, the philosophy, science and art of things natural.

"Have you more faith in a spoonful of medicine than in the power than animates the living world?"
-- BJ Palmer

Indeed, the adjustment is intended to reduce stress and interference to a natural, innate expression of life.

Spiritual traditions have eternally exploited the idea that there is a relationship between our behaviors and our quality of life – what goes around comes around, whether you call it karma, providence, or fate. Our actions matter.

"Never give a sword to a man who can't dance." – Confucius

So then, our destiny is therefore partially under our control – the part we can do something about. Of course, there are unseen forces and inexplicable mysteries that elude human intellect. Why some live and some die, some celebrate and some suffer, is beyond our grasp to fully understand – but it seems to me like our best shot is to do as much good as possible.

We cannot know what lies around the next bend. We only know that we have a moment of now, to be invested as we see fit. Will you perform with magnificence, exhibiting the finest attributes of humanity? Or will you bring something less than your best and roll the dice?

I've had periods in my life when I felt persecuted, unsupported, and alone. I've worked hard only to have my feelings dashed to the ground repeatedly. I've been on top, and I've discovered that it just meant I had farther to fall.

"You are so weak. Give up to grace.
The ocean takes care of each wave till it gets to shore.
You need more help than you know." – Jalaluddin Rumi

At no point did I quit – but I did surrender. Surrender does not mean capitulate – it means to allow what is naturally right to transpire. Participate in it, let it carry you along for a while if need be, and bring everything you can to facilitate it, but relinquish the need to control everything – you simply won't be able to, and you'll miss out on this miracle of grace.

It doesn't happen to you – it happens in you. It grows from a seed of awareness and blossoms into a magnificent bouquet of love, consciousness and esteem.

And then, the invitation – will you just be carried by the wind, or will you work your sails to tack against it and manage it so you travel as you please?

What better way to be thankful for the amazing lives we lead than to make the most of them? That's grace in action.

"By 'guts' I mean, grace under pressure" – Ernest Hemingway

Bring more grace into your life. Let your experience of grace make room for more grace. Be grateful for what you have. Move with poise and center, through yoga, t'ai chi, moving meditation or good posture. And welcome your many blessings by paying attention to how blessed you already are. Grace begets grace.

"God, give me grace to accept with serenity the things that cannot be changed,
Courage to change the things which should be changed,
and the Wisdom to distinguish the one from the other.
Living one day at a time, enjoying one moment at a time,
Accepting hardship as a pathway to peace." -- Reinhold Niebuhr

And whatever your personal beliefs, it just makes sense that in an environment that is made of matter and energy, the vibrations we generate with our intentions and our actions have to land somewhere – energy can't be created or destroyed, it just changes form, Einstein tells us. So, there are quantum explanations for our experiences – ultimately, our good fortune, and our reward for an ethical, service-oriented life, earns us a proverbial smile from on high.

And, when you tap into that unlimited resource, the manifestation is grace.

Bereavement   August 2017

It seems to me that there's been a lot of dying recently. There's so much violence and turbulence, we risk growing numb to yet another fatal tragedy, man-made or organic in origin, bombing or mudslide, car attack or hurricane.

And the celebrities -- comedy icons Jerry Lewis and Dick Gregory pass away days apart after distinguished, service-oriented and meaningful careers. Mary Tyler Moore, Glen Campbell, Don Rickles, Chuck Berry, Gregg Allman – tile after tile in the mosaic of my adolescence, the faces and voices of my youth fading into oblivion, all gone in 2017.

And Regina's two pussycats, Skitty and Squirty, left us within weeks of each other. They weren't very noisy, but it's a different kind of quiet in our house now.

It's clear that there's nothing more natural than death, an unavoidable eventuality of birth and life. When it occurs at the cellular level, it's part of normal physiological maintenance, but when the organism itself perishes, it's customary in our culture to take note and react.

Technically, the way we experience others is a construct in our own minds, hearts and bodies, so it seems reasonable to expect those imprints to remain with us, even after those others are no longer physically present, and indeed this is the case. My mom's gone five years and my dad two, yet I can summon them in my imagination as if they were still here, and I have frequently capitalized on their sage counsel even in the absence of their corporeal selves.

But we attach great importance to the feelings of grieving and sadness we associate with a loved one's departure, a complex pattern of beliefs, emotions and values we refer to as bereavement.

Bereavement is a state of intense grief or mourning upon the loss of someone (or something) significant. For some, it borders on or enters into the realm of depression. For others, there's a philosophical shrug with a gesture toward the inevitability of it all. And, of course, there's everything in between, a spectrum of sensations each of us perceives in our own way.

Here's my take on it.

When Einstein published his "Theory of Relativity," he knew that it addressed not only issues of physics but of cosmology as well. If energy can't be created or destroyed, but only changes form, is that true about spiritual energy, the vibration of life itself? Isn't it logical that upon death, that bit of life energy would have to land somewhere?

My favorite poem to this effect is called "A Parable of Immortality" by Henry van Dyke, a nineteenth century author, educator and clergyman. I believe it was my dear friend Dr. Barry Warren who first shared it with me.

"I am standing by the seashore.
A ship at my side spreads her white sails to the morning breeze
and starts for the blue ocean.
She is an object of beauty and strength,
and I stand and watch
until at last she hangs like a speck of white cloud
just where the sun and sky come down to mingle with each other.

Then someone at my side says, 'There she goes!"
Gone where? Gone from my sight -- that is all.
She is just as large in mast and hull and spar
as she was when she left my side
and just as able to bear her load of living freight
to the places of destination.
Her diminished size is in me, not in her.

And just at the moment when someone at my side says,
'There she goes!',
there are other eyes watching her coming,
and other voices ready to take up the glad shout:
'Here she comes!' "

When we feel a sense of bereavement, the focus of that is in us. And for that reason, we have some degree of control as to how to respond to it.

To put this in perspective, we chiropractors work with the subtle substance of the soul, harvest the fruits of Innate, marvel at the Bigness of the Fellow Within. And those chiropractic greats who have gone to their reward have left an indelible impression Every day I use the gifts I received from Tom Whitehorne, or Richard Van Rumpt, or M.L. Rees, or Dick Versendaal, or Joe Flesia, or Reggie Gold, among many others.

And someday it will be your turn, and someday it will be my turn – what will be our legacy, for future generations to reflect upon and grow from? The powerful play goes on, and you may contribute a verse – we all stand on the shoulders of giants, the next generation is looking for us to pay it forward.

I've concluded that feelings of bereavement may start with sadness or loneliness, but they either fade to imperceptibility, or they mature and evolve into a lifelong appreciation for those who have influenced us, never to be diminished while we keep that inner flame ablaze.

Many years ago, I composed this eulogy song, which I sang at the memorial services for my parents and grandparents. To sort through my feelings, I wrote:

"When Someone You Love Is Gone,
Got to find the will to carry on,
When Someone You Love Is Gone,
There'll be one more star to wish upon,
You'll miss the smile, the tender touch,
But know (s)he loved you just as much,
When Someone You Love Is Gone, carry on."

Bereavement is a personal and intimate experience – it gives us an opportunity to get to know ourselves better, especially how we show up in the face of adversity. Learn, learn, learn the many lessons built into this uniquely human slice of life, our own mortality. Don't hide from it – embrace it, and it will reveal universal secrets you cannot grasp any other way. And remember to tell people you love them while they're still around. They'll feel good about it, and so will you.

First Responders September 2017

With all the turmoil being caused by the over-the-top natural disasters, I have marveled at the army of unsung heroes who deserve our praise and acknowledgment – it's the first responders, the extraordinarily dedicated rescue artists who put their own lives on the line to help those in dire need.

Some are highly trained at their craft, professionals who have committed to a career of running into fires, digging through wreckage looking for survivors, and working thirty-six-hour shifts or until reinforcements make it to the scene.

And some are volunteers, neighbors, not especially skilled but armed with the intense passion to help where help is called for. Often simple townspeople, they rise to the occasion, outperforming their personal best with little or no acclaim, just because they were needed and they answered the call. Amazing.

Hurricanes, earthquakes and the like are too gigantic for us to wrap our minds around – the force is so dynamic, enough to rip our lives out by their very roots, and often we can't do anything but wait it out and hope for the best. But the first responders, they are the trail-blazers who risk their own safety to help those in distress, saving lives and putting themselves in the line of fire to make a difference.

What does it take to be a great first responder? A first responder needs the iron will of determination, and the raw fearlessness of the daredevil. Yet, a first responder can be driven by the compassion of assisting someone in trouble, and the service-orientation that is required to plow through adversity while exhibiting an endearing attitude.

It takes guts, grace under pressure, and the strength and resiliency of an endurance athlete. It takes faith to keep going when the muscles are aching and the eyes are burning, and a deep love for humanity to rationalize the pain, suffering and sacrifice. It takes self-esteem and integrity to be willing to raise standards this high, and it takes a high form of confidence and leadership to put their heads in the lion's mouth and expect to come out whole.

My college roommate and one of my dearest friends, Dr. Clifford N. Conarck, may he rest in peace, ran the Smithhaven Veterinary Hospital for many years, but when the planes hit the World Trade Center towers, he decided he was going to do something to help, and he headed for Ground Zero with service dogs trained to locate victims under the rubble. Sadly, he died soon thereafter in a motorcycle accident, but the work he did in the months after 9/11 helped dozens of families to connect with their loved ones and their personal effects and memories, easing the burdens of such untold tragedy.

I think about the NYPD and NYFD, who ran up the stairs while the hoards, crazed with fear, were streaming down to seek cover. What could have driven them to such acts of selflessness, overcoming their instinctual impulse for self-protection, and instead giving everything to save someone they didn't know? For some, it was the last thing they did.

I saw the footage of the floods in Texas and Florida, where police, firefighters and other public servants threw caution to the wind and went out into torrential rain and destructive wind to look out for those who were struggling. People brought their boats from miles around to pluck people from the rising waters and spirit them off to a safe haven -- strangers helping strangers, the courage and generosity of the first responders.

I also saw the coverage of the Mexico City earthquake, where schools, apartment buildings and hospitals collapsed from the shocks. The community quickly organized into a bucket brigade, moving supplies and water to where it was needed. Citizens quickly devised a system where, if they heard any signs of life, any sounds beneath the broken buildings, they instantly raised their fists, signifying that everyone must be silent so the front line of rescuers could hear the subtlest noises. They pulled little kids from their devastated schoolrooms with that kind of bravery, patience and teamwork.

And remember, when the body gets into a tough spot, we also have first responders in our physiology. Sometimes they are local cells or molecules, sometimes the brain steps in immediately and calls the shots, but there is a syntax and hierarchy of response, always a perfect response given the circumstances, as Dr. Morter taught us. The point is, as long as our bodies are working well, they are designed for instantaneous response with hair-trigger precision, to address emergencies, heal injuries and illnesses, maintain normal function and generate wellness.

And finally, there may well come a time when instead of people waiting until the crisis conditions in their body necessitate heroic intervention, they opt for a first response of things natural, where they visit their chiropractors not just to address painful disorders, but the prevent them, or better, to create a reality where they do not exist. It once sounded like a fantasy, but the day is coming when people will pursue vitality and quality of life more than they fight illness, pain and disease. And when they do, chiropractors will be there to light the way.

Hospitality   October 2017

In his book "Setting The Table," restauranteur Danny Meyer, renowned for upscale New York City dining establishments like Union Square Café and Eleven Madison Park, as well as his trade-at-shoulder-level fast food chain Shake Shack, differentiates between service and hospitality.

"Understanding the distinction between service and hospitality has been at the foundation of our success. Service is the technical delivery of a product. Hospitality is how the delivery of the product makes its recipient feel. Service is a monologue – we decide how we want to do things and set our own standards for service. Hospitality, on the other hand, is a dialogue. To be on the guest's side requires listening to the person with every sense, and following up with a thoughtful, gracious, appropriate response. It takes both great service and great hospitality to rise to the top."

So, for our Winners Circle Personal Growth Weekend, we visited a one-of-a-kind resort and spa on the Yucatan Peninsula, Nizuc in Cancun. Though the crystal turquoise waters, pristine white sand beaches and perfect weather can be found throughout the Riviera Maya, there was more to Nizuc than just magnificent geometric stone architecture and breath-taking Caribbean vistas.

Nizuc's claim-to-fame is the finest service, with an elaborate hiring and training process which cultivates a bright, happy, fully engaged team member who sees the importance of making guests feel great.

Now, producing this good feeling in the person you serve can take myriad forms. At Nizuc, as those of you who were there already know, the staff had the unique protocol of greeting each guest by name, with visual contact, a warm smile and a hand over the heart, a charming and uplifting greeting to be sure. Some even added a nod or a slight bow – weird at first, but somehow delightful.

This may seem over-the-top on paper, but in actuality it came to be expected and appreciated. We even found ourselves returning the compliment, which clearly illustrated that their methods were effective – we gave honor back, as they were honoring us. That is the essence of relationship, connection and mutual support, and also a strategy guaranteed to generate hospitality.

In fact, the participants in the event got an inside the skin example of this – we built bicycles to donate to underprivileged children in a nearby community, and while we were assembling the bikes, we wished for the opportunity to see the looks on the faces of these kids – and when they did indeed surprise us and show up to receive their gifts, the energy field was palpable, lush with joy, compassion and gratitude, far outdistancing any generosity and service on our part – it was about how the youngsters were made to feel that really mattered.

How can you amplify your hospitality in your practice, business, home or community? Practice seeing the world through someone else's eyes – by putting yourself in others' positions, you walk a mile in their proverbial moccasins, and experience the world more like they do. This shift in viewpoint provides insight into what it might take for that other to feel good, and therefore it offers guidance about how you need to show up and what you need to do to contribute to that outcome.

Shape your discoveries into procedures and policies that are likely to bring about warm, happy feelings in those you serve. At a vacation resort, it's a very short relationship, so name recognition, broad smiles and instant attention to detail are all there's time for. But when the encounter will last longer than that, as in a doctor-patient relationship over a period of months and years, hospitality can start with those tools, but can be further developed by matching your style with the optimal expectations of the health care consumer in general and that specific family in particular.

Do you address your patients, clients and customers as if they are guests? Do you call them by name? Do you look them in the eye? Do you smile authentically? Have you asked them enough questions to elicit their key values, so you can be sure to echo them and avoid stepping on any unnecessary land mines?

Producing good feelings in people is not only good for that person in that moment – it's the surest way to generate both repeat business and abundant referrals. Notice, I was so impressed with Nizuc, I am writing about my experience so you can get a glimpse of what makes it so special. They left me with residual good feelings which

I am conveying to you – isn't that what you want with those you serve, for them to be inspired to talk about you and recommend you?

Mastermind with your team about ways to demonstrate your hospitality to your end users, and ask good questions to find out how they want to feel. The sum total of these discussions, with a little humility and proactivity, will yield a formula for forging an indelible relationship with those you touch and serve – and a great likelihood that they will project to others how they feel about you.

Coping   November 2017

We are all invariably called upon to deal with adversities, and most of us have learned to take things in stride, at least most of the time. But at extremely challenging times, it's especially important to have a mechanism for defusing the intensity, and responding to the opportunities that miraculously appear in every crisis. We need to be able to cope.

Dictionary.com defines coping as "facing and dealing with responsibilities, problems, or difficulties, especially successfully or in a calm or adequate manner." Coping is not avoiding, nor is it over-engaging – coping has a quality to it that smacks of reason, of acceptance, and yet of determination to succeed no matter what the odds.

With our studies into stress and the assortment of causes built into our society, we need to thoroughly understand the coping mechanism, and recognize the action steps required to handle stress, for ourselves and for those who count on us.

Active stress tends to take one of four forms – physical/mechanical stress, chemical/nutritional stress, mental/emotional stress, and vibrational/energic stress. It's easier to cope when the interventions are an optimal fit for the types and degrees of stress.

For example, if someone is suffering from a gluten or sugar sensitivity, then it would be helpful to get some chiropractic, to use BrainTap or to exercise – but the most direct way to shut down the stress is to intervene with chemical/nutritional methodology – in this case, reducing or eliminating the intake of gluten or sugar.

That individual copes by maintaining a good attitude, but also by choosing the right lifestyle considerations and staying consistent with the dietary alteration, so the body can respond as completely as possible, preventing unnecessary prolonged coping.

So, when someone comes to your office, there may be physical, chemical, emotional and/or vibrational components to their problem, and it's up to your artistry and clinical scope to decide on the appropriate blend of approaches – but while the patient is responding to your care, they must learn to cope with the time and cost it takes to heal, with the inconvenience of changing their habits, or the pressure of going through whatever refinements they need to achieve their goal.

The CDC actually has some constructive advice for coping with stresses, calling for "engaging in healthy activities" and "getting the right care and support." They go on to recommend eating well and exercising, getting sufficient sleep and rest, taking breaks when called for, sharing your stresses with others, and avoiding drugs and alcohol. They are also clear that if the stress gets too difficult to handle, seek professional counseling with an expert who can help shape the movement toward a swift resolution when possible.

One of the great challenges with coping occurs when the coper chooses a less than resourceful or healthy way to deal with problems, for example, drinking alcohol to forget a failed relationship. While it may have the immediate effect of temporary amnesia and relief, it's like using pain killers to cope with painful disorders -- it requires constant replenishing, and has concomitant detrimental effects in addition to the pleasant feelings of avoidance. Instead, designing a constructive means of coping helps the person get through the tough time without creating additional side issues.

The ability to cope turns out to be a predictor for patient success in your practice, too. Some people over-report their suffering, while others may under-report the way they feel. Patients who can cope with their health problems may seem better sooner, while someone who tends to be more reactive may take longer to acknowledge their progress, based on their interpretations of their condition and symptoms. Use objective assessment and analysis to calibrate each person's response, and it will evolve into an empirical measure of their ability to cope.

Obviously, it's useful to develop tools to help people cope better, based not only on your clinical advice, but also on how to handle the healing process. Because it varies from patient to patient, have an assortment of coping techniques in your bag of tricks – affirmation, visualization, and relaxation technology, for example, or massage, or ice, or heat, or anti-inflammation counseling, in addition to your typical program of care.

Often, just producing more optimism gives the coping patient what is needed to succeed. Other times, their complaining is part of the healing, similar to what John Gray refers to as "grumbling" in "Men Are From Mars, Women Are From Venus," and should then be taken in stride.

But the combination of ultra-competence in canceling the impact of stress and assisting the patient in getting through the ordeal makes for a happy practice and an enthusiastic staff, because the practice that copes together, hopes together.

We all work really hard, and find ourselves confronting significant hardship each day – learn and master the coping process, and minimize your stress while you maximize your results. Ueshiba, founder of Aikido and master of balance, was asked why he never gets knocked off center, and retorted, "I do get knocked off center – I just recover so quickly no one can tell."

That should be our target for coping – handle stuff as expediently as possible, to preserve time, energy and resources to move forward.

Dreaming   December 2017

"The Dreamer has a Dream. The Thinker has a Vision. The Storyteller has a Purpose. The Leader has a Mission. Liberate yourself from your present and past… by inventing your own options, which is what entrepreneurs do." -- Michael Gerber, author of "The E-Myth" series and founder of "The Dreaming Room"

Those of you who have given me the privilege of coaching you probably remember that at the very beginning of our work together, I ask you to write a dream, the answer to the question, "If there were no rules and you couldn't fail, what would your practice be like?"

When we do this exercise, I am careful to discern between a dream and a goal. Goals have details and time frames and action steps and stress, while dreams have none of those things – they're dreams. No planning, no pressure, no disappointment, no need to do anything at all, and that freedom gives us unique opportunity within the dreaming process – to discover who we would have to be or become to execute on that dream, and then to make it a goal if we desire, having already reaped the great benefit of enhancing our identity.

Some of you may remember the story of Steve, a chiropractor who sought me out at Parker years ago to interview me about taking him on as a member. It seems that he had lost his ability to dream, and wondered if I was the one to help him rediscover it.

Our conversation went well, and we began to work together. At first, I felt we were getting somewhere, but he resisted and recoiled before he re-engaged, telling me the following story.

"Dennis," he said, "I haven't been completely honest with you. About twenty years ago, I invested $100,000 in a new company whose name I can't tell you, but you would surely recognize."

"Last year," he continued, "I cashed out… for over a billion and a half dollars."

My mouth hung open, and he went on to say, "You know, after you've given your wife a hundred million dollars, and each of your five kids a hundred million dollars, and you still have almost a billion dollars left, where do you go from there?"

I said simply, "I've never heard of anything quite like that."

And he said "Yeah, Coach, what do you think? Nice dream, huh?"

That's my all-time favorite, but I've heard tales of splitting time between a penthouse office in New York City and skiing the slopes of Grenoble, opening free mega-clinics in impoverished neighborhoods nationwide, seeing one patient each month and charging $1,000,000, and growing extra arms to double their adjusting potential – try it on for yourself, it's fun and productive, especially if you use your dream as a catapult toward your best self.

The point of this aspect of dreaming is to use it as leverage to generate specific elements of personal growth. "The dream" invites the follow-up question, "Who would you need to be or become to have that practice?" and that initiates a journey of personal growth, driven by pursuit of the identity that would be most likely to make your dreams come true.

This is where you can build a foundation with Gerber's model by crystallizing your dream, creating your vision, establishing your purpose and choosing your mission. The way I conceptualize this introspective research is that your vision is your big "What," your purpose is your big "Why," and your mission is your big "How."

Gerber also differentiates between "incremental" dreaming, which is dreaming dreams that you accomplish and move on to other dreams, and "intentional" dreaming, which is to open yourself to pure potentiality and see what manifests.

Either way, you'll be compelled to develop an identity profile that is consistent with the realization of your dreams, whether you achieve them or not. It's the journey, and building yourself continuously in strong and noble thought is its own reward, triggered by the dreaming process.

And, you will fulfill some or even most of these dreams if you show up as that kind of person who would. This explains why identity and dreaming are so intimately related – your identity determines what you dream, and your dream demonstrates who you are.

My favorite quote on dreaming comes from Johann Wolfgang von Goethe, who famously said, "Whatever you do or dream you can do — begin it. Boldness has genius and power and magic in it."

This helps us avoid the pitfall of procrastination, which implies being satisfied by the dream alone. By creating a vision, purpose and mission, and by sketching out your dream and your identity profile, you'll move the process along. You'll discover that dreams do come true, if and when we take action on bringing them into reality.

The Second Puzzle   January 2018

No doubt when you discuss your approach with those you touch and serve, you orchestrate a program based on that individual's start point, and where you want to go from there.

If it's a chiropractic patient, you might talk about three phases of care, first to relieve, then to correct, finally to grow and expand. For a weight loss client, you might need to get the person out of trouble by slamming on the dietary brakes, then develop better habits to establish a new normal, and finally plan a healthy lifestyle to enhance quality of life.

Everything we experience along the way has stages and gradations, and that is true even about life itself. Childhood into adolescence into early adulthood, adulthood into maturity into seniority, we create our own standards to measure our movement throughout those periods, based on our own personalized expectations and self-assessment.

So then, when someone gets to a point, regardless of age, that they reach a milestone of completion by their definition, that metaphorically puts a piece of the puzzle in place, and when enough puzzle pieces are in place, that solves the first puzzle.

The first puzzle can have many different configurations, depending on values hierarchy, beliefs and priorities. One typical example might be someone who has good health and good self-esteem, has the desired significant other and/or family relationships, enjoys work and play and generates enough income to live as he or she wishes.

Now, this may not be the definition of your first puzzle – that's up to you to clarify and refine. Frankly, many people never solve, or even fully understand, their first puzzle.

But you probably have at least some of the pieces of the first puzzle in place, and you may even feel relatively complete with this first set of worthy objectives.

And that invites discussion of the second puzzle.

When I graduated from New York Chiropractic College in 1977, I was thrilled to begin practicing, and I woke up every morning excited to take care of people. I soon thereafter married the girl of my dreams, started a beautiful family, and after a substantial and challenging learning curve, got some coaching and guidance and built a thriving practice, yielding a very satisfying income and lifestyle.

But about ten years into this wonderful and fulfilling period, I started to get itchy, like there was something else I was supposed to notice and act on that wasn't immediately apparent. I realized that no matter how many hundreds of people I saw each week, I still felt like I had so much more to give. I needed a bigger game – I wanted a greater sphere of influence, and I was ready to leap toward a new reality where I could have more impact.

My quest led me to The Masters Circle, and I have had the rare and precious experience of overseeing about a thousand Masters Circle members attracting 120,000 new patients and delivering almost six million adjustments in a single year. Now that's a practice!

The point is, as I lived my life, I learned and applied first puzzle principles and distinctions that brought me to where I was in 1987. From there, the beginning of my second puzzle, I confess that I was probably more courageous than I should have been. I went from being a successful expert in practice to becoming a novice consultant and speaker, working for a small fraction of my previous compensation, with no promise of abundant return, going from owner and entrepreneur to employee and part of a team, relinquishing much of my control.

Yet, I knew I was on the right track, and that inner knowing is an important component to the second puzzle. Innate thot flashes are part of second puzzle discovery, transcending educated mind to reveal some vital direction toward fulfillment.

Tony Robbins taught me that we tend to overestimate what we can do in a year, but underestimate what we can do in a decade. Adjust your perceptions of time and space accordingly – sometimes second puzzle outcomes are gradual and methodical, sometimes they are immediate and quantum – that's part of the fun with the second puzzle. There's a less clearly elucidated pathway, because it is a road less traveled.

I mean, think about it – people who solve the first puzzle are already big winners in life, by their own definition. For many, that's good enough, and they ride out their excellent lifestyles for the rest of their days, nothing wrong with that.

But some have a quirk of spirit that causes them to always think bigger, to create a grander vision and grow into it, and those are the ones who explore the second puzzle. Teaching, writing, leading, researching, reworking, inventing, associate doctors, entrepreneurial pursuits, or just a more elegant balance of your time and energy – it's not for everyone, but for those who have an internal crusade that gnaws at them, perhaps these thoughts will prove useful.

It's when we realize we've done all we can from our current vantage point that we move to investigate new territory of doing good. It may be about sharing your wisdom with a mastermind or group of students. It may be mastering other healing approaches, or pursuing philanthropic or charity community service. It could be meditation, or yoga, or martial arts, or fitness, as some reflections of a new identity.

Advanced citizens know that there is more to an extraordinary life than just the material trappings of success. Think one step bigger than you seem, look for the next opportunity to make a difference, and let the magic of the second puzzle come through you. It can take years to manifest, or it can happen in an instant – listen for the wee small voice inside, and prepare to be awed by the result.

World Class   February 2018

No doubt you're aware of the Winter Olympics in Pyeongchang, South Korea, and you've witnessed some of the amazing accomplishments these young people are achieving. They have worked so hard for most of their lives to reach world class status.

It seems logical that if you do good work, you should get good results, and if you do great work, you should get great results.

But I learned from Tony Robbins many years ago that this is not generally the case.

If you do good work, you typically get… fair results. Now, this is better than if you do fair work, in which case you would ordinarily get poor results or no results at all – but if you want good results, you'll have to do great work.

And, if you want great results, you'll have to do outstanding work.

And, if you want outstanding results, you'll need to do… world class work. And if you do world class work long enough and consistently enough, you become world class.

What does it mean to be world class?

James Collins, in "Good to Great," described enduring success as a function of three factors – the third is, what are you passionate about? Second, what turns your economic engine? And the first question he asks, is… what can you be the best in the world at?

Answer these questions and take action on what you discover, and you'll be on the path to becoming world class.

"While their competition is asleep, world-class leaders are up -- and they're not watching the news or reading the paper. They are thinking, planning and practicing."
-- Robin Sharma

Bob Hoffman tells us, "Proper planning prevents poor performance," and suggests that every ten minutes of planning saves back an hour of wasted time.

Decide how much imagining and planning to schedule each day or week, and your work will be more fulfilling and your results more satisfying.

"Only through focus can you do world-class things, no matter how capable you are."
– Bill Gates

All of us have more than enough potential. But the amount of our potential we gain access to is called our capacity, which depends on our ability to find limitations and weaker areas that impede our progress and build resources to handle them.

And that requires focus, to evaluate and act on the many details of success. You'll need to develop a fine focus and self-discipline to keep your attention on the road ahead, despite any adversities and distractions along the way.

"Almost all world-class athletes and other peak performers are visualizers. They begin with the end in mind." – *Stephen Covey*

One of the tools used to activate the law if attraction is visualization. You could increase your skill at visualization through Silva Mind Control, or by studying the work of Joe Dispenza, John Demartini, or Tony Robbins.

All of us can visualize – when you dream, that stuff isn't happening in the room, is it? You are visualizing. But to willfully visualize may take rehearsal. For example, look at a brightly colored object, and then close your eyes while maintaining the image. This wakes up your dormant capability and before long, you'll develop more skill and precision.

"Quality training is what I do now; before it was a combination of both quality and quantity. Now I'm not trying to be a world-class athlete, I don't need to train at that level. It's about being fit, fit for life."
-- Jackie Joyner-Kersee

Know your outcome and adapt your intensity to match it. When your purpose is clear, your decision-making gets black-and-white, so you can decide how hard to push and when. If you go all out every minute, you could exhaust your resources and might not have the "kick" left you may need when approaching a critical crossroads.

Many years ago, Guy Riekeman invited Al Ries and Jack Trout, marketing and positioning experts, to do a private workshop for $40,000, but they declined. When pressed for an explanation, they responded that they didn't see how it advanced their purpose. Now that's congruency, and that's part of how they got to be world class.

Adjust your approach to suit your desires and expectations. Save bandwidth for your most important goals and follow David Allen's 4 D's from "Getting Things Done" -- do it, delay it, delegate it, or dump it.

All world class performers look to guidelines like these (but not limited to them) to keep themselves on point. Ironically, some decide to be world class, while others at some point discover that they already are.

"In cognitively demanding fields, there are no naturals. Nobody walks into an operating room straight out of a surgical rotation and does world-class neurosurgery."
-- Malcolm Gladwell

But all of us have the raw ability to play at a world class level – it's only a matter of how much of that potential you can gain access to. This cracks the code of ongoing growth – build capacity and fill it with attraction. Then build more capacity, and fill that with attraction. Then repeat as long as you feel like playing.

In doing so, you adopt the habits and behaviors that other world class performers choose, and that offers you your best opportunity of being world class yourself.

Inertia   March 2018

Those in the know make every effort to understand and live consistently with things natural. Learning to marvel at and apply universal laws is part of a winning strategy, whatever your chosen field.

For example, consider the concept of inertia. Inertia is the resistance to changes in motion – in other words, a body in motion tends to remain in motion, and a body at rest tends to remain at rest, unless acted upon by outside forces strong enough to redirect such movement or lack thereof.

Isaac Newton is credited with noticing this phenomenon and stated in his "first law" that "every object will remain at rest or in uniform motion in a straight line unless compelled to change its state by the action of an external force," which is generally accepted as the definition of inertia.

We're accustomed to thinking about this in physics classes, as pertains to inorganic systems, but inertia relates to living systems as well -- busy people tend to get things done, creative people tend to create, athletes tend to work out, lazy people tend to underperform, and so on.

When it comes to the definition of inertia, most people focus on the "remain in motion" part, but the key phrase is "unless acted upon by an external force" – this is where you can influence your forward thrust, increased if you engage and reduced if you slack off.

So, you can look for effective interventions and appropriate entry points, to recognize when an outside force could be applied to the system to alter the course and move you toward desired outcomes. Reframing or redirecting your course of action is a great way to capitalize on the law of inertia – get the forces lined up so you are naturally supported by your own flow, a sort of energic tensegrity, like birds flying in formation. Just remember, it will take enough force to overcome the inertia of the system and initiate the changes you seek.

Inertia is resistance, by definition, and resistance is stress – it can be distress or eustress, but either way it's stress, and as such it may have a physical, chemical, emotional and vibrational component. So, if you're in a physical pattern that serves you, you'll tend to perpetuate it, and likewise, if you're in a pattern that doesn't serve you, you'll tend to perpetuate that. Chemically, your dietary discretions and indiscretions will tend to repeat, and it's obvious that our emotional palette often replicates itself. And vibrationally, you've no doubt had the experience of being on a roll, where everything you touched turned to gold – and surely, you've had the experience of things not going your way for what seemed like too long. That vibrational inertia is a kind of microcosmic karma that rides the rhythms of your congruency and integrity.

There is clearly inertia to a patient's condition, and the response to your care – if you can get the person moving in the right direction, there will be a tendency for that constructive movement to continue. And likewise, if the person has a long history of poor health and destructive lifestyle decisions, there will be a pull for the patient to maintain those faulty patterns until and unless you work steadily to break them.

This helps you establish your optimal program of care for each patient – it's the program that most effectively capitalizes on the inertial tendencies of their healing process. While there may be fits and starts at times, when a patient generates a trend of getting better, they usually follow that path to resolution – and likewise, if they never catch the wave of healing, they may not respond as you would prefer.

That's why this discussion of inertia is so critical – by acting on systems to alter their trajectory, and then by knowing what type of intervention or when no more intervention is called for, you operate the mechanisms of both success and healing with certainty and optimization.

We may also develop philosophical inertia – for example, I once believed that chiropractors who adjusted below the axis were mixers. Exposure to brilliant chiropractic minds served as an "external force" that changed my path to include a spectrum of chiropractic approaches. Purists may miss out on opportunities to grow because of their dogma – and sometimes, it may be desirable and self-preservational to do so, while at other times, it could oppose valuable growth.

It's up to you if you want to practice progressively or traditionally. But recognize that you have choice at every juncture, and can change at will, as long as you are aware of your tendency to stay the way you have been.

This universal principle affects your ability to heal, learn, earn, love, be happy and have fun – it offers you a method of surfing the crests of excellence, and of transcending the troughs of tragedy and disappointment. Look for the presence of inertia in your own life and practice – knowing when to stay the course and when to shift gears is an often-overlooked finesse point of success and fulfillment.

Structure   April 2018

"One cannot help but be in awe when [one] contemplates the mysteries of eternity, of life, of the marvelous structure of reality." -- Albert Einstein

Everything we do requires structure. Breathing occurs when the molecular structure of air engages the anatomical structure of our respiratory tract. To counteract the relentless downward pull of gravity, our spinal structure is designed to flexibly withstand many directions of engineering stress, protecting its precious contents, as long as healthy biomechanics are preserved.

To succeed, we use goal structure to frame our forward thrust. Without structure, measurement is difficult, often impossible. You might use the Six P's – Purpose, Personal Goals, Professional Goals, People Goals, Prosperity Goals, and Play Goals. Or, you may chunk your goals by time – right now goals, one-week goals, one-month goals, three-month goals, six-month goals, one-year goals, two-year, five-year and ten-year goals and so on.

A successful practice has a structure, too -- attracting the right number of the right kind of new patients, compelling them to comply and establishing a fair method of exchange all takes structure, not to mention the structure of the identity, personality and practice philosophy that would direct such achievements.

"Thought changes structure... I saw people rewire their brains with their thoughts, to cure previously incurable obsessions and trauma." -- Norman Doidge

Catherine Ponder's "Dynamic Laws of Prosperity" and Bruce Lipton's talks on epigenetics and consciousness helped me understand that thoughts are things -- and that means that when they move they bump into other thoughts and objects and that creates an impact, as we see demonstrated in the law of attraction.

The manifestation of that impact is structure. It's the way things fit together. It's why neuro-linguistic programming (NLP) is so powerful – it dials into the structure of language to generate new patterns of thinking that work better, given the circumstances.

There are two primary tools in NLP, anchoring and reframing -- anchoring is creating associations between thoughts and/or actions, and reframing is changing the meaning of associations between thoughts and/or actions. This offers a model for the structure of successful behavior of all kinds.

Tony Robbins talks about the structure of internal processing, the way we think – we systematically ask ourselves three questions, which shape our interpretation of our reality and our response to it.

"What do I focus on? What does it mean? What do I do?" All of our actions and behaviors hatch from this process, and this structure is necessary for all sensible thought.

"Whatever affects one directly, affects all indirectly. I can never be what I ought to be until you are what you ought to be. This is the interrelated structure of reality."
-- Martin Luther King Jr.

Neale Donald Walsch talks about the relationship between TOM and MARY to be more than TOM + MARY, but rather, TOMARY, a new entity where both contribute their wholeness to a new whole. This suggests that what affects me also affects you, based on the intimacy of our relationship, and provides structure for all ecumenical philosophies and a model for world peace. Once we grasp our connectedness, we'll gravitate toward less conflict and stress and more commonality and love.

Simon Senzon teaches about BJ Palmer's structure of consciousness, in which Universal Intelligence doles itself out in smaller parcels to each individual in the form of Innate Intelligence, which then filters into Educated Intelligence -- and finally, this cycle comes to fruition, with Self-Creation, where Educated is reflecting Innate expression.

"I don't think that scheduling is uncreative. I think that structure is required for creativity." -- Twyla Tharp

302

So, when you are attempting to invent, build, create or develop something, tap into the available structure and use the assets you have.

You might want to use the Results Quinary -- start with an idea, specify it into a goal, assemble a plan, take action on your plan, and that would create a result. If it's the desired result, good -- pick another target. If not, go back through the process to see where it fell short. Drive the system with a strong why (leverage) and a solid how (strategy), and you possess a direct and scalable way to accomplish your outcomes.

Or, if you need better time structure, you could consider a 7-Pager – print out seven blank daily sheets and insert all your weekly responsibilities and obligations, so you can accurately assess your time management. Repurpose time as you wish or recognize when you are overprogrammed and make tough decisions about your priorities. That's how you make the structure of time and energy work for you, instead of being victimized by it.

"Those with the courage to explore the weave and structure of the Cosmos, even where it differs profoundly from their wishes and prejudices, will penetrate its deepest mysteries." -- Carl Sagan

It's worth your attention to look at structure and see how it serves you, as you are using it constantly. From the infinitesimal forces intertwining the most miniscule bits of matter, to the universal laws governing celestial interaction, it's structure that holds all of it together. Whether you are aligning a spine, repairing a shaky table or organizing a movement to change the world, structure makes it all possible.

Authorship   May 2018

"Every human being is the author of his own health or disease." -- Buddha

Your worldview will define the degree to which you believe your own vision and effort will alter the course of your destiny.

Some people see themselves at the mercy of a deterministic universe, where our path and our fate are pre-ordained by genes, deities, karma or some other personal interpretation of choice. Others feel more vital and responsive, an epigenetic manifestation where they can adapt to conditions and find opportunity to prosper in spite of whatever obstacles.

No one really knows which is more correct, since powerful arguments have been made from both sides for centuries, from Socrates and Plato up through current-day mechanism and vitalism.

Some, like Mother Teresa, describe themselves as "a pencil in God's hand." Others may feel more like the New England farmer who was out tilling his field when a city slicker came passing through town. The friendly stranger stopped and called out, "Hey there, what a beautiful farm God has blessed you with!" And the farmer paused and shrugged, "Ayuh, but you should have seen it when He had it all to Himself."

"To master magical realism, one must make the real seem unreal but, more importantly, make the unreal seem real." – Kevin Ansbro

Only you can decide how much to leave to divine intervention and how much to take command, and the formula you select will lead to your degree of authorship. If you believe your direction is predetermined, as many have good reason to do, then you may choose to relinquish ownership of your story in favor of trust and faith in the grace of a higher power.

But if you want to write, or at least co-write the script of your best life, it requires a willingness to take some authorship, a responsibility to guide yourself toward what you really desire through creativity, focus and self-discipline, resilience and perseverance.

It seems obvious to me that both of these perspectives are necessary. To believe in something greater than yourself, however you choose to frame it, opens up vistas of potential that might not be available without this point of view, not to mention making a space for the concept of "miracles." Yet, applying your tools of mastery to build capacity and attraction, even if it is all part of your spiritual evolution, will still be enhanced by your effective investment of attention and energy.

I contend that these viewpoints are not in opposition, but rather, work together. Ultimately, either alone might fall short of any sufficiently exhaustive philosophical inquiry, but each individual's mixture points at answers to his or her own otherwise unanswerable questions, based on the balance of Innate and Educated Minds. Are we in charge of our lives? What is our future? Why do bad things happen to good people and vice versa? Do we need to have goals and plans, and how committed should we be to achieve them?

"The finder of his theme will be at no loss for words." – J. V. Cunningham

When we recognize our level of authorship, these dilemmas begin to clarify. It's apparent that there are some things that are under our control, and some that are not. Staying focused on what we can do something about is the best way to preserve energy and resist wasteful or unproductive behavior at times of adversity.

If we are more deterministic, then we believe it's as it should be, regardless of personal suffering, and we can rationalize that it's in the cards for us. Or, if we believe we can change the outcome, we can see that we need to concentrate our power in places where it will do some good.

Buddha points out that our level of healthful expression is a response to the recipe we write for ourselves, and this is a key point we need to get across to the patients we serve. We can assume that this means healers need to inspire in their clientele a willingness to do what it takes to move into the space they wish to inhabit.

Patients have been enticed into seeking cures. What we can offer them is healing, which invariably requires a shared responsibility, where doctors do the doctor things and patients do the patient things.

"Don't be 'a writer.' Be writing." – William Faulkner

Remember that from the same root as "authorship" comes "authority" and "authorized" – the doctor must accept and act on the authority to guide the doctor-patient relationship, and the patient must authorize the doctor to be that guide and follow accordingly, partnering by contributing real-time feedback and intuitive insight.

By those rules and standards, you and your patients can co-author the healing process, with a little help from Innate Intelligence, where you and they collaborate based on the deal you strike. Some doctors do much of the heavy lifting themselves, while others prefer a health and wellness cooperative relationship. Again, these are reflections of your own sense of authorship.

As Dr. Hoffman says, we are all under constant, chronic low levels of physical, chemical, emotional and vibrational stress, which invariably leads to damage, degeneration, disease and ultimately death. Find your preferred blend of guidance from above down and from inside out, and you'll be reflecting the authorship that resonates with who you really are.

"As a writer you try to listen to what others aren't saying...and write about the silence." – N.R.Hart

Zero-Sum   June 2018

You may remember Paul Zane Pilzer's comments on economics, classically defined as "the distribution of scarce resources." It insinuates that there is only so much wealth to go around, and if you have it, there won't be enough (or any) for me.

This worldview is referred to as "zero-sum," and its misguidedness is a root cause for a lot of the problems we face in our current culture. Much of the greed in our society comes from the notion that wealth is limited by the number of gold doubloons and green pictures of dead presidents available, which flies in the face of what truly evolved entrepreneurs know, and what Pilzer reminds us of – that there is an unlimited amount of wealth, more than enough to go around, and your massive success in no way affects my ability to flourish, prosper and thrive.

Albert Einstein said, "The most important decision we make is whether we believe we live in a friendly or hostile universe." The thought that we would inhabit a place that had too little or barely enough riches and sustenance to nurture all of the planet's residents does not make sense, especially when you look at the already well-established bountiful rhythms of Nature -- there's an organizational, Universal Intelligence that keeps things in proper order and balance.

Do expectations and results vary? Of course, it's not guaranteed, since at times, there may be a bigger, grander purpose affecting the outcomes than just your desires. But the possibility always exists -- you must play well enough to qualify, and then take your best shot to capitalize on the clues that success leaves for you,

Decades ago, the Club of Rome, a think-tank of scientists and dignitaries from all over the world convened to discuss the future, and worried that the world's oil reserves would quickly be expended, which could signal brutally hard times – when they met in the late 1960's, they predicted that within ten years of that gathering, the world would be out of energy.

But when they reassembled ten years later, much to their amazement, they realized that they now had 90 years of resources to draw upon – what happened?

They hadn't considered the advances in technology, like better pipelines, more efficient gas consumption in cars, more effective heating, and so on – it led to a greater capacity even despite the increased demand.

That's where zero-sum thinking falls short – advances in technology invite a new use of present resources, or sometimes entirely new resources, to be repurposed creatively and appropriately, leading to a greater result than previously understood or expected.

I mean, computers are the centerpiece of one of the world's most dominant industries – and what is the chip, the computer's brain, made out of? Silica. And what is silica? It's sand! Scientists found a way to turn sand into a trillion-dollar business, through ingenuity and vision. It's another example of using technology to expand what seems like a zero-sum game with limited opportunity into an open-ended upward spiral of accomplishment.

This is true about human resources as well. We don't need to settle for our current level of achievement – we can make ourselves better, build additional skills and resources, and perform at a higher level because of it, using human technology like affirmation, visualization, goal-setting, resource-building, beliefs and values, organizing principles and habits of excellence, to name just a few tools and methods.

Therefore, we can change the rules of the game we play in two steps. First, we must adopt a mindset of growth that allows for many winners and many victories. Second, we must acknowledge that we are not bound by genetics, physical stature, intellect or any other common measurements that tend to stifle people and restrict their progress – rather, we inhabit an epigenetic world where genes respond to circumstance and conditions, in a competition that challenges you to triumph over your current reality and previous best, not over your adversaries. In fact, "compete" actually means "to conspire together," meaning that when you go up against someone, you strive to do your best and inspire the best in your opponent, so everyone registers their own personal win.

This applies in the context of healing, too. Donny Epstein talks about reorganizational healing, suggesting that what we interpret as disease may actually be an opportunity for the system to reorganize better than before. He comments that it's not about returning to pre-disease status, another zero-sum phenomenon -- it's more about using the disease and the healing experience as a springboard to greater consciousness and expression of your potential. Healing is a quantum experience, not a linear one, and that's why anyone can heal from anything, given the right conditions and approach.

Carol Dweck told us the difference between a fixed mindset and a growth mindset – a growth mindset makes room for evolution and positive change. Live out your dream by transcending zero-sum thinking – there's more than enough to go around for you, your loved ones, your competitors, and everyone else, too. In the final analysis, it turns out that we live in a friendly universe. A life and career of abundance is possible for all of us. Einstein would be proud.

Priorities   July 2018

"Most of us spend too much time on what is urgent and not enough time on what is important."
-- Stephen R. Covey

How do we decide what to do? How can we tell what's really important to us? What do we cherish most, despise most, seek most, or avoid most, and why?

There are really only two reasons we do or don't do anything – it's either because we want to or because we have to.

"Action expresses priorities." -- Gandhi

Tony Robbins says that there are three questions that shape our internal processing – what do I focus on? What does it mean? What do I do?

We interpret our experiences using this process, so we know which actions to take, and why. Your particular process will be based on your perceptions – what you choose to focus on, what meanings you assign based on your worldview, and then which actions seem like the best response to that meaning.

In neurolinguistic programming (NLP), we learn about generalized behavior patterns known as metaprograms. For example, the "direction" metaprogram, moving towards or moving away, refers to people's tendency to be influenced more by benefits or consequences. This is why people take action either because they want to or they have to – they will tend to move toward pleasure or away from pain.

David Simon, author of "The Ten Commitments" and Deepak Chopra's partner until his untimely demise in 2012, appeared on our SuperConference stage over a decade ago, teaching us that human beings are simple creatures with only two settings -- yum and yuk.

Simon's point was that we decide what to do or not do based on how it "tastes" to us, yummy or yucky. This is not usually as linear as we would hope for, despite the simplicity of Simon's message.

"What counts can't always be counted; what can be counted doesn't always count."
-- Albert Einstein

We have a densely interwoven system of values, beliefs and personality traits which determine what we focus on and what it means to us. Those foundational elements, filtered through the conditions of the present moment, define the relative importance of the various aspects of our lives. This relative importance generates a personal hierarchy that defines our priorities.

"Resolve to perform what you ought; perform without fail what you resolve."
-- Benjamin Franklin

We do what we do because of our priorities. And each of us has our own unique set. This is the basis for community -- we find commonality by coming together around major key values (like freedom, spirituality, or fitness, for example) with those who share (or somewhat share) those values.

Then, since it's unlikely that everyone in the community will have the exact same priorities, we embrace certain shared norms, and then set about the process of expressing ourselves to play our role, to add something to our communities.

There is indescribable magic in tribe, in aggregating a community's power to enact positive change, and provide a platform for people to shine. It taps both the group energy field and the individuals' vibrations as well. That is why we work so hard as chiropractors and advanced citizens – we sense that our priority of a healthy brain and constructive lifestyle decisions is an idea whose time has come, and we continue to refine our mastery so that when the stars align, we are prepared.

"You can't move so fast that you try to change the mores faster than people can accept it. That doesn't mean you do nothing, but it means that you do the things that need to be done according to priority."
-- Eleanor Roosevelt

How many people do you know who have a profound commitment to make the world a better place? It's only rare because most do not prioritize unconditional love and dedicated service high enough compared to their own survival and success. But this can change, as more of us awaken to the opportunity of working together for the betterment of all.

"Remember that you have only one soul; that you have only one death to die; that you have only one life…If you do this, there will be many things about which you care nothing." -- Saint Teresa

We all want our own creature comforts and achievements, and that is completely understandable and quite appropriate. But when we prioritize doing as much good as possible, we not only enjoy our own success, but we can also feel like we are contributing to the greater consciousness of our world.

Or not. That's the beauty of priorities – it's one place where you are utterly, completely and eternally in charge of your own goals and perspectives.

"This above all, to thine own self be true." -- William Shakespeare

And that's what free will is really all about – please use the privilege well.

Stress Patterns   August 2018

With all the talk about Brain-Based Wellness, the concept of stress is front and center in our awareness. We watch for the effects of stress in our own lives, and we observe and comment on the impact of stress in the lives of those we touch and serve.

Bob tells us that people suffer from constant, chronic low levels of physical, chemical and emotional stress, which invariably leads to damage, degeneration and disease. Further analysis uncovers another form of stress, vibrational stress, which occurs as energic or cellular disruption when we are bombarded with electromagnetism, cosmic rays, ultraviolet light and so on.

The assault on our brains and nerve systems is relentless and potentially devastating – unless precautions are taken to preserve them, and radical measures pursued to rehabilitate them when necessary. This, then, turns out the be the health challenge of the Twenty-First Century – whoever conquers stress will own the future of health care.

The way we look at it, healthy people become less so as they fail to adapt to the stresses they encounter – and doctors who address this pandemic will become the healers of our culture. Fighting disease hasn't worked out well – it's too deep in the un-health cycle to be truly effective except in certain heroic circumstances.

The solution lies in understanding stress patterns and differentiating those that can be dealt with from those that must be coped with. So, for each of the four major types of stress, there will be some stresses that can be reduced or eliminated, and others that require adaptation and accommodation.

For example, if patients have physical stresses because their feet are not striking the ground squarely, then orthotics may alleviate that stress. But if someone has physical stress because of a physically demanding job they wish to continue, then you'd need to figure out how to fix or handle the net effects of that ongoing stress – for example, regular adjustments, supports, massage and/or personal training.

Likewise, if someone has chemical stress because of poor diet, it can be rectified with nutritional counseling – eating better will reduce chemical stress. But what if they work with toxic substances? If you can't prevent that, this patient needs regular cleanses and detoxification, as well as proactive positive nutrition to build immune function, an alkalizing green shake as an anti-inflammatory and a probiotic to streamline the purge of poisons.

Along the same lines, if someone is suffering from emotional stress from unresourceful self-talk, bad attitude or other forms of self-sabotage, they can learn not to self-flagellate and thereby reduce their emotional stress. If, though, they are subject to an irritating or abusive environment at work or with family or friends, they may not be able to avoid or even diminish the noxious input. That means they have to develop better coping mechanisms, like meditation, breathing, martial arts training, yoga or BrainTap.

Finally, vibrational stress may be more insidious – it could come from hair dryers, cell phones and tablets, microwave ovens, power lines or satellite dishes, for example, not to mention the myriad celestial particles that constantly bombard us, including a hundred trillion neutrinos passing through us every second. Does that do anything? We don't yet know, but like gravity is a universal phenomenon that contributes to our physical stress, a shower of infinitesimal bits of stuff could be a universal phenomenon that could be contributing to our vibrational stress. Like excessive sun exposure over time, it can manifest in undesirable ways unless it is addressed.

There's obviously a way to limit your exposure to dangerous radiation, for example by wearing a hazmat suit or a hat in the sun, or for common types of electromagnetic stress by using a Q-Link or some other EMF shielding device. But for vibrational stresses you cannot avoid, you may need to establish a habit of grounding or energy cleansing. Soaking in Epsom salt and water, fasting, walking barefoot outside or using ionic foot baths may be helpful, as well as light therapy, vibration plates, laser, pulsed electromagnetism and frequency specific microcurrent.

Here's where it gets interesting – because no one has a pure form of stress. All of us are a composite of the three (plus one) types of stress, and our lifestyle considerations need to be shaped around our stress patterns. That analysis is a major clue to the type of health habits and care necessary for each of us, helping us shape our own health and lifestyle decisions to suit our best interests, and preparing us to similarly guide others.

Given that all of us have all four types of stress, we can establish relativity – is someone a physical stress major with a chemical minor? An emotional major with a physical minor? Are you a CEV, or a PECV? This simple new language gives us a way to classify patients based on meaningful information more than just a symptom profile. It streamlines communication in multi-doctor offices. It helps us to organize a patient's or a family's program of care, because it is tuned to their typical stress patterns.

This changes the conversation about health and wellness, evaluating underlying stresses to design proactive care, rather than only a systems analysis and differential diagnosis. By focusing on causes and interrupting the causative rhythms earlier, we can avoid illness and promote wellness.

There may be patterns within families, tribes, social movements, clubs, or not. Everyone has their own stress fingerprint and their own formula for coping and resolution, and this calls for healing artistry. Can you construct a recipe of stress reduction and adaptation methodologies that will solve the riddle of your subject's stresses?

This is the cutting edge of healing – practical techniques of facilitating good function, instead of merely fighting already-developed disease processes. It starts with understanding and responding to the impact of stress in all its permutations and combinations. Whoever conquers stress owns the future of health care.

Brain-Based Wellness   September 2018

From the beginning, the Palmers talked about connection between brain cell and tissue cell. They concentrated on the neurological basis of chiropractic. In fact, Tim Faulkner, author of "The Chiropractor's Protégé," reported that DD Palmer, circa 1899, began his students' education by teaching them that "every action of the body is done by and through the nerves." But somehow, our profession got sidetracked and started focusing more on the nerve root and pain relief than on the astonishing neurological circuitry that brings about the miraculous healing and wellness benefits chiropractic is famous for.

It's time to use the progress we've made as chiropractic functional neurologists to move our profession forward, retaining the traditional lexicon, but adding jargon that today's health care consumers understand and relate to. We must adapt.

In the first hundred years, chiropractic fought for credibility, and earned respect by resolving painful problems naturally, without drugs or surgery. Millions got well, and a small army of passionate chiropractors told the story – subluxations are bad, correcting them is good, and our communities got healthier because of it.

But there is unrest to this day about the way we explain and represent the entirety of our services to the public. It eludes all but the most committed and enthusiastic patients when we talk about wellness, about prevention, about personal growth – people can understand chiropractic as a remedy for their conditions, but it's hard for them to grasp health advantages beyond the relief of pain.

This is because we spend the bulk of our patient education time talking about spinal nerve interference, an important concept to be sure, but a narrow perspective that invites discussion of pinched nerves, radicular pain and other disorders, focusing on the superficial issue yet ignoring the deeper opportunities -- to help the body respond appropriately to stress, to balance the physiology to facilitate natural healing and recovery, and to establish a foundation of consistent good function that enhances longevity and quality of life.

All chiropractors have patients who receive benefits that are not confined to their chief complaint, yet we have never developed an effective way to communicate that – until now.

Over the last eight years, a movement has been developing to explain chiropractic without the need for any advanced scientific knowledge or philosophical leaps of faith. In masterminds and seminars created by Drs. Barwell, Hoffman, Porter and Perman, distilled in part from the research and perspectives of dedicated chiropractic neuroscientists like Haavik, Carrick, Gonzales, Demartino, Melillo, Brock and Kharrazian, among others, the concept of Brain-Based Wellness™ was born -- a simpler, more direct way to describe chiropractic care and help people realize why they need a Doctor of Chiropractic on their health and wellness team. It's time to change the conversation.

We'll touch more people and get better acceptance if we can change the way we communicate our message. We still need chiropractic terminology, but more between doctors and select patients and enthusiasts, not as our profession's unique selling proposition – that simply hasn't worked. It's hard for people to comprehend an esoteric concept like vertebral subluxation, but it's easier for them to understand stress. It's hard for them to grasp the concept of spinal nerve interference, but it's easier for them to see that a healthy brain is necessary for a healthy body.

And that is the connector we've been seeking – dating back to the "simple safety pin cycle" that BJ used to explain the relationship between brain cell and tissue cell, the brain has always been the central factor in chiropractic physiology, yet it's become de-emphasized in our patient education. No more!

When you talk about stress, the brain and the positive impact of your care, you shift your focus from pain to brain. It's completely consistent with chiropractic philosophy, yet it's more accessible for your patient. It's a new language, easy to learn and apply, derived from the principles of Brain-Based Wellness™.

All of us are under stress. We deal with the physical stress of injury, postural distortion and the relentless downward pull of gravity. We suffer chemical stress from poor diet, environmental pollution, and accumulated toxicity. We feel emotional stress from our work, our relationships, our finances, or our health. We even have to withstand vibrational stress from being continuously bombarded with electromagnetism and cosmic radiation. These stresses keep your body pinned in sympathetic overload, preparing for fight or flight, instead of balancing properly with parasympathetic healing and recovery. These constant, chronic low levels of physical, chemical and emotional stress always lead to damage, degeneration and disease.

In a Brain-Based Wellness™ practice, you can evaluate your patients' brain function and develop corrective and wellness procedures for handling your patients' physical, chemical and emotional stress, in addition to relieving the painful or bothersome condition that brought them to you.

Your recommendations will transform from predicting a number of adjustments to designing a program of brain rehabilitation and care, where you train your clientele to eliminate the stresses they can avoid and adapt to those they cannot change. In this way, you become their most trusted health and wellness advisor, and you help them make lifestyle decisions that support optimal neurological expression, the chief aim of chiropractic care.

The hundreds of doctors who are changing the conversation are noticing that more patients are embracing wellness care, more referrals are being attracted before they suffer needlessly, and more of their neighbors are seeing value in regular chiropractic care where before it was relegated to emergency musculoskeletal crisis intervention.

This is the dawning of a new era of chiropractic practice, where the original intentions of our chiropractic pioneers will come to fruition, above down inside out. Brain-Based Wellness™ is a quiet revolution, based on a singular premise -- that those who conquer stress most skillfully will be the influencers who usher in the golden age of the chiropractic wellness lifestyle.

Violence   October 2018

Over twenty years ago, I discovered the writing of Neale Donald Walsch, and his refreshing worldview helped me formulate many of the philosophies that have shaped my maturation as an educator and thought leader.

Walsch explains that we live in the world of the relative, where we require contrast to interpret our reality. For us to experience what we call "up," there must be something called "down;" for us to experience "light," there must be "darkness," and so on. Thus, it stands to reason that for there to be peace, something contrary to peace must also exist.

Which brings me to a sad report of horrific violence this past week. A crazed lunatic, unable to break into a black church in Kentucky, invaded a local Kroger's, slaughtering two innocent shoppers – another maniac shot up a synagogue in an idyllic community in Pittsburgh, literally Mr. Rogers' neighborhood – and a psychopathic pipe-bomber tried to assassinate over a dozen past and current US leaders and influencers. While such tragedy has become commonplace, these events seemed particularly hurtful and heinous.

I once heard Walsch quote Jean Houston, saying "Often our weaknesses are our strengths turned up too high." As such, important values such as self-preservation and security can be over-inflated into paranoia and wild-eyed survival, neither of which matches the underlying intention.

Self-protection is built into our genetic code – we learned in junior high school biology that irritability, avoiding unpleasant input, is a basic drive of life, right down to one-celled organisms. We also heard about cells using phagocytosis to envelop and destroy any foreign matter perceived to be an invader, a violent act to be sure, justified though it may be.

The instinct of self-defense on a cellular or societal level is understandable. And the purpose of such activity is generally to obliterate any potential dangers, up to and including demolishing the ostensible source of fear -- which may become the seed of violent behavior.

So, if such tendencies are hard-wired in our DNA, how can we reasonably expect to avoid descending into a cesspool of tribal conflagration, much as we are witnessing at this turbulent time? Is it just part of life that at times we will act badly, succumbing to our basest human compulsions?

It reminds me of the Native American story, where a young brave approached his father the chief to inquire about the meaning of life.

The chief responded, "You have two wolves inside of you, always at war. One is angry, vicious, spiteful and filled with hate, and one is gentle, loving, compassionate and kind. They constantly battle for control of your mind and heart."

"Which one wins?" the curious youngster asked.

"The one you feed," the chief calmly answered.

This parable may seem simplistic, given the complexities of modern living. But how could it be otherwise, at a micro or a macro scale? Where your attention goes, your energy flows, and so it is up to each of us to monitor our own emotions, to demonstrate our inclination toward peace, and to watch carefully when circumstances prod us to turn our feelings up a little too high.

This invokes the first key to Capacity Technology™ -- that there are only two kinds of things, things we can do something about and things we can't do anything about, and we need to stay focused on things we can do something about. We may not be able to control all the events of our lives, but we can surely control how we show up and what we do.

The root cause of violence is stress – unresolved physical, chemical, emotional and vibrational stresses that fester inside of us. And that is why brain-based wellness care is an uncelebrated and under-appreciated key to reducing the violence in our world – enhanced adaptation from brain-based chiropractic leads to better overall function of the pre-frontal cortex, which then leads to better executive decision-making, which then leads to less friction and better conflict resolution.

And then there are the drugs that list aggressive behaviors as side effects. How many violent actors have had their body chemistry altered by medications and/ or illicit substances? And how many of them might have chosen differently if not for those poisons?

Everyone must forge a path of self-direction that not only provides for their own needs, but also the best interests of society and the greater good. To take responsibility for such self-direction, we must exercise presence of mind, a close cousin of consciousness. There have been times when I was so angry or so unhappy that I found myself capable of unspeakable and mortifying acts, of hostility, retribution, gluttony, pick your sin. Sometimes I was nasty and didn't bite my tongue before I said something I should have held back. But on my better days, I come to my senses in time to avoid throwing myself off the ledge.

This is the quality we need to nurture in ourselves and our sphere of influence -- breathing, thinking, visualizing, considering the net impact of our actions, so we can select the healthiest and most productive strategies to handle our stresses. That is the only way for us to feed the right wolf – to respect each other's differences and aim for commonality while staying true to our fundamental standards and ideals.

That congruency and collaboration will ultimately serve us well and reduce the probability of unwarranted violence. So remember, while the tendency may be hard-wired, the behavior is always a choice. Choose well.

Polarity   November 2018

In the late Seventies, when I was avidly studying advanced technique, I had the good fortune to live near a grand old man of Directional Non-Force Technique, Dr. William Ajosa. A 1922 graduate of Lincoln-National College of Chiropractic and a contemporary of his mentor Dr. Richard Van Rumpt, he was already close to eighty when I met him, another in a long succession of enthusiastic young DNFT practitioners itching to work with one of the few remaining early masters.

Ajosa lived in a spooky mansion in Malverne NY that served as his home/office, a few miles from my apartment in Lynbrook, so it was natural that when Doc needed someone to come over and adjust him, I was elected for proximity if not skill.

Visiting Ajosa was a trip unto itself. His wife Anna, a brilliant and pioneering chiropractor in her own right over five decades, was an Alzheimer's sufferer who spewed a stream of gibberish, a thin and ghostly figure with scraggly white hair roaming the dark halls in a pale loose-fitting night gown. I'd sit in his reception area waiting for him to finish with his patients, while Anna would be trying to smooth out the carved wooden arms of their antique furniture. The last patient would leave, Doc would bark at Anna to get back in her room, and I would enter his healing chamber.

Ajosa had Marie-Strumpell Disease, ankylosing spondylitis, so though he was close to six feet tall, his spine was fused in flexion -- he was bent over from the waist at ninety degrees and had to look up to have a conversation, so he didn't say much. Sixty years of leaning over adjusting tables twelve to fifteen hours a day took its toll, and his body had adapted so he could still adjust patients, which was all he wanted to do.

He greeted me with his customary grunt and slid onto the adjusting table. I knew the drill – he would test areas on himself, I would measure his legs and report "short" or "even", and he would describe the adjustment he wanted me to make, based on this pure and innate method of analysis.

I learned so much from Ajosa's reasoning and logic, including his unique style of sub-occipital fiber analysis, which gave me a clear window into real-time body function.

One of his most practical tools was finger polarity. He showed me how adjacent fingers carry opposite charges, and to develop his adjusting strategy, he would test by touching with an attracting or repelling finger to activate the short-leg reflex, to establish the listing and the desired line of drive for adjustment.

Why is that important? Because learning to question the body about the optimal, most effective intervention is the key to safe and consistent support of things natural – healing is then a facilitation more than a treatment, asking the body what it wants and delivering that. This was a seminal period for me as an energetic healer, learning about the polarities available to use as a vibrational asset.

When John Demartini spoke at The Winners Circle years later, he explained his philosophy of balance, where there is a center line of light and love, and any deviation from it calls for an equal and opposite response, based on the laws of physics. So, when something disrupts the balance, like a harsh or violent act, there will be a natural tendency toward an equal and opposite act of good to balance out the disruption.

These two examples illustrate how polarity shows up in microcosm and in macrocosm. At all times, there are mighty polarities in play, wrestling for control, while the only resolution is balance. All factions are entitled to exist, but not more than other factions, since that's what maintains the balance, and is the cause for polarity in the first place – to re-establish a homeostasis, a steady state where everything contributes to the best of its ability.

We see it in politics – the divisions are deep, and people more dug in than ever on their point of view. It seems futile and inert, like the butterfly stalling in its struggle to burst free from the cocoon. But that's often how progress manifests, rough and dirty, as a tug of war, pressure gradually turning coal into diamonds, a confluence of the concepts of thought leaders, voicing their positions until consensus emerges as the next best idea, and the process begins anew.

In his landmark philosophy book "Conversations With God," Neale Donald Walsch depicts our world of the relative as the contrast between "isness and isnotness." This is the first polarity, existence – either something exists, or it does not. And from that framework of relativity, we construct our current experience out of binaries, ups and downs, ins and outs, ons and offs, rights and lefts and yeses and nos.

So, polarity is normal, yet we have no obligation to linger in any one extreme. The nature of reality is equilibrium, and even chaos tends back toward equilibrium, the expression of polarities interacting – pendulums swinging, galaxies exploding and resolving in peace eons later, black holes absorbing everything in their vicinity and big-banging new universes.

It's like the great martial artist Ueshiba, when asked why he never gets knocked off center – he admitted that he does get knocked off center, but he recovers so quickly no one can tell.

And that is the secret to polarity – like a judo grapple, it can seem motionless, arduous and frustrating. But through an elegant exchange, a magical dance generates energy, produces movement, and ultimately leads to a steady state that works for all concerned, at least until the next quantum leap presents itself. And so, we continue to grow, and need to learn not to despise the turbulence or lack of obvious progress, but to respond to it and make the most of it. That's how we use polarity instead of being used by it.

Evolution December 2018

"There's a theory that says that life is based on a competition and the struggle and the fight for survival, and it's interesting because when you look at the fractal character of evolution, it's totally different. It's based on cooperation among the elements in the geometry and not competition."
— *Bruce Lipton*

When we think about evolution, our first thought is Darwinism, survival of the fittest, the classical sense of evolution.

But evolution is where growth meets adaptation. "Evolution" insinuates constructive change. "Survival of the fittest" implies positive movement – that which evolves, survives and thrives. This differentiates evolution from other mutations or combinations with less favorable outcomes.

In microcosm, each cell divides its resources between growth and function, and innate consciousness determines the balance. An effective cell grows to maturity and functions as intended – early in its life, more focus on growth, later in its life, more focus on function, in dynamic equilibrium.

When a cell's balance shifts too far toward function at the expense of growth, we call that aging. When the balance shifts too far toward growth at the expense of function, we call that hypertrophy. Because this is an innate homeostatic process, we'd expect the balance for any given cell at any given time to always be naturally right.

But cells can be out of coordination, out of communication, not working together, and when that happens, the cells may act on their own behalf rather than supporting the integrated whole. Chiropractors call that a subluxation, and simply, it is unresolved stress, disrupting the system.

When growth and function operate in harmony, the organic response is evolution. Aging gracefully softens into maturity and mastery, and growth manifests as neuro-plasticity, neurogenesis and rejuvenation.

When the balance is right, growth and function work together. Unresolved stress distorts that balance. And the healing process resets it – or improves upon it.

Donny Epstein calls this phenomenon "reorganizational healing" – he explains that while many healers think of healing as restoring the patient to pre-condition status, he looks at the healing process as an opportunity to evolve. Rather than returning to a prior state, healing can and should be a springboard to a better place. We can use illness, injury and disease to reorganize ourselves.

For example, Stephen Hawking lived forty or fifty years longer than most ALS sufferers, pouring his growth and function into the faculties he had instead of succumbing to the burden of those he lacked, leaving a world class intellectual legacy though he couldn't walk, move or speak. And Beethoven composed his most beautiful and powerful music after he had lost his hearing – something new had awakened in his inner sound when he no longer had the outer.

Such stories give new meaning to the disease process. We get sick for a reason and we get well for a reason, and we can use the healing process to build momentum, re-balance growth and function and move toward even greater well-being.

And that is the trajectory of evolution. To grow in function, to function in growth, to have your cells dance in synergy to the eternal symphony. That shows up as wellness in cells and also in groups of cells, like tissues, organs, systems and people.

"The first step in the evolution of ethics is a sense of solidarity with other human beings."
-- Albert Schweitzer

Now, in macrocosm, we humans are like cells in the organism of our world. We too must strike the right balance between growth and function, physically, chemically, emotionally and vibrationally.

When we are functioning well, we can refine or accelerate our growth. Physically, we can add chiropractic, exercise, massage, yoga, or martial arts. Chemically, we could detoxify with a cleanse, stop poisonous habits, develop a better diet, alkalize to decrease inflammation, or take nutritional and metabolic supplements. Emotionally, we can pursue nurturing relationships, life coaching and counseling or neuro-linguistic programming, or practice breathing, meditation or prayer; and vibrationally, you can tune your energy with acupuncture, electromagnetism, laser, light and sound, affirmation and visualization or frequency-specific microcurrent, for example.

When we avoid the stresses we can avoid, and adapt to and cope with those we can't, innate consciousness can balance our growth and function. And the same reasoning can be applied to groups of people, the tribes that make up society.

Like with cells, people can fall out of communication and coordination with each other, and when this happens, more energy goes to self-preservation, ego and dogma and less to the greater good. It is only through social harmony that a new dynamic equilibrium can be established, a higher vibration that generates the growth/function ratio for optimal evolution. But how?

"Non-violence leads to the highest ethics, which is the goal of all evolution. Until we stop harming all other living beings, we are still savages." -- Thomas A. Edison

Our greatest thought leaders agree that transcending violence is a key to evolving as individuals and as a culture. Every spiritual tradition evolves from '"an eye for an eye" to "love your neighbor as yourself." King Solomon, Buddha, Jesus, Gandhi, Martin Luther King Jr., Mother Teresa, across all perceptible tribal boundaries over the last three thousand years, non-violence appears to be based on universal principles.

So, when we get out of the way of this relentless evolutionary process, our cells, ourselves, our tribes and our culture will be the beneficiaries, propelling us into a Golden Era of Peace, Love, Wellness and Prosperity, the open-ended upward spiral of evolution. Nature needs no help, just no interference.

Fitness   January 2019

"Physical fitness is not only one of the most important keys to a healthy body, it is the basis of dynamic and creative intellectual activity." -- John F. Kennedy

It was just after the turn of the millennium, but I remember it like it was yesterday. Regina had just made a Homer Simpson joke, and as I was walking past a store window, I glanced up to notice a fat guy inside – only it was my own reflection I saw.

Gross!. There was no getting around it, I was overweight. Approaching middle age, I was showing my age around my middle.

I had heard Tony Robbins speak about Bill Phillips and his "Body for Life" program, and one of our early Winners Circle members, Doug Cox was crushing it with those protocols. One serious and slightly terrifying conversation later, I was determined to go from pear-shaped to V-shaped, and I began my private twelve-week exercise and diet revolution.

Well, you know what, it worked – I lost pounds and inches, transcended my distaste for fitness regimens, and while I haven't maintained the formal program, I still exercise almost every day, I eat a mostly healthful plant-based diet and adhere to many of the same principles that helped me reset my course toward fitness all those years ago.

That's because at its best, fitness is integrated as consciousness, not just a series of mechanical procedures. I don't especially like to exercise, but I like what happens when I do. It took a while before I found the right routine, but once I did, I was able to commit to the habit.

As long as I'm confessing, I love sugary treats and adult beverages and chips and cookies and ice cream and all the stuff I shouldn't have – but while I do cheat with some regularity, I maintain the consciousness of fitness, so I rarely go too far outside reasonable boundaries.

What are your rules around fitness? What will you always do? What will you never do? Are you clear on your "shoulds" and "musts?" How would you rate your current level of fitness? What would be the first thing you would change to improve?

"If we could give every individual the right amount of nourishment and exercise, not too little and not too much, we would have found the safest way to health." -- Hippocrates

Even twenty-five centuries ago, the prevailing wisdom was that providing good fuel and maintaining a good working order made sense, and even more so today, given the modern stresses we contend with. In ancient Greece, they knew that proper nutrients and raw materials coupled with effective body function would surely be reflected in health and vitality.

By the mid-Nineteenth Century, Charles Darwin was advancing his theories on the survival of the fittest, meaning that those individuals who were blessed with superior genes would flourish at the expense of their weaker neighbors. For its time, this was profound though it would ultimately be recognized to be too simplistic and linear a worldview to explain all of nature, as it was initially reputed.

At the dawn of the Twentieth Century, the Palmers were exploring the connection between "man the physical and man the spiritual," introducing a new paradigm that integrated consciousness into fitness. The philosophy said that the Innate Intelligence that animates the body is connected to a source, Universal Intelligence, and that fitness, more than merely big muscles and stamina, referred to fit function. This notion that has been progressing for over a hundred years, manifesting as today's wellness movement.

As Bruce Lipton tells us, today we understand that there are factors that aren't governed by the individual's heredity, but rather the interplay between their genetic code and the environment. This cements the significance of consciousness in the discussion of fitness, not just a musclebound-run-a-four-minute-mile kind of fitness, but real fitness, meaning that you fit into the reality you wish to create for yourself, which evolves as you invest in it.

These were the underpinnings of brain-based wellness, where fitness meets consciousness, and from that, a new perspective on becoming fit takes shape – the invitation to develop a natural, organic way to feed, run, repair and grow yourself as a person, playing your chosen roles.

"For years, I always thought it was hilarious that I was this fitness guru, because fitness was just a tool I utilized to help people improve their confidence. For me, it's never been about fitness. It's always been about helping to empower people." -- Jillian Michaels

So when we embark upon a journey of personal fitness, or when we guide our loved ones or our patients to embrace this way of life, we'll do better to realize that it is more than hard-won victories over our resistance and the sculpting of a great beach body. There is an esoteric side to fitness, a phenomenon of natural rightness and physical, chemical, emotional and vibrational grace that dissipates stress and establishes wellness. When we acknowledge and act on these distinctions, we open ourselves to a world of beauty, glory, success and fulfillment, and those who master that become the fittest of all.

Winning   February 2019

Consider the way you would play the game of life, depending on which of these two worldviews about winning you choose to subscribe to:

"Winning isn't everything, it's the only thing." -- *Vince Lombardi*

"A champion needs a motivation above and beyond winning." -- *Pat Riley*

These are two of the greatest winners of all time, with radically conflicting positions on the thing that made them great – which concept matches better with what you personally think?

Project for a moment what these ideas mean in real life.

If winning is the only thing, what are you willing to commit to accomplish it? What would you do, change, stop, or amplify to win? It's quite clear that with this much intensity around winning, an individual or team will do a fair share of winning, and be frustrated and miserable when that doesn't occur.

If there is a motivation that lies beyond winning, this individual might not have quite the same intensity around winning, but may have more intensity about cause, vision or purpose.

Twentieth Century sportswriter Grantland Rice coined the phrase "It's not whether you win or lose, it's how you play the game." Yankee manager Joe Torre said, "Competing at the highest level is not about winning. It's about preparation, courage, understanding and nurturing your people, and heart. Winning is the result." And the inimitable Yogi Berra said, "I tell the kids, somebody's gotta win, somebody's gotta lose. Just don't fight about it. Just try to get better."

So these models illustrate the nuances of winning – I wouldn't suggest that any of these remarks are wrong. They came from people who proved themselves over and over and speak from personal experience. They can't all be right – or can they?

Yogi points out that the key competition is with yourself, to improve your own personal best. Rice suggests that competitors are actually co-conspirators, in it together to produce the most satisfying outcome unrelated to the final score. The rising tide floats all the boats, and raising the level of play makes all players better.

It's clear that sometimes raw aggressive power wins, and sometimes subtle elegance wins – that tug-of-war has defined and redefined humanity throughout the ages. There's a right time for strength, and a right time for finesse – if you're not sure, watch an aikido demonstration and get a clear image of effortless ease in action.

This reminds me of the story of the two wolves. A young man approached a wise elder and asked, "what is the meaning of life?" The elder said, "You have two wolves inside you. One is angry, violent, and powerful, and one is gentle, loving, and supportive, and they are constantly at war.

"Which one wins?" the young man asked. The elder calmly responded, "The one you feed."

While I do believe that in the final analysis love will conquer all, that is no excuse to live wimpy, weak or unfocused. That is not winning behavior. You must bring enough personal power to win, whether it's aggressive power or subtle power.

To win, you must develop your weaker areas and strengthen them enough so they no longer hold you back. This creates an organic forward thrust, a momentum based on natural forces and not arbitrary decisions. Sometimes this means you need to build new resources. Sometimes it means you have to wind something back a bit – Jean Houston says that often, our weaknesses are our strengths turned up a little too high.

Sadly, we can't control who wins, but we can control how we show up – that's what Joe Torre was talking about. It's preparation, courage, team-building, and heart, which then leads to winning, no matter the outcome.

In the best business deals, everyone walks away from the table slightly dissatisfied – if anyone is overjoyed, someone got beat. It is in compromise, Covey's Third Alternative, where the greatest victories can be earned – that when the most people benefit.

So we may not be able to control the result, but we can be determined to show up as a winner.

"The will to win, the desire to succeed, the urge to reach your full potential, these are the keys to personal excellence." – Confucius

So, when you help someone else win, are you a winner? When you step aside to let someone else shine, are you a winner? What does winning mean to you?

If you play professional baseball and get three hits out of every ten at bats, you go to the Hall of Fame – but that means you walk back to the dugout cursing and fuming 70% of the time. Defining what winning means for you is critical – it may be the difference between being mostly in agony or frustration and being mostly in ecstasy or bliss.

Following her successes in track and field in the 1956 and 1960 Olympic Games, world-record-holder and international sports icon Wilma Rudolph said, "Winning is great, sure, but if you are really going to do something in life, the secret is learning how to lose. Nobody goes undefeated all the time. If you can pick up after a crushing defeat, and go on to win again, you are going to be a champion someday."

We all have our own stories to tell – tell yours. It's the surest way to win.

Surprise   March 2019

As many of you may know, my lovely wife and I have participated in many kinds of adventure trainings – jumping out of planes, walking 45 feet of hot coals, high ropes courses, climbing a 55 foot telephone pole and leaping off the top toward a trapeze ten feet away, playing paintball till dawn in the mountains of Maui, bungee jumps, zip lines, water slides – we've done a lot of cool stuff and lived to tell the tale, which is why we were so excited to go to Paws Up, a winter wonderland resort outside of Missoula, Montana.

We were thrilled to be staying in the pristine wilderness, and jazzed about going dog sledding, skeet shooting and snowmobiling in this frozen northwestern paradise.

"We plan, God laughs." -- Yiddish Proverb

So you also may already know that in the first half hour of our first event, Regina, an experienced and skillful driver, plowed her snowmobile into a tree at 40 MPH and broke both wrists, narrowly escaping much more serious injury. To say this was a surprise is an understatement – remember, we've done plenty of extreme stuff and emerged unscathed. This hardly seemed like the most dangerous activity – famous last words, I suppose.

But that's the way it is with surprise – if you saw it coming, it wouldn't be a surprise.

"I have seen many storms in my life. Most storms have caught me by surprise, so I had to learn very quickly to look further and understand that I am not capable of controlling the weather, to exercise the art of patience and to respect the fury of nature." -- Paulo Coelho

How do you take the world's most self-sufficient woman and render her instantly dependent on others to open a door, comb her hair, eat – there's no way to prepare for such an eventuality, even when it's temporary like Regina's situation. Yet, I've seen her adapt over these couple of weeks, learning to use the fingertips of her left hand, pretty much all the movement she has had, to begin to take on the tasks previously assigned to her right hand – heck, she used chopsticks lefty tonight, I'm not sure I can do that, perhaps because I've never needed to.

And maybe that's the point. Necessity is the mother of invention, and surprises often necessitate innovation -- new tools, techniques, methods and strategies, neuroplasticity in action.

Then why do some of us handle or even relish surprises, while other feels ruffled and unsettled in the face of them? I learned many years ago from Tony Robbins that nothing has any meaning except the meaning you give it, and that means you can view surprises through any filters you choose.

If Regina framed her "surprise" as "OMG, I have two broken arms, I can't do anything, woe is me," she'd have a completely different experience from the one she is having. Rather, every day she adds motion and patterns of movement so she keeps her fingers functional, and that should reduce her time for healing and incapacity.

"Life is what happens to you while you're busy making other plans." -- John Lennon / Allen Saunders

So then, you may wonder, if a surprise can come along and radically alter the course of our destiny, is it worth it to plan at all? My impression is that it still makes sense to set a course in the direction you wish to travel. Intention matters, and you can put yourself in a better position to win, given whatever unforeseen circumstances.

You might need to tack against the wind, since a direct route may or may not be available – but given Mama Nature's tendency to do as she pleases on behalf of the greater good, we must each seek the right balance between faith and fortune, between hard work and effortless ease, between making things happen and allowing them to happen, between pushing and attracting.

This prepares us to handle whatever stresses accompany the unexpected, so we can appreciate the joys and challenges of surprise.

"The fact that I exist is a perpetual surprise." -- Rabindranath Tagore

Surprises are obviously not all abrupt wake-up calls – some are fun, joyful expressions of creativity and playfulness. I love to surprise my wife with some little token of my esteem. But the ultimate surprise is when I open my eyes in the morning and I realize I am above ground – any day above ground is a great day.

So being surprised by little wondrous occurrences is an abundant way to live – appreciating the nice things that may not be gaudy and expensive, but are no less meaningful when you look at them right. A smile from a grandchild, a good licking by your dog, the flavor of a new ice cream you've never tried before – seek out and participate in surprises, to keep life interesting and to avoid boredom and stagnation.

"Life is like a box of chocolates – you never know what you're going to get."
-- Forrest Gump

The Curse Of Knowledge   April 2019

Leaders invariably find themselves in a position of authority, and what we do with that authority determines the scope and level of influence we attain. So, effective communicators must provide the appropriate guidance to move the process forward, whatever that process may be.

This depends on clear understanding on the part of the followers – thus, a leader must offer direction in a form that is comprehensible to even the least engaged and least skillful teammate, to get sufficient buy-in and execution, and ultimately achieve the desired results.

It's common for such inspired leaders to fall into a trap of their own making, where they attempt to deliver a message that is only partially received – and that communications gap is the subject of this discussion.

Conceptualize it this way – if our relatively masterful degree of awareness could be quantified as "Level 10," we recognize that as experts we may need to adjust our method of disseminating our philosophy so it's easier for people to grasp – and so we make an effort to simplify our approach, perhaps to a "Level 6," which seems uncomplicated enough from our point of view.

The problem is, a typical patient, prospective patient or staff member may be operating at a "Level 1 or 2" by comparison – they are not dumb, they are simply under-informed, and ill-equipped to interpret the complexities of our more evolved thinking.

This phenomenon is referred to as the "curse of knowledge," first noted by economists Colin Camerer, George Loewenstein and Martin Weber in their 1989 article in the "Journal of Political Economy." It's the distance between what a master believes is basic and what an ordinary individual can absorb and utilize, like when a college professor forgets what it was like to be a student learning new material for the first time. It is a cognitive bias, in other words a misconception, where the communicator erroneously and unwittingly assumes that the audience has sufficient background to incorporate the message being presented.

Another way of saying this is that when someone is very experienced on a particular topic, he or she may find it difficult to translate it into common language, to appreciate the perspectives, problems and issues of those who are less experienced. This develops into a communications rift, where the leader "talks over people's heads" which causes a diminished understanding.

If this amounted to mere holes in the person's awareness, that would be bad enough, but the mind resists a vacuum, so the listener will tend to "make stuff up" to fill in what they didn't catch, which creates a brand new set of glitches – the communicator thinks the communication was received a certain way, while the receiver gets and then conveys a somewhat altered message, like the proverbial "telephone game," where the information is garbled and distorted, unrecognizable as the original transmission.

So how do we avoid being trapped by the curse of knowledge? Blogger Giovanni Segar suggests six quick pointers that will help you develop a better match between your message and your audience's capacity to learn.

1. Cut out technical jargon and speak simply. When you use an unfamiliar word, the listener goes into a "search" pattern which commandeers their thinking for a few seconds or longer. This interrupts their ability to follow your communication and widens the information gap. Pick easier words.

2. Get a reality check from someone who doesn't know what you know. By "trying on" your message with someone who resembles your audience, you can gain clarity and certainty that you are speaking at a level the target receiver can interpret properly.

3. Express yourself clearly using concrete words. Stay away from fluffy or obscure references and use analogies people can easily assimilate.

4. Prepare far enough in advance so you can review your work and match it to the least common denominator of your participants. When you "sleep on it," you may reconsider some of your approach to make it more accessible.

5. Choose the scope of your material carefully, so you don't aim too high and try to cover too much. Pick appropriate stories and metaphors. Usually, if you focus on three well-designed major points, you'll keep it clear enough for your group to follow.

6. Be present – just knowing about the curse of knowledge will help to prevent any slipping down that slope. Tune your communication to dovetail with the needs, intentions and emotional level of your listeners, as well as the intellectual track that will work best – it makes you a better presenter overall, with individuals as well as groups, and avoids missed opportunity that can cost you in the long run.

Great communicators are sensitive to the curse of knowledge, and find ways to change the conversation to connect with people viscerally and emotionally, not just logically. Pay attention to the way you educate your patients and train your team – a refined technique will not only grow your practice, it will also serve the greater good by moving more people toward the chiropractic wellness lifestyle.

Elegance   May 2019

I didn't think much about elegance until I started studying the work of Anthony Robbins in 1985. Before then, elegance brought up mental pictures of an old-time movie with rich people at gala occasions, couples in tuxedos and evening gowns, accessorized with a cane, top hat and diamond necklace, hair impeccably slicked back or piled magnificently atop the head, most of which I could barely relate to.

Tony introduced me to a whole new context for the word – elegance is reflected in concise and thorough self-expression, with language that is descriptive without being self-indulgent, with attitude that is impressive without being overwhelming. Elegance is subtle, clean, and dignified, and it is not gaudy, overstated or tacky.

"Elegance is not about being noticed, it's about being remembered." -- *Giorgio Armani*

We can learn to be more elegant, and in doing so, refine our approach and enhance our results. Elegance is the shortest distance between two points, getting to your outcomes and conclusions through an artful investment of resources.

That is not to say that elegance is independent of appearance – in fact, appearing elegant is a pleasant side effect of being elegant. Tony showed us an exercise where we walked around the room in an imaginary cape, not like a super-hero (though that would have been fun too), but rather a deluxe, jet black cape one might wear to a formal night out at the theater in the fanciest of times.

Capewalking is more strut than stroll, a definitive stride that announces that you have arrived. It's not about acting a part, but rather about showing up confident, self-assured and authentic.

"Simplicity is the ultimate sophistication." -- *Leonardo da Vinci*

So elegance doesn't require overemphasis – in fact, it is the opposite of it. Showy and spectacular has its place, but elegance requires taste and class, to discern what is just enough without being too much.

Consider the masterfully executed upper cervical specific adjustment, for example – the mindset, visualizing the atlas in its articulation with the axis and the occiput and the line of drive called for to set it into motion – adapting your posture, taking out the tissue slack, setting the contact on the transverse process with Nail Point One, rolling the indifferent pisiform into the anatomical snuffbox, aligning the episternal notch directly above, cocking the elbows, and then…

At the exact moment of maximum focus and presence for the doctor and optimal receptivity from the patient, the magical thrust is delivered, with speed, precision and torque, a concussion of forces that Innate Intelligence knows exactly how to use, poetry in motion, HIO, the proverbial Hole In One.

A thing of beauty – and, a portrait of elegance in real time.

"The elegance of a mathematical theorem is directly proportional to the number of independent ideas one can see in the theorem and inversely proportional to the effort it takes to see them." -- George Polya

Elegance hits its stride in mastery of communication. Many of the language constructions used in neurolinguistic programming (NLP) were derived by Richard Bandler from Plausibility Patterns that were based on the insights of renowned Hungarian mathematician George Polya. So, the essence of hypnosis, gaining rapport with the subconscious mind so hypnotic suggestions are accepted without friction or defensiveness, manifests from skillfully engaging the client to produce the optimal conditions for change.

Persuasion depends on being able to transcend mere logic to produce an emotional or visceral response, which only occurs when there is an internal agreement deeper than reason.

That's how Tony Robbins, Milton Erickson and Virginia Satir, among the greatest therapists of all time, got rapid responses to their interventions, sometimes in a single session – they tapped into a secret inner place that opens the subconscious trap-door, and develops ultimate leverage to cause the subject to move right now, the pinnacle of elegance.

"Self-command is the main elegance." Ralph Waldo Emerson

So in the final analysis, it's what happens between our ears and in our hearts that determines our degree of elegance. In "Outliers," Malcolm Gladwell said that it takes 10,000 hours to become a master, regardless of our chosen path. But to begin your journey toward elegance, all it takes is a concept and a little determination.

The lyricism of a Mozart piano concerto – the cubist strokes of a Picasso charcoal – the seventeen syllables of a thought-provoking haiku -- elegance is everywhere in the world of art and culture. But it is also in the gym, in your local restaurant, and of course, in your office.

Choosing to practice and perform elegantly is more than a good idea – it will set you apart from your competition, position you as a thought leader, and help you break through to new levels of accomplishment. Elegance conserves time and energy; it exploits strengths and minimizes weaker areas, so it expands your capacity and streamlines your pursuit of your personal best.

It takes raising your standards and preparing to make good on your promise, but behaving and living elegantly will reward you and fortify you, and help you rise to your highest echelon of achievement. Then, you can make your greatest contributions, with style and grace.

Endurance   June 2019

"A man may die, nations may rise and fall, but an idea lives on. Ideas have endurance without death."
-- John F. Kennedy

Over the ten years I have been writing The Advanced Citizen, I have made many distinctions about personal power, identity, values and virtues, and the standards leading to growth, happiness, success and fulfillment. It has been a labor of love, and my nature would be to keep writing it indefinitely. Ideas have endurance without death, something no individual could claim.

So I have done my best to provide you, beloved reader, with ideas, some perhaps more timeless than others, but all intended to contribute in some constructive way.

Life is more marathon than sprint, and while you may have to act quickly at times, the biggest decisions and actions need to be tailored to the long run. Eating bags of chips now may feel satisfying, but leads to poor physiology, obesity and disease later on -- it was the faulty decision-making that was the underlying culprit.

Making better decisions for your ultimate well-being necessitates a vision of your best future, and you'll need persistence and drive to get there.

"Come what may, all bad fortune is to be conquered by endurance." *-- Virgil*

We've all taken some lumps along the way, some more than others, but we all know what it's like – and we've all found a way to keep going forward, continuing to broadcast our ideas, as a doctor, a teacher, a spouse, a parent, a friend, a thought leader, an advisor, an entrepreneur and a human being. It's common sense why we do this – we inherently know our ideas may endure far beyond our physical selves.

Tony Robbins taught me that there are four levels of leadership. First, to lead yourself, a trait many never master. Second, to lead another, and then third, to lead a group.

But the fourth level of leadership is to lead without being physically present. Your ideas lead -- others hear them, respond to them and share them with their sphere of influence. That is a higher form of leadership with more impact, because it transcends you and your life, and expands the boundaries for others with whom you may never directly interface.

"A man on a thousand mile walk has to forget his goal and say to himself every morning, 'Today I'm going to cover twenty-five miles and then rest up and sleep.'" -- Leo Tolstoy

Those who endure may not be any stronger than you. They have learned that if they think only of the great distance that needs to be covered, it robs momentum and diminishes enthusiasm. So if you break up the task at hand into manageable pieces, it is more likely that you can maintain the energy required to persevere.

This process is known as "chunking" – for example, if you have a cord of firewood delivered to your house, you can't pick up all the wood at once to stack it, but if you move one stick of kindling at a time it will take hours. So, you choose a "chunk" size, two or three or four logs or whatever you can carry, the most efficient way to do it without undue stress. Thus, chunking is the antidote to overwhelm – whenever you find the current difficulty too great, chunk it down and you'll find it easier to handle.

"Endurance is patience concentrated." -- Thomas Carlyle

When I first went scuba diving, I was instructed not to breathe fast or heavy in the beginning, because it would use up my air and reduce the time I could stay down there. Likewise, we must learn to pace ourselves, which takes patience and restraint.

It's like, when I was a teenager, I was convinced that my parents were the dumbest people on earth. Funny, as I got older, they got smarter.

And looking back, I realize that they didn't overreact to my insolence and disdain – they saw discretion as the better part of valor. They let me have a little space while I sorted through my adolescent emo-spasms, and I did indeed come around. Maybe something like this has happened to you or someone you know.

"Foolish consistency is the hobgoblin of little minds." -- Ralph Waldo Emerson

Endurance is not banging your head against the wall. It is not mindlessly following a preconceived pursuit. Endurance requires presence of mind, contemporaneous focus, and openness. You must be able to maintain what my old friend Seth Lederman called "double vision" – to see the end in mind while fully engaging the current moment. This is the surest way to endure – to light the fire of purpose inside of you and to express it by disseminating your best truth and taking your best actions right now.

This gives you a chance to evaluate your use of the present moment in the context of your ultimate objectives.

Endurance may not be endless. Having endured, sometimes you reach a point that feels like an end point. When nearing completion, endurance has served its purpose. To the degree that you can say that to yourself, you should be proud indeed, for those who follow through are few and far between.

And anyway, it's the ideas that endure, not the individual – ashes to ashes, dust to dust, we'll all be pushing up daisies somewhere along the line. But to have left an idea that someone can refer to, apply, make their lives better because of, that is the ultimate endurance. It's how you lead without being physically present. And maybe one or more of your ideas will endure, as the verse you wrote for the song of life.

Share your ideas. It's your shot at immortality and eternal influence.

Completion   July 2019

"All things must pass." -- George Harrison

"One door closes, and another bigger door opens." -- L. T. Markson

"One man's ceiling is another man's floor." -- Paul Simon

I have never subscribed to the notion that "all good things must come to an end" -- I see so many good things hard-wired into our world that will keep rocking and rolling into perpetuity. The mountains and the sea, the undying love of one for another, the eye-to-eye, heart-to-heart contact between parent and child, the flavor of victory and the indomitable human spirit -- there are many good things that will not come to an end.

But not so this humble newsletter. It has been a privilege to impart my perspectives over these ten-plus years. And, true to form, it invites an exploration of the final play within the play -- it calls for a discussion of completion.

People who are wired like me tend to appreciate process more than station to station movements. I don't love beginnings or endings, as they are confrontational, unpredictable, uncomfortable.

Fortunately, some goals are outcome goals, that have an endpoint and a moment of celebration, while others are process goals, where the goal is the continuation of the constructive habit or protocol with ongoing celebration. Daily meditation or exercise, reading, personal hygiene or writing a newsletter are all examples of process goals, where as long as you're participating and growing in the process effectively, you're achieving the goal. That's how I've been able to preserve my forward thrust to write 130 editions, over a hundred thousand words, there's a lot of inertia that keeps that kind of a process progressing.

So it took some introspection to avoid falling into the abyss of unending mechanical performance, well-executed but somehow lacking a certain spark of spontaneity and full engagement. I could continue to assemble these offerings forever, but I realize that it's time for me to bring this particular process to a close, and invest the six-to-eight hours a month it takes to write these thousand words or so into another, fresher, more compelling project.

"Good to Great" by James Collins shows us how visionaries preserve their core values and ideologies, and then vary their strategies to suit the current marketplace. So, my intent is to maintain the excellence deserved and expected by The Winners Circle, and also morph this service and energy center into a new form that accomplishes everything these words are supposed to deliver, but is a better fit for today's advanced citizen, half a score later.

In fact, if you are reading these final words and you are not a Winners Circle member, then it means you have in your hands (or on your screen) the anthology of a decade of essays designed to examine the human condition from every angle. Member or not, I thank you for the honor of sharing my thoughts. And how fitting to come to conclusion by looking at the remarks of some great thinkers about completion.

"One's not half of two; two are halves of one." -- e.e. cummings

"Good business leaders create a vision, articulate the vision, passionately own the vision, and relentlessly drive it to completion." -- Jack Welch

"There's always a group of songs that I'm working at. Some of them are 10 years old, and some of them are just a few weeks old. I'm always trying to adjust these songs to some position where I can bring them to completion." -- Leonard Cohen

"It has nothing to do with me, the way I look, my hair wrap, my style, it's about you and what you feel for my music. If I can make you feel like the way that people who influenced me made me feel, that's completion." -- Erykah Badu

"Always aim at complete harmony of thought and word and deed.

Always aim at purifying your thoughts and everything will be well." – Mahatma Gandhi

"We come this way but once. We can either tiptoe through life and hope we get to death without being badly bruised or we can live a full, complete life achieving our goals and realizing our wildest dreams." -- Bob Proctor

"There are very few human beings who receive the truth, complete and staggering, by instant illumination. Most of them acquire it fragment by fragment, on a small scale, by successive developments, cellularly, like a laborious mosaic." -- Anais Nin

"Man learns through experience, and the spiritual path is full of different kinds of experiences. He will encounter many difficulties and obstacles, and they are the very experiences he needs to encourage and complete the cleansing process." -- Sai Baba

"A whole is what has a beginning and middle and end." -- Aristotle

"This is my charge to everyone. We have to be better. We have to love more, hate less. We've got to listen more and talk less. We've got to know that this is everybody's responsibility. Every single person here. Every single person who is not here. Every single person who doesn't want to be here. Every single person who agrees and doesn't agree, it's our responsibility to make this world a better place." – Megan Rapinoe

"This is my wish for you:
Comfort on difficult days,
Smiles when sadness intrudes,
Rainbows to follow the clouds,
Laughter to kiss your lips,
Sunsets to warm your heart,
Hugs when spirits sag,
Beauty for your eyes to see,
Friendships to brighten your being,
Faith so that you can believe,
Confidence for when you doubt,
Courage to know yourself,
Patience to accept the truth,
Love to complete your life." - Anonymous

Epilogue: Accountability and Truth   August 2019

Looking back over eleven years of compiling these ideas, it occurs to me that there was a reason I indulged myself and my readers in this glimpse into my innermost conceptual sanctum.

I love to inspire and lead others toward productivity and fulfillment. I come from a line of teachers and businesspeople, so I have always felt a sense of accountability to become a thought leader, and to present what I learn and discover, for fun and profit. Our perspectives are our legacy, our effort to contribute our verse to the song of life. "Ideas have endurance without death," JFK reminds us. We all stand on the shoulders of giants – at some point, we may become the shoulders others stand upon.

Is that pompous? Perhaps, and I would be remiss if at this late date I didn't confess to a degree of intellectual arrogance. At times, I do take myself a bit too seriously. If you've read this far, no doubt you've detected that.

But that doesn't mean that ideas are not our most profound and useful currency – they evolve our opportunities, and offer us a way to break through to higher consciousness and greater achievement.

"If it is to be, it is up to me." -- William H. Johnson

It has been joyful and immensely satisfying to engage you in this intimate fashion – but only you can decide if it has been a fun academic exercise or a legitimate call to action. In my humble opinion, we need to do something, to pull together to help our culture metamorphose into coherence, appreciating and honoring all the different nuances and diversities that make us who we really are. The whole is truly more than the sum of the parts.

I have made so many incredible friends along the Winners Circle path -- Brad Kirzner, Jared Leon, Julia and Kevin Keiser, Jon Bergrin, Tom Salmon, Jimmy Leonette, Deborah Morrone, Bryan Natusch and Amber Mc Lelland, Eric Nepute, Joe Di Carlo, Steve Swain, Manuel Mazzini, Tod Pelly and so many more of the hundreds of members who exemplify advanced citizenry, and motivate me daily.

"The buck stops here." -- Col. A. B. Warfield / Harry S. Truman

Drawing this formal "Advanced Citizen" process to a close shouldn't reduce the development or outflow of creative material. I feel accountable to continue to offer what I have, I just want to take a breather – as Bob Weir croons in "Jack Straw," "We can share what we got of yours, 'cause we done shared all of mine…"

At age 66, I still have considerable tread left on me -- but that doesn't mean I need to race around the same track indefinitely. Accountability does not require blind faith or trust, nor tireless monotony. Accountability insists that we keep delivering, but there can be some flexibility on the shape it assumes. Jackie Joyner-Kersee, Olympian champion, remarked on her evolution out of the spotlight, "Quality training is what I do now; before it was a combination of both quality and quantity. Now I'm not trying to be a world-class athlete, I don't need to train at that level. It's about being fit, fit for life."

And so, beloved readers, don't be surprised to see some of these insights, and probably some new ones, morph into another form. I can't tell you for sure, and a brief sabbatical is called for – but make no mistake, the truth (as I see it, of course) is relentless and invincible. It outlasts any resistance, laziness, indifference or explosive rebellion. Truth will out. It always comes to the forefront sooner or later. As Schopenhauer says, truth is at first ridiculed, then violently opposed, and finally accepted as self-evident. Literally, nothing can stop it.

Now, as I suggested, this content may simply entertain you, or you could assimilate it into a code of identity, ethics and behavior that compels you to express more of the greatness you have inside.

No one can decide that for you, and no one can do it for you. Success leaves clues, but only you can determine what to do with this time lapse chronicle of the last decade's highest virtues, intended to be a roadmap to your personal growth and development.

Are you willing to be an advanced citizen? If you have read this far, you have been exposed to myriad tools and techniques for becoming a better you, investing your surplus energy and love in noble and worthy causes. Here's one last distinction that, when properly applied, can be a catapult to massive impact and global relevance.

If you want to play a bigger game, you may not be able to do it alone, so you'll need to comprehend and apply the dynamics of team-building. Bruce Tuckman told us that groups start by **forming**, when the players who will participate come together. Once the team forms, the next phase is **storming** – differing factions express their point of view, and a cohesive vision is painfully but inexorably pursued and forged. Many teams and relationships don't survive the storming process, but if you are tough enough and persistent enough, you get to **norming** – standards are established, objectives are identified, and strategies crystallize. Only then is the team ready to excel at **performing**.

These four phases – forming, storming, norming and performing – may repeat cyclically, so be prepared for changes in personnel (more forming), conflicts of opinion (more storming), the need for mediation and problem solving (more norming) and the will to put everything you've learned into consistent action (more performing.) That's where real progress comes from.

Needless to say, our world is now undergoing some intense storming – it's painful, but it is necessary for the next phase of norming and ultimately the performing we all aspire to and will surely enjoy.

So if we hold ourselves accountable to do our part, based on our best interpretation of our truth, what more can we ask of ourselves? And what more could you ask of me, or I of you?

Bob Hoffman tells us that the one quote that changed everything for him is "Ultra-successful people are uncommonly skilled at execution." They just get things done.

That's what accountability is for, getting things done and doing as much good as possible. And that's the truth.

Final Reflections   September 2019

The concept of being an advanced citizen was inspired by a talk delivered by Guy Riekeman, Chancellor of Life University in 2007. It means to do all the things citizens do – work, play, marry and raise families for some, develop careers, and so on.

Advanced Citizens, though, go the extra mile. They are involved in meaningful causes. They make their voices heard in some dignified yet penetrating way. They are thought leaders. They make a difference in the world.

The point of writing this monthly newsletter was to offer some guidance to evolving influencers, to give them a toolbox, a reservoir of distinctions to draw upon when called for. In that way, we grow the leaders of tomorrow, the visionaries of the next generation, by preserving the core values and ideologies, but varying the strategies to meet the new marketplace.

Great American novelist Toni Morrison said, "There is no time for despair, no place for self-pity, no need for silence, no room for fear. We speak, we write, we do language. That is how civilizations heal." So the words we put together have power, and grace, and potential to make a significant difference.

"The pen is mightier than the sword." -- Edward Bulwer-Lytton

As Tony Robbins teaches, to create lasting change we must raise our standards, choose empowering beliefs, and apply winning strategies. When we direct this process toward the most significant virtues of life, we become Advanced Citizens.

I hope and expect that something in this collection resonated with you – if so, please share it with someone you care about. A candle loses nothing by lighting another candle. We're all in this together, hence the need for Advanced Citizens – someone must take responsibility to lead the way.

Thanks for being or becoming one of the few who do.

Acknowledgments

Special thanks to The Winners Circle, a constant source of inspiration and vitality.

Thank you to my lovely wife Regina Perman, whose patience and support have always been a cornerstone in my success.

Thanks to Dr. Bob and Sharon Hoffman, who masterfully run The Winners Circle with passion and dexterity.

Thank you to the historical leadership of The Winners Circle, Dr. Larry Markson and Dr. Janice Hughes, whose creativity and guidance formed the early incarnations of The Winners Circle.

Thank you to online resources Brainyquotes.com, Dictionary.com, Goodreads.com, Google.com, Wikihow.com and Wikipedia.com.

And thank you to the following advanced citizens, who were quoted or mentioned in "The Advanced Citizen."

Jay Abraham 316 (month 3 of year 16, so March 2016)
Patch Adams 813 (month 8 of year 13, so August 2013)
Aesop 216
Anna Ajosa 1118
William Ajosa 1118
C. P. Alderfer 213
David Allen 517, 218
Woody Allen 113
Greg Allman 817
Chris Anderson 117
Mario Andretti 1213
Butch Andrion 1009
Maya Angelou 216, 816, 916
Kevin Ansbro 518
Aristotle 212, 719

Alejandra Robles Arizmendi 813

Giorgio Armani 519

Thomas Armstrong 1113

Arthur 712

Sebastian and Isabella Artois 1016

Mary Kay Ash 414

Sai Baba 719

Erykah Badu 719

Marty Balin 615

Richard Barwell 715, 818

Michael Bennett 1015

Michael Bergdahl 513

Jon Bergrin 819

Yogi Berra 219

Chuck Berry 817

Steve Bourdage 911

Andrew Boyd 216

A Drayton Boylston 111

brainyquotes.com 1213

Nathaniel Branden 309, 114, 1214

Breakthrough Coaching 212

Brandon Brock 818

Buddha 808, 216, 518, 1218

Warren Buffet 114

Edward Bulwer-Lytton 919

Noel Burch 512

Edmund Burke 614

Krista Burns 517

Leo Buscaglia 216, 816

Colin Camerer 419

Glen Campbell 817

Albert Camus 114, 216

Jack Canfield 517

Thomas Carlyle 619

Ted Carrick 818

Peter Carstens 911

Jimmy Carter 1216

Gary Chapman 713

Lord Chesterfield 310

Michael Chiarello 615

Frederic Chopin 814

Deepak Chopra 1208, 709, 111, 312, 1215, 117, 718

Winston Churchill 414

Robert Cialdini 1014

James Cima 109

Gerry Clum 1209, 911, 813, 416

Paulo Coelho 1213, 319

Leonard Cohen 719

James Collins 212, 218, 719

Erin Collins 1014

Cliff Conarck 917

Confucius 814, 717, 219

Calvin Coolidge 1213

Stephen Covey 212, 816, 218, 219

Stephen R. Covey 1016, 718

Doug Cox 119

e.e. cummings 719

Jeff Cumro 1015

J. V. Cunningham 518

Mary Curtis 111

Dalai Lama XIV 216

Matt Damon 411

Charles Darwin 1218, 119

Sindre Daugstad 911

Leonardo DaVinci 916, 117, 814, 417, 519

Jason Deitch 115

Major DeJarnette 109

John Demartini 611, 113, 515, 716, 218, 1118

Rob Demartino 818

Billy DeMoss 911

David Denton 109

Joe Di Carlo 819

Charles Dickens 1213, 1016

dictionary.com 413, 114, 1117

Joe Dispenza 218

Norman Doidge 418

Peter Drucker 614

Carol Dweck 713, 618

Wayne Dyer 413, 114, 815, 1016

Thomas Edison 213, 916, 1218

Albert Einstein 413, 114, 314, 814, 515, 216, 916, 1116, 817, 418, 618, 718

Dwight D. Eisenhower 213

Queen Elizabeth II 414

Ralph Waldo Emerson 310, 512, 114, 414, 916, 519, 619

Donny Epstein 618, 1218

Milton Erickson 519

Euripides 916

Tim Faulkner 718

William Faulkner 518

Leon Festinger 213

Joe Flesia 817

Michael Flynn 911

Henry Ford 414

Pope Francis 915, 216, 816

Anne Frank 815

Ken Frank 615

Benjamin Franklin 1016, 718

Fujibushi 615

Robert Fulghum 314, 1016

Mahatma Gandhi 1215, 718, 1218, 719

Howard Gardner 1113

Bill Gates 218

Antoni Gaudi 1112

Michael Gelb 117

Patrick Gentempo 911

Michael Gerber 1217

Kahlil Gibran 1214, 814

Chuck Gibson 813

André Gide 310

Malcom Gladwell 513, 714, 516, 218, 519

Reggie Gold 817

George Gonzalez 818

George Goodheart 109

goodreads.com 114

Jenna Goudreau 113

Jason Gould 911

Katherine Graham 111

John Gray 1117

Dick Gregory 817

Wayne Gretzky 310

Peter Guber 513

Forrest Gump 319

Heidi Haavik 818

Thich Nhat Hanh 216

Rob Hanopole 115

Mark Victor Hansen 1013

George Harrison 719

N. R. Hart 518

Stephen Hawking 1218

helpguide.org 114

Ernest Hemingway 816, 717

Mike Hernacki 910

Napoleon Hill 1212, 217

Hippocrates 119

Bob Hoffman 808, 1109, 1110, 611, 1111, 712, 912, 313, 713, 913, 1013, 115, 415, 416, 1116, 218, 518, 818, 819

Karen Horney 1114

Jean Houston 818

Russ Hudson 915

Janice Hughes 808

Victor Hugo 916

Aldous Huxley 414

innerfrontier.org 113

Otto Janke 1009, 111

Thomas Jefferson 916

Jesus 1218

Derek Jeter 1014

Steve Jobs 814

William H. Johnson 819

Samuel Johnson 310

Michael Jordan 1113, 414

Jackie Joyner-Kersee 111, 218, 819

C. G. Jung 517

Jon Kabat-Zinn 114

Helen Keller 1213, 314

Brian Kelly 911, 813

Julia and Kevin Keiser, 615,819

John F. Kennedy 119, 619, 819

Robert F. Kennedy 310

Christopher Kent 813

Datis Kharrazian 818

Martin Luther King Jr. 114, 314, 116, 1216, 418, 1218

Brad Kirzner 819

Austin Komarek 813

Seth Lederman 619

Bruce Lee 814

Miriam Leean 810

Jonah Lehrer 1216

John Lennon 314, 319

Jared Leon 819

Jimmy Leonette 1015, 416, 819

Jerry Lewis 817

Harvey Lillard 516

Abraham Lincoln 114

Bruce Lipton 418, 1218, 119

Jim Loehr 510, 615

George Loewenstein 419

David Logan 1209

Vince Lombardi 1213, 414, 219

Italo Magni 111

Larry Markson 808, 416, 719

Stacey Marshall 810

Abraham Maslow 512, 213, 416

The Masters Circle Global 212, 819

Denise Mathre 1009, 1110, 111, 213

Manuel Mazzini 911, 1111, 816, 819

Linda McCartney 814

Ross McDonald 911

Heath McKinley 810, 111

Amber McLelland

Robert McIver 310

Rob Melillo 818

Danny Meyer 1017

Jillian Michaels 119

Brad Miller 911

Joan Miro 1112

Mary Tyler Moore 817

Toni Morrison 919

Deborah Morrone 819

M.T. Morter 715, 917

Sue Morter 808

Red Motley 210

Per Munksgaard 911

Dan Murphy 813

Bryan Natusch 819

Eric Nepute 911, 819

Martha Nessler 111

Isaac Newton 814, 318

Reinhold Niebuhr 717

Anais Nin 719

Wes Nyberg 911

Rebecca Nystrom 615

Eugene O'Neill 1216

Yoko Ono 1016

Suze Orman 1214

Thomas Paine 916

BJ Palmer 109, 511, 212, 312, 413, 216, 717, 418, 918, 119

DD Palmer 1011, 212, 516, 718, 119

Jim Parker 416

Dolly Parton 1216

Bo Peabody 412

Norman Vincent Peale 213, 414

Tod Pelly 819

Bill Perman 615

Daniel Perman 615

Doria Perman 317

Eileen Perman 812

Regina Perman 615, 417, 617, 817, 319

Steven Perman 317, 617

Bill Phillips 119

Picasso 1112

Vern Pierce 109, 715

Paul Zane Pilzer 618

Plato 212, 815, 216

Plutarch 1216

George Polya 519

Catherine Ponder 418

Cynthia Porter 115, 818

Patrick Porter 115, 818

Colin Powell 1213, 915

Kurt Price 810

Bob Proctor 719

Ayn Rand 114, 915

Megan Rapinoe 719

Amit Ray 216

M. L. Rees 109, 817

Steven Reiss 213

Matthieu Ricard 416

Grantland Rice 219

Don Rickles 817

Guy Riekeman 808, 514, 218, 919

Al Ries and Jack Trout 218

Pat Riley 219

Don Richard Riso 915

Eric Roach 911

Tony Robbins 808, 509, 909, 210, 311, 1111, 112, 213, 313, 513, 1213, 314, 614, 1014, 416, 516, 716, 1216, 617, 118, 218, 418, 718, 1218, 319, 519, 619, 919

Carl Rogers 517

Haavard Rognerud 911

Jim Rohn 213

Eleanor Roosevelt 114, 718

Theodore Roosevelt 816

Alan Rousso 410

J. K. Rowling 1016

Wilma Rudolph 219

Don Miguel Ruiz 912, 114

Jalaluddin Rumi 717

Carl Sagan 418

Tom Salmon 1015,819

George Santayana 614

Virginia Satir 519

Allen Saunders 319

Robert Scheinfeld 314

Arthur Schopenhauer 216, 819

Tony Schwartz 510, 615

Norman Schwartzkopf 513

Albert Schweitzer 216, 1218

Giovanni Segar 419

Meridee Lynn Senick 911

Simon Senzon 511, 418

Dr. Seuss 411, 712

William Shakespeare 718

Robin Sharma 515, 218

George Bernard Shaw 916

John A. Shedd 310

Skitty and Squirty 817

Carly Simon 112

David Simon 117, 718

Paul Simon 719

David Singer 212

Jeff Smith 813

Socrates 610, 713

King Solomon 1218

Bruce Springsteen 112

Myles Starkman 1015

Anton Stas 810, 911

John Steinbeck 816

Gloria Steinem 1016

Stephenson 212

Glenn Stillwagon 611, 715

Harriet Beecher Stowe 916

Joe Stuckey 109

Steve Swain 911, 819

Rabindranath Tagore 319

Mother Teresa 814, 815, 216, 518, 718, 1218

Twyla Tharp 418

Henry David Thoreau 814, 1216

Leo Tolstoy 814, 619

Joe Torre 219

Aura Tovar 317

Brian Tracy 815

Harry S. Truman 819

Gary Trupo 115

Bruce Tuckman 819

Desmond Tutu 815

Lao Tzu 114, 814, 815, 617

Morihei Ueshiba 915, 1115, 616, 1117, 1118

Jim Valvano 414

Henry van Dyke 817

Richard Van Rumpt 109, 611, 817, 1118

Iyanla Vanzant 517

Vauvenargues 310

Dick Versendaal 817

Virgil 619

Diane Von Furstenberg 814

J. W. von Goethe 1217

Denis Waitley 1012, 317, 418, 1018, 1118

Sam Walton 513

Charlie Ward 813

Col. A. B. Warfield 819

Barry Warren 912, 817

Simone Weil 717

John Wesley 1215

Edith Wharton 816

Tom Whitehorne 109, 817

Walt Whitman 514

Wikihow.com 916

wikipedia.com 714

Oscar Wilde 815

John William Ward 310

Martin Weber 419

Jack Welch 719

Bob Weir 819

Robin Williams 411, 514

Sid Williams 416

Marianne Williamson 613, 813, 617

Colin Wilson 111

Oprah Winfrey 114, 816, 617

Tiger Woods 1113

Zig Ziglar 114, 915

Rhea Zimmerman 813

In "*The Advanced Citizen*" Dr. Perman defines a forward path for thought leaders, a training ground for visionaries based on his 32 years studying and coaching high achievers in action.